Revelation

ABOUT THE AUTHORS

General editor:

Clinton E. Arnold (PhD, University of Aberdeen), professor and chairman, department of New Testament, Talbot School of Theology, Biola University, Los Angeles, California

Revelation:

Mark W. Wilson (DLitt et Phil, University of South Africa), adjunct professor of New Testament, Regent University, Virginia Beach, Virginia

Zondervan Illustrated Bible Backgrounds Commentary

Revelation

Mark W. Wilson

Clinton E. Arnold   *general editor*

ZONDERVAN®

ZONDERVAN.com/
AUTHORTRACKER
follow your favorite authors

ZONDERVAN®

Zondervan Illustrated Bible Backgrounds Commentary: Revelation
Copyright © 2002 by Mark Wilson

Requests for information should be addressed to:

Zondervan, *Grand Rapids, Michigan 49530*

Library of Congress Cataloging-in-Publication Data
    Zondervan illustrated Bible backgrounds commentary / Clinton E. Arnold, general editor.
       p.cm.
    Includes bibliographical references.
    ISBN-10: 0-310-27832-5
    ISBN-13: 978-0-310-27832-0
    1. Bible. N.T.—Commentaries.   I. Arnold, Clinton E.
    BS2341.52.Z66 2001
    225.7—dc21
                                             2001046801
                                           CIP

Printed in China

Interior design by Sherri L. Hoffman

07 08 09 10 11 12 13 • 12 11 10 9 8 7 6 5 4 3 2 1

CONTENTS

INTRODUCTION

All readers of the Bible have a tendency to view what it says it through their own culture and life circumstances. This can happen almost subconsiously as we read the pages of the text.

When most people in the church read about the thief on the cross, for instance, they immediately think of a burglar that held up a store or broke into a home. They may be rather shocked to find out that the guy was actually a Jewish revolutionary figure who was part of a growing movement in Palestine eager to throw off Roman rule.

It also comes as something of a surprise to contemporary Christians that "cursing" in the New Testament era had little or nothing to do with cussing somebody out. It had far more to do with the invocation of spirits to cause someone harm.

No doubt there is a need in the church for learning more about the world of the New Testament to avoid erroneous interpretations of the text of Scripture. But relevant historical and cultural insights also provide an added dimension of perspective to the words of the Bible. This kind of information often functions in the same way as watching a movie in color rather than in black and white. Finding out, for instance, how Paul compared Christ's victory on the cross to a joyous celebration parade in honor of a Roman general after winning an extraordinary battle brings does indeed magnify the profundity and implications of Jesus' work on the cross. Discovering that the factions at Corinth ("I follow Paul . . . I follow Apollos . . .") had plenty of precedent in the local cults ("I follow Aphrodite; I follow Apollo . . .") helps us understand the "why" of a particular problem. Learning about the water supply from the springs of Hierapolis that flowed into Laodicea as "lukewarm" water enables us to appreciate the relevance of the metaphor Jesus used when he addressed the spiritual laxity of this church.

My sense is that most Christians are eager to learn more about the real life setting of the New Testament. In the preaching and teaching of the Bible in the church, congregants are always grateful when they learn something of the background and historical context of the text. It not only helps them understand the text more accurately, but often enables them to identify with the people and circumstances of the Bible. I have been asked on countless occasions by Christians, "Where can I get access to good historical background information about this passage?" Earnest Christians are hungry for information that makes their Bibles come alive.

The stimulus for this commentary came from the church and the aim is to serve the church. The contributors to this series have sought to provide illuminating and interesting historical/cultural background information. The intent was to draw upon relevant papyri, inscriptions, archaeological discoveries, and the numerous studies of Judaism, Roman culture, Hellenism, and other features of the world of the New Testament and to make the results accessible to people in the church. We recognize that some readers of the commentary will want to go further, and so the sources of the information have been carefully documented in endnotes.

The written information has been supplemented with hundreds of photographs, maps, charts, artwork, and other graphics that help the reader better understand the world of the New Testament. Each of the writers was given an opportunity to dream up a "wish list" of illustrations that he thought would help to illustrate the passages in the New Testament book for which he was writing commentary. Although we were not able to obtain everything they were looking for, we came close.

The team of commentators are writing for the benefit of the broad array of Christians who simply want to better understand their Bibles from the vantage point of the historical context. This is an installment in a new genre of "Bible background" commentaries that was kicked off by Craig Keener's fine volume. Consequently, this is not an "exegetical" commentary that provides linguistic insight and background into Greek constructions and verb tenses. Neither is this work an "expository" commentary that provides a verse-by-verse exposition of the text; for in-depth philo-

logical or theological insight, readers will need to have other more specialized or comprehensive commentaries available. Nor is this an "historical-critical" commentary, although the contributors are all scholars and have already made substantial academic contributions on the New Testament books they are writing on for this set. The team intentionally does not engage all of the issues that are discussed in the scholarly guild.

Rather, our goal is to offer a reading and interpretation of the text informed by what we regard as the most relevant historical information. For many in the church, this commentary will serve as an important entry point into the interpretation and appreciation of the text. For other more serious students of the Word, these volumes will provide an important supplement to many of the fine exegetical, expository, and critical available.

The contributors represent a group of scholars who embrace the Bible as the Word of God and believe that the message of its pages has life-changing relevance for faith and practice today. Accordingly, we offer "Reflections" on the relevance of the Scripture to life for every chapter of the New Testament.

I pray that this commentary brings you both delight and insight in digging deeper into the Word of God.

Clinton E. Arnold
General Editor

LIST OF SIDEBARS

Revelation

LIST OF CHARTS

INDEX OF PHOTOS AND MAPS

ABBREVIATIONS

1. Books of the Bible and Apocrypha

1 Chron.	1 Chronicles	Josh.	Joshua
2 Chron.	2 Chronicles	Jude	Jude
1 Cor.	1 Corinthians	Judg.	Judges
2 Cor.	2 Corinthians	Judith	Judith
1 Esd.	1 Esdras	Lam.	Lamentations
2 Esd.	2 Esdras	Lev.	Leviticus
1 John	1 John	Luke	Luke
2 John	2 John	Mal.	Malachi
3 John	3 John	Mark	Mark
1 Kings	1 Kings	Matt.	Matthew
2 Kings	2 Kings	Mic.	Micah
1 Macc.	1 Maccabees	Nah.	Nahum
2 Macc.	2 Maccabees	Neh.	Nehemiah
1 Peter	1 Peter	Num.	Numbers
2 Peter	2 Peter	Obad.	Obadiah
1 Sam.	1 Samuel	Phil.	Philippians
2 Sam.	2 Samuel	Philem.	Philemon
1 Thess.	1 Thessalonians	Pr. Man.	Prayer of Manassah
2 Thess.	2 Thessalonians	Prov.	Proverbs
1 Tim.	1 Timothy	Ps.	Psalm
2 Tim.	2 Timothy	Rest. of Est.	The Rest of Esther
Acts	Acts	Rev.	Revelation
Amos	Amos	Rom.	Romans
Bar.	Baruch	Ruth	Ruth
Bel	Bel and the Dragon	S. of III Ch.	The Song of the Three Holy Children
Col.	Colossians	Sir.	Sirach/Ecclesiasticus
Dan.	Daniel	Song	Song of Songs
Deut.	Deuteronomy	Sus.	Susanna
Eccl.	Ecclesiastes	Titus	Titus
Ep. Jer.	Epistle of Jeremiah	Tobit	Tobit
Eph.	Ephesians	Wisd. Sol.	The Wisdom of Solomon
Est.	Esther	Zech.	Zechariah
Ezek.	Ezekiel	Zeph.	Zephaniah
Ex.	Exodus		
Ezra	Ezra		
Gal.	Galatians		
Gen.	Genesis		
Hab.	Habakkuk		
Hag.	Haggai		
Heb.	Hebrews		
Hos.	Hosea		
Isa.	Isaiah		
James	James		
Jer.	Jeremiah		
Job	Job		
Joel	Joel		
John	John		
Jonah	Jonah		

2. Old and New Testament Pseudepigrapha and Rabbinic Literature

Individual tractates of rabbinic literature follow the abbreviations of the *SBL Handbook of Style*, pp. 79–80. Qumran documents follow standard Dead Sea Scroll conventions.

2 Bar.	*2 Baruch*
3 Bar.	*3 Baruch*
4 Bar.	*4 Baruch*
1 En.	*1 Enoch*
2 En.	*2 Enoch*
3 En.	*3 Enoch*
4 Ezra	*4 Ezra*

3 Macc.	3 Maccabees
4 Macc.	4 Maccabees
5 Macc.	5 Maccabees
Acts Phil.	Acts of Philip
Acts Pet.	Acts of Peter and the 12 Apostles
Apoc. Elijah	Apocalypse of Elijah
As. Mos.	Assumption of Moses
b.	Babylonian Talmud (+ tractate)
Gos. Thom.	Gospel of Thomas
Jos. Asen.	Joseph and Aseneth
Jub.	Jubilees
Let. Aris.	Letter of Aristeas
m.	Mishnah (+ tractate)
Mek.	Mekilta
Midr.	Midrash I (+ biblical book)
Odes Sol.	Odes of Solomon
Pesiq. Rab.	Pesiqta Rabbati
Pirqe. R. El.	Pirqe Rabbi Eliezer
Pss. Sol.	Psalms of Solomon
Rab.	Rabbah (+biblical book); (e.g., Gen. Rab.=Genesis Rabbah)
S. ʿOlam Rab.	Seder ʿOlam Rabbah
Sem.	Semahot
Sib. Or.	Sibylline Oracles
T. Ab.	Testament of Abraham
T. Adam	Testament of Adam
T. Ash.	Testament of Asher
T. Benj.	Testament of Benjamin
T. Dan	Testament of Dan
T. Gad	Testament of Gad
T. Hez.	Testament of Hezekiah
T. Isaac	Testament of Isaac
T. Iss.	Testament of Issachar
T. Jac.	Testament of Jacob
T. Job	Testament of Job
T. Jos.	Testament of Joseph
T. Jud.	Testament of Judah
T. Levi	Testament of Levi
T. Mos.	Testament of Moses
T. Naph.	Testament of Naphtali
T. Reu.	Testament of Reuben
T. Sim.	Testament of Simeon
T. Sol.	Testament of Solomon
T. Zeb.	Testament of Zebulum
Tanh.	Tanhuma
Tg. Isa.	Targum of Isaiah
Tg. Lam.	Targum of Lamentations
Tg. Neof.	Targum Neofiti
Tg. Onq.	Targum Onqelos
Tg. Ps.-J	Targum Pseudo-Jonathan
y.	Jerusalem Talmud (+ tractate)

3. Classical Historians

For an extended list of classical historians and church fathers, see *SBL Handbook of Style*, pp. 84–87. For many works of classical antiquity, the abbreviations have been subjected to the author's discretion; the names of these works should be obvious upon consulting entries of the classical writers in classical dictionaries or encyclopedias.

Eusebius

| Eccl. Hist. | Ecclesiastical History |

Josephus

Ag. Ap.	Against Apion
Ant.	Jewish Antiquities
J.W.	Jewish War
Life	The Life

Philo

Abraham	On the Life of Abraham
Agriculture	On Agriculture
Alleg. Interp	Allegorical Interpretation
Animals	Whether Animals Have Reason
Cherubim	On the Cherubim
Confusion	On the Confusion of Thomas
Contempl. Life	On the Contemplative Life
Creation	On the Creation of the World
Curses	On Curses
Decalogue	On the Decalogue
Dreams	On Dreams
Drunkenness	On Drunkenness
Embassy	On the Embassy to Gaius
Eternity	On the Eternity of the World
Flaccus	Against Flaccus
Flight	On Flight and Finding
Giants	On Giants
God	On God
Heir	Who Is the Heir?
Hypothetica	Hypothetica
Joseph	On the Life of Joseph
Migration	On the Migration of Abraham
Moses	On the Life of Moses
Names	On the Change of Names
Person	That Every Good Person Is Free
Planting	On Planting
Posterity	On the Posterity of Cain
Prelim. Studies	On the Preliminary Studies
Providence	On Providence
QE	Questions and Answers on Exodus
QG	Questions and Answers on Genesis
Rewards	On Rewards and Punishments
Sacrifices	On the Sacrifices of Cain and Abel
Sobriety	On Sobriety
Spec. Laws	On the Special Laws
Unchangeable	That God Is Unchangeable
Virtues	On the Virtues

Worse	That the Worse Attacks the Better

Apostolic Fathers

1 Clem.	First Letter of Clement
Barn.	Epistle of Barnabas
Clem. Hom.	Ancient Homily of Clement (also called 2 Clement)
Did.	Didache
Herm. Vis.; Sim.	Shepherd of Hermas, Visions; Similitudes
Ignatius	Epistles of Ignatius (followed by the letter's name)
Mart. Pol.	Martyrdom of Polycarp

4. Modern Abbreviations

AASOR	Annual of the American Schools of Oriental Research
AB	Anchor Bible
ABD	Anchor Bible Dictionary
ABRL	Anchor Bible Reference Library
AGJU	Arbeiten zur Geschichte des antiken Judentums und des Urchristentums
AH	Agricultural History
ALGHJ	Arbeiten zur Literatur und Geschichte des Hellenistischen Judentums
AnBib	Analecta biblica
ANRW	Aufstieg und Niedergang der römischen Welt
ANTC	Abingdon New Testament Commentaries
BAGD	Bauer, W., W. F. Arndt, F. W. Gingrich, and F. W. Danker. Greek-English Lexicon of the New Testament and Other Early Christina Literature (2d. ed.)
BA	Biblical Archaeologist
BAFCS	Book of Acts in Its First Century Setting
BAR	Biblical Archaeology Review
BASOR	Bulletin of the American Schools of Oriental Research
BBC	Bible Background Commentary
BBR	Bulletin for Biblical Research
BDB	Brown, F., S. R. Driver, and C. A. Briggs. A Hebrew and English Lexicon of the Old Testament
BDF	Blass, F., A. Debrunner, and R. W. Funk. A Greek Grammar of the New Testament and Other Early Christian Literature
BECNT	Baker Exegetical Commentary on the New Testament
BI	Biblical Illustrator
Bib	Biblica
BibSac	Bibliotheca Sacra

BLT	Brethren Life and Thought
BNTC	Black's New Testament Commentary
BRev	Bible Review
BSHJ	Baltimore Studies in the History of Judaism
BST	The Bible Speaks Today
BSV	Biblical Social Values
BT	The Bible Translator
BTB	Biblical Theology Bulletin
BZ	Biblische Zeitschrift
CBQ	Catholic Biblical Quarterly
CBTJ	Calvary Baptist Theological Journal
CGTC	Cambridge Greek Testament Commentary
CH	Church History
CIL	Corpus inscriptionum latinarum
CPJ	Corpus papyrorum judaicorum
CRINT	Compendia rerum iudaicarum ad Novum Testamentum
CTJ	Calvin Theological Journal
CTM	Concordia Theological Monthly
CTT	Contours of Christian Theology
DBI	Dictionary of Biblical Imagery
DCM	Dictionary of Classical Mythology.
DDD	Dictionary of Deities and Demons in the Bible
DJBP	Dictionary of Judaism in the Biblical Period
DJG	Dictionary of Jesus and the Gospels
DLNT	Dictionary of the Later New Testament and Its Developments
DNTB	Dictionary of New Testament Background
DPL	Dictionary of Paul and His Letters
EBC	Expositor's Bible Commentary
EDBT	Evangelical Dictionary of Biblical Theology
EDNT	Exegetical Dictionary of the New Testament
EJR	Encyclopedia of the Jewish Religion
EPRO	Études préliminaires aux religions orientales dans l'empire romain
EvQ	Evangelical Quarterly
ExpTim	Expository Times
FRLANT	Forschungen zur Religion und Literatur des Alten und Neuen Testament
GNC	Good News Commentary
GNS	Good News Studies
HCNT	Hellenistic Commentary to the New Testament
HDB	Hastings Dictionary of the Bible

HJP	*History of the Jewish People in the Age of Jesus Christ*, by E. Schürer
HTR	*Harvard Theological Review*
HTS	Harvard Theological Studies
HUCA	Hebrew Union College Annual
IBD	Illustrated Bible Dictionary
IBS	Irish Biblical Studies
ICC	International Critical Commentary
IDB	*The Interpreter's Dictionary of the Bible*
IEJ	*Israel Exploration Journal*
IG	*Inscriptiones graecae*
IGRR	*Inscriptiones graecae ad res romanas pertinentes*
ILS	*Inscriptiones Latinae Selectae*
Imm	*Immanuel*
ISBE	*International Standard Bible Encyclopedia*
Int	*Interpretation*
IvE	*Inschriften von Ephesos*
IVPNTC	InterVarsity Press New Testament Commentary
JAC	*Jahrbuch für Antike und Christentum*
JBL	*Journal of Biblical Literature*
JETS	*Journal of the Evangelical Theological Society*
JHS	*Journal of Hellenic Studies*
JJS	*Journal of Jewish Studies*
JOAIW	*Jahreshefte des Osterreeichischen Archaologischen Instites in Wien*
JSJ	*Journal for the Study of Judaism in the Persian, Hellenistic, and Roman Periods*
JRS	*Journal of Roman Studies*
JSNT	*Journal for the Study of the New Testament*
JSNTSup	Journal for the Study of the New Testament: Supplement Series
JSOT	*Journal for the Study of the Old Testament*
JSOTSup	Journal for the Study of the Old Testament: Supplement Series
JTS	*Journal of Theological Studies*
KTR	*Kings Theological Review*
LCL	Loeb Classical Library
LEC	Library of Early Christianity
LSJ	Liddell, H. G., R. Scott, H. S. Jones. *A Greek-English Lexicon*
MM	Moulton, J. H., and G. Milligan. *The Vocabulary of the Greek Testament*
MNTC	Moffatt New Testament Commentary
NBD	*New Bible Dictionary*
NC	Narrative Commentaries
NCBC	New Century Bible Commentary Eerdmans
NEAE	*New Encyclopedia of Archaeological Excavations in the Holy Land*
NEASB	Near East Archaeological Society Bulletin
New Docs	*New Documents Illustrating Early Christianity*
NIBC	New International Biblical Commentary
NICNT	New International Commentary on the New Testament
NIDNTT	*New International Dictionary of New Testament Theology*
NIGTC	New International Greek Testament Commentary
NIVAC	NIV Application Commentary
NorTT	*Norsk Teologisk Tidsskrift*
NoT	*Notes on Translation*
NovT	*Novum Testamentum*
NovTSup	Novum Testamentum Supplements
NTAbh	Neutestamentliche Abhandlungen
NTS	*New Testament Studies*
NTT	New Testament Theology
NTTS	New Testament Tools and Studies
OAG	*Oxford Archaeological Guides*
OCCC	*Oxford Companion to Classical Civilization*
OCD	*Oxford Classical Dictionary*
ODCC	*The Oxford Dictionary of the Christian Church*
OGIS	*Orientis graeci inscriptiones selectae*
OHCW	*The Oxford History of the Classical World*
OHRW	*Oxford History of the Roman World*
OTP	*Old Testament Pseudepigrapha*, ed. by J. H. Charlesworth
PEQ	*Palestine Exploration Quarterly*
PG	*Patrologia graeca*
PGM	*Papyri graecae magicae: Die griechischen Zauberpapyri*
PL	*Patrologia latina*
PNTC	Pelican New Testament Commentaries
Rb	*Revista biblica*
RB	*Revue biblique*
RivB	*Rivista biblica italiana*
RTR	*Reformed Theological Review*
SB	Sources bibliques
SBL	Society of Biblical Literature
SBLDS	Society of Biblical Literature Dissertation Series

SBLMS	Society of Biblical Literature Monograph Series
SBLSP	*Society of Biblical Literature Seminar Papers*
SBS	Stuttgarter Bibelstudien
SBT	Studies in Biblical Theology
SCJ	*Stone-Campbell Journal*
Scr	*Scripture*
SE	*Studia Evangelica*
SEG	*Supplementum epigraphicum graecum*
SJLA	Studies in Judaism in Late Antiquity
SJT	*Scottish Journal of Theology*
SNTSMS	Society for New Testament Studies Monograph Series
SSC	Social Science Commentary
SSCSSG	Social-Science Commentary on the Synoptic Gospels
Str-B	Strack, H. L., and P. Billerbeck. *Kommentar zum Neuen Testament aus Talmud und Midrasch*
TC	Thornapple Commentaries
TDNT	*Theological Dictionary of the New Testament*
TDOT	*Theological Dictionary of the Old Testament*
TLNT	*Theological Lexicon of the New Testament*
TLZ	*Theologische Literaturzeitung*
TNTC	Tyndale New Testament Commentary
TrinJ	*Trinity Journal*
TS	*Theological Studies*
TSAJ	Texte und Studien zum antiken Judentum
TWNT	*Theologische Wörterbuch zum Neuen Testament*
TynBul	*Tyndale Bulletin*
WBC	Word Biblical Commentary Waco: Word, 1982
WMANT	Wissenschaftliche Monographien zum Alten und Neuen Testament
WUNT	Wissenschaftliche Untersuchungen zum Neuen Testament
YJS	Yale Judaica Series
ZNW	*Zeitschrift fur die neutestamentliche Wissenschaft und die Junde der alteren Kirche*
ZPE	*Zeischrift der Papyrolgie und Epigraphkik*
ZPEB	*Zondervan Pictorial Encyclopedia of the Bible*

5. General Abbreviations

ad. loc.	in the place cited
b.	born
c., ca.	circa
cf.	compare
d.	died
ed(s).	editors(s), edited by
e.g.	for example
ET	English translation
frg.	fragment
i.e.	that is
ibid.	in the same place
idem	the same (author)
lit.	literally
l(1)	line(s)
MSS	manuscripts
n.d.	no date
NS	New Series
par.	parallel
passim	here and there
repr.	reprint
ser.	series
s.v.	*sub verbo,* under the word
trans.	translator, translated by; transitive

Zondervan
Illustrated
Bible
Backgrounds
Commentary

REVELATION

by Mark Wilson

Early Christianity and Ephesus

On his second ministry journey Paul attempted to preach in Asia but was prevented by the Holy Spirit (Acts 16:6). On his return to Jerusalem, he stopped briefly at the synagogue in Ephesus (18:19–21). Paul finally came to Asia during his third journey, making Ephesus his base for about two and a half years. Through his ministry the entire province was reached with the gospel (19:1–41, esp. v. 10). During his subsequent imprisonment in Rome, Paul wrote three letters to the Christians in Asia—Colossians, Philemon, and Ephesians. After his release he stopped briefly in Ephesus, leaving Timothy to deal with problems in the church there (1 Tim. 1:3). He later wrote two letters to Timothy in Ephesus.

ISLAND OF PATMOS

A view of the bay.

Revelation
IMPORTANT FACTS:

- ▪ **AUTHOR:** John.
- ▪ **DATE:** c. 69 (early date) or 95 (late date).
- ▪ **OCCASION:**
  - To prepare believers in Asia for the coming of Jesus.
  - To expose false teaching and ungodly behavior in the seven churches.
  - To reveal the divine judgments to fall on the unrepentant.
  - To exhort believers to persevere despite persecution and hardship.
- ▪ **THEMES:**
  1. God, ruling from his divine throne, is the sovereign Lord of history.
  2. Jesus as the sacrificial Lamb is victorious over Satan and the world.
  3. The world system typified by Babylon and the two beasts is opposed to God and his people.
  4. The saints who overcome will receive eternal rewards in the new heaven and new earth.

How Peter developed a relationship with the church in Asia is unknown. Although the New Testament never states that Peter traveled through Asia Minor (also called Anatolia, modern Turkey), he most likely did on his way to Corinth (1 Cor. 1:12) and Rome (1 Peter 5:13). Peter later wrote to the church in Anatolia, with the province of Asia named specifically in his greeting (1 Peter 1:1).

The New Testament is also silent on how John came to reside in Asia. Church tradition relates that a community of Christians migrated to Asia from Judea in A.D. 66 at the beginning of the Jewish revolt. Philip and his daughters settled in Hierapolis, while John and his community located around Ephesus. The early church fathers, such as Polycrates and Irenaeus, provide the literary evidence for John's ministry in Asia. The book of Revelation, along with the Gospel and Letters of John, all have their provenance in and around Ephesus.[1]

Historical Background

The writing of Revelation has been placed either in the decade of the 60s or the 90s of the first century A.D. The later date is suggested in a statement by the church father Irenaeus (late second century) that Revelation was seen at the end of the reign of the emperor Domitian (A.D. 81–96).[2] Domitian's cruelty is well documented by Roman historians, and the church historian Eusebius calls him a second Nero because of his persecution of the church.[3] Revelation's portrait of mass martyrdom appears to link it historically to a persecution by Domitian. However, late twentieth-century historians have proven convincingly that no persecution of the church occurred under Domitian, only one limited to the Roman aristocracy in his immediate circle.[4]

The early date places the composition of Revelation between Nero's death in

MODERN PATMOS
Orthodox monastery of St. John with its massive fifteenth-century walls and seventeenth-century battlements.
▼

A.D. 68 and the fall of Jerusalem in 70. The *Sitz im Leben* (life setting) depicted in Revelation better accords with the historical situation of the Roman empire during the 60s. After the fire in Rome in 64, Nero began to persecute the church. Many Christians, including Peter and Paul, lost their lives during this time. The late 60s was one of the most turbulent periods in Roman history. In 66 the Jews revolted in Judea, and over one million Jews died during Titus's siege of Jerusalem in 70.[5] Other revolts broke out in Gaul, Batavia, and Dacia. Most serious was the struggle among the Roman generals and their legions for control of Rome following Nero's suicide. In 68–69 the reigns of Galba, Otho, and Vitellius followed in quick succession. In July 69 Vespasian was proclaimed emperor by his supporters in Egypt and Judea, but not until December 20 were his troops able to occupy Rome and kill Vitellius. During the "Year of the Four Emperors" the Roman empire appeared to be self–destructing and its famed *Pax Romana* (Roman peace) lost.

How is this internal evidence to be reconciled with the explicit statement of Irenaeus that Revelation was seen during Domitian's reign? Like Eusebius, Irenaeus may have misunderstood his sources because, at the time he wrote, the identity of 666 was already forgotten. Since Domitian ruled in Rome for nearly a year in the absence of his father Vespasian, perhaps the historical tradition became confused.[6] Because I believe the evidence favors an early date, this commentary will presuppose a date of composition around 69.

Prophetic Background

A prophet named John receives this revelation while experiencing persecution because of his Christian witness. As John considers the present situation of the Asian churches in light of the history of God's people, many parallels present themselves. Moses, the first prophet, led Israel to her freedom after a series of ten plagues forced Pharaoh to free them. Isaiah prophesied during the exile of the northern kingdom (Israel) after its capital, Samaria, fell to the Assyrians in 722 B.C. Jeremiah, Ezekiel, and Daniel were all prophets of the Exile who experienced the capture of Jerusalem and the destruction of the temple by the Babylonians in 586 B.C. The prophet Zechariah saw the Jews return from the Exile and rebuild the temple in 516 B.C.

John sees himself standing in the line of these great prophets, who spoke to God's people during similar turbulent times. He reflects this by drawing much of his language and imagery from Old Testament prophetic literature. Revelation has approximately 150 allusions and near quotations of Old Testament texts, a literary phenomenon called intertextuality. These references are not prefaced with such typical introductions used in the New Testament as "It is written" or "The Scripture says." John presumes his

JOHN

An icon of St. John receiving his revelation on the island in the monastery at Patmos.

▼

audience is familiar with the Old Testament and can recognize the historical and theological background for these allusions. This is why we should be familiar with the Old Testament, because New Testament books like Revelation cannot be understood apart from that background.

The prophetic situation of Revelation's initial audience is politically and spiritually precarious, and these early Christians need encouragement to persevere in the face of overwhelming odds. This has been the power of Revelation's message for Christians throughout church history. Each generation has faced its own unique prophetic situation that has tested its resolve to uphold the word of God. Because the church has entered the new millennium, it will see fresh challenges arise as it moves closer to that final generation that will not only see the rise of the Antichrist but will also witness the return of Christ.

Interpreting Revelation

As the last book of the New Testament and of the Bible, Revelation's position in the canon makes it one of the most important books in Scripture. Many biblical themes introduced in Genesis, such as the creation, garden, Fall, and promise of a Messiah, find their fulfillment in Revelation.

Besides the Gospels and Acts, Revelation is the only other place in the New Testament where Jesus speaks directly and extensively. Bibles that use red letters have Revelation 1:17b–3:22 all in red! Revelation is the only New Testament book where Jesus speaks to churches from heaven as the ascended Lord.

Many readers of the New Testament, however, approach the book of Revelation with great apprehension. Not only are its language and imagery difficult to understand, but its interpretation has generated much controversy. Prophecy teachers present various charts on Revelation that purport to hold the key to interpreting the book. Scholars often differ on how to understand the basic issues surrounding the book. How then is the average reader supposed to make any sense of this book? Certainly the original audience would have understood most of the book. Otherwise John would not have chosen this way to communicate to the seven churches.

JOHN'S GRAVE

(left) Traditional site of the burial place of St. John near Ephesus.

(right) An icon of St. John's burial (in the Monastery of St. John on Patmos).

▼

Throughout church history Revelation has come to be the Bible's most abused book. Numerous sects and cults have had an unhealthy preoccupation with its contents and often claimed to be its only true interpreters. Often such claims have led to tragedy. An example is the Branch Davidian leader, David Koresh, who claimed to be the Lamb of God. His fanaticism led to the disastrous events at his compound, Ranch Apocalypse, at Waco, Texas, in April 1993. Many Christian leaders have used Revelation to speculate about the coming end of the world, particularly with the turn of the new millennium. Numerous popular books and movies have derived end-time themes from its contents. Unfortunately the historical background and audience of the book is often ignored or forgotten in the discussions. By discovering the meaning of John's revelation to the first churches, we will better understand its relevance for us as Christians today.

Prologue and Greeting (1:1–8)

The revelation of Jesus Christ (1:1). This opening phrase functions as the title of the book. The Gospels of Matthew and Mark begin with similar introductory titles. It also declares that this divine revelation is from Jesus (its source) and about him (its content). The Greek word *apokalypsis*, from which we derive the book's other name (the Apocalypse), means "unveiling" or "revelation." Today the word "apocalypse" has negative connotations and specifically suggests end-time cataclysmic events. However, in the early church, prophets commonly received revelations, which were then shared with others (1 Cor. 14:30–31). Paul himself received the gospel he preached through a revelation of Jesus Christ (Gal. 1:12, 16).

The phrase "revelation of Jesus Christ" already had end-time connotations in the Asian church John served. Both Paul (1 Cor. 1:7) and Peter (1 Peter 1:7, 13) used the phrase to speak of the future *parousia*, a Greek word often simply transliterated as Parousia, which means Christ's second coming. This is likewise an emphasis in Revelation, which repeatedly declares that Jesus is coming soon (cf. Rev. 1:1, 7; 22:7, 12, 20).

Sending his angel (1:1). Angels play a prominent role in mediating this revelation vision to John. Angelic mediation is frequently found in other prophetic and apocalyptic literature. In the Old Testament angels are sent to interpret the visions given to Ezekiel (Ezek. 40–48), Daniel (Dan. 7–12), and Zechariah (Zech. 1–6). Angelic intermediaries often appear in intertestamental apocalypses as well. Uriel, Raphael, Raguel, Michael, and Enoch are angels mentioned in *1 Enoch*, while Uriel and Ezra are named as mediators in *4 Ezra*. Angels were important to the religious life of the people in Asia Minor. Numerous Jewish and Christian inscriptions found in Turkey call on angels for protection and assistance. A

grave inscription from Eumena, northeast of Laodicea, declares, "If anyone inters another [here], he will have to reckon with God and the angel of God."[7] These angels were thought to serve as supernatural servants and messengers for God. However, these inscriptions provide no evidence that angels were called on in a mystical sense for visionary revelation.

His servant John (1:1). John identifies himself first as a "servant" (cf. 22:9), a designation used by such apostles as Paul (Rom. 1:1; Gal. 1:10), Peter (2 Peter 1:1), and James (James 1:1). "Servants" (used eleven times) and "saints" (used twelve times) are the two most frequent designations for Christians in Revelation. The author also identifies himself as John on three other occasions (Rev. 1:4, 9; 22:8). Which "John" he is has been debated throughout church history. The most prominent John in the Synoptics was the son of Zebedee and brother of James. John was a fisherman in Galilee when Jesus called him to become one of his first disciples (Mark 1:19–20). He was later named as one of the twelve apostles (Mark 3:17). John and Peter were frequent companions in ministry (Acts 4:1–23; 8:14–25). Justin Martyr, speaking to the Jew Trypho in Ephesus (c. A.D. 135), identified the author of Revelation as one of Christ's apostles. Irenaeus claimed that the beloved disciple who wrote the Gospel of John in Ephesus was the same John who authored Revelation.[8]

However, as early as the third century, Christian writers like Dionysius, bishop of Alexandria (190–264), began to deny that John the apostle wrote Revelation.[9] They noted its thematic and stylistic differences with the Gospel and the first letter, but these can be attributed to factors other than different authors. Papias (A.D.

60–135), also a disciple of John and bishop of Hierapolis, further confused the issue by appearing to mention a second John called "the elder." This seemed to confirm an early tradition of two tombs in Ephesus, each called John's. The early church historian Eusebius mistakenly used Papias's statement to identify this second John as the author of Revelation.[10]

Despite these objections, no explicit internal or external evidence exists to rule out John the apostle, author of the Gospel and 1, 2, and 3 John, from being the author of Revelation. Today in Ephesus there is only one grave site for John, found in the central section of the remains of the cross-shaped Basilica of St. John. This magnificent church was built by the emperor Justinian (527–65) over the site of an earlier church that also marked John's grave.

Blessed is (1:3). This is the first of seven unnumbered beatitudes in Revelation (cf. 14:13; 16:15; 19:9; 20:6; 22:7, 14). Their form resembles the beatitudes spoken by Jesus: "Blessed are the poor in spirit. . . . Blessed are those who mourn," and so on (Matt. 5:3–11). The beatitudes in Revelation are all eschatological; that is, they relate to Christ and his second coming and to the blessings promised to believers in the new heaven and new earth. Their predominance in the second half of the book suggests that the original Asian audience was in view throughout the book, not just in chapters 1–3.

The one who reads . . . those who hear (1:3). The lector of Revelation was undoubtedly John's close associate, who was entrusted with delivering the scroll to the churches. (This assumes that John was still on the island of Patmos when the document was circulated.) Reading

Scripture aloud by a lector was a common practice in the early church, as Paul wrote to Timothy: "Devote yourself to the public reading of Scripture" (1 Tim. 4:13). It followed an established custom in the Jewish synagogues, where Moses was read on every Sabbath (Acts 15:21; cf. 13:15).

There was a practical reason for reading aloud publicly: Only about fifteen percent of the general populace in cities such as Ephesus were literate. Scholars make this estimate based on the large number of extant inscriptions. A casual walk through the site of Ephesus today confirms this abundance of inscriptions. In fact, over 3,750 Greek inscriptions from Ephesus are catalogued, the largest number from any city in antiquity apart from Athens and Rome.[11] In the churches, however, the literacy percentage would likely be higher because of the presence of Jewish believers. The Jews of the Diaspora taught their children to read so they could read the Greek Old Testament, known as the Septuagint (abbreviated LXX). In the remote Galatian city of Lystra, Timothy was taught the Scriptures from infancy by his grandmother Lois and his mother Eunice (2 Tim. 1:5; 3:15).

This prophecy (1:3). Genre is the literary classification to which a particular document belongs. Revelation is an example of mixed genre because it shares characteristics with prophetic, apocalyptic, and epistolary literature. Like the Old Testament prophets, the author of Revelation identifies himself by name. He links himself to these prophets through shared prophetic experiences, commissions, acts, and curses (to be highlighted in the commentary). The Greek phrase *tade legei* ("These are . . ."), found at the beginning of each message in chapters 2–

3, is used over 300 times in the LXX to introduce prophetic declarations (e.g., Zech. 1:3). Its only other use in the New Testament occurs when the prophet Agabus addressed Paul (Acts 21:11).

Often Revelation is categorized as apocalyptic because it shares with other intertestamental literature such features as visions, cosmic dualism, symbolism, angelic mediation, transcendent reality, and imminence of time. Such similarities are readily apparent. But unlike other apocalypses, Revelation is not pseudonymous; that is, it does not claim its author to be a departed saint such as Enoch or Ezra, and it contains paraenesis, or words of exhortation. By calling his work a "prophecy" six times (1:3; 19:10; 22:7, 10, 18, 19), John clearly puts his work in the same literary stream as its Old Testament predecessors, particularly Ezekiel, Daniel, and Zechariah.

The province of Asia (1:4). When the New Testament uses the word "Asia," it does not mean the present continent that includes China. Rather it refers to a Roman province located across the western

REFLECTIONS

BIBLICAL ILLITERACY IS A PROBLEM NOT ONLY IN society at large but also in the church. Most Christians have never read the Old Testament in its entirety. Surveys indicate that few can name the Ten Commandments or the Beatitudes. Such lack of Bible knowledge produces believers who may be ignorant of God's will, dependent on feelings, and vulnerable to false teaching. Revelation's first audience was promised a blessing for reading and obeying its prophetic word. A similar blessing is likewise available for today's readers of the Bible. A renewed emphasis on Scripture reading, both public and private, has the potential to produce in our generation believers who are not only biblically literate but spiritually mature.

third of the peninsula called Asia Minor or Anatolia, the modern country of Turkey. The province was formed about 129 B.C. after the Attalid king Attalus III bestowed on the Romans his kingdom based in Pergamum. Asia included such former Greek regions as Mysia, Lydia, Phrygia, and Troas as well as the islands of Lesbos (Mitylene its chief city), Kios, Samos, and Cos—all places mentioned in Acts.

Asia was one of the richest provinces under Rome's hegemony, and Roman officials eagerly plundered its wealth. In 88 B.C. the Asians joined the revolt of Mithridates, the king of Pontus, and massacred in one day over 80,000 Italian residents of Asia. After order was restored and the Roman republic gave way to the principate in 27 B.C., the Asians became enthusiastic supporters of the first emperor Augustus and his policies. Because of its wealth and secure location, the province fell under the jurisdiction of the Roman Senate, which annually appointed a proconsul to govern Asia.

Grace and peace (1:4). This apostolic greeting is identical to that found in the

ROMAN PROVINCE OF ASIA

▼

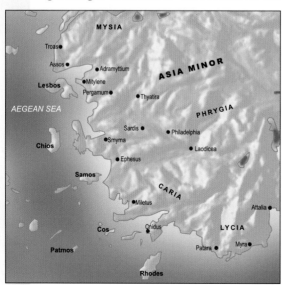

letters that Peter and Paul wrote to the Asian churches (except 1 and 2 Tim.). When these believers heard Revelation's typical apostolic greeting, they would naturally associate it with the letters received earlier from these apostles. These letters were undoubtedly still being read in the congregations. Like other ancient letters, Revelation contains an opening (Rev. 1:4–5) and a closing (22:21) that frame the body of the letter.

From him who is, and who was, and who is to come (1:4). This unique phrase, alluding to the Septuagint reading of Exodus 3:14, focuses on God's eternal nature of past, present, and future (cf. Rev. 1:8; 4:8). As the sovereign God who controls the future, he now uses his knowledge to inform and encourage his people about their destiny on earth and in heaven. Part of this name, written on a carnelian gemstone, was apparently found in Ephesus. The Greek magical inscription includes the words, "for you are him who is," with the wording from Exodus 3:14 in Hebrew on the reverse.[12] The addressees learn that this prophetic writing is from God, who identifies himself in a unique trinitarian way.

From the seven spirits before his throne (1:4). Whether this imagery refers to the Holy Spirit is difficult to determine. However, the parallel prepositional construction with the Father and Son strongly points to such an identification. These seven spirits (or sevenfold Spirit; see NIV note) are seen in 4:5 before the throne blazing as lamps. In 3:1 Jesus says he holds the seven spirits of God along with the seven stars, or angels, the two being closely linked here. Later these seven spirits are described as the Lamb's seven eyes sent out into the earth (5:6).

A possible Old Testament background for this striking image is Zechariah 4:1–10, where the seven lights on a gold lampstand seen by the prophet are said to be "the eyes of the LORD, which range throughout the earth" (4:10). Another possible source is the LXX reading of Isaiah 11:2, where a seventh attribute of the Spirit—the Spirit "of the fear of the LORD"—is added to the other six. The Holy Spirit in his sevenfold ministry is thus presented as the omniscient enabler for the omnipotent God. Since the plurals of Revelation 1—seven spirits, seven churches, and seven angels—all become singular in chapters 2–3, John's emphasis may also be on the distinctive ministry of the Holy Spirit to each church.

From Jesus Christ (1:5). Three phrases follow that describe Jesus: "faithful witness," "firstborn from the dead," and "ruler of the kings of the earth." Each title emphasizes a distinctive theme related to Christ's work and ministry—the cross, resurrection, and ascension—developed later in the book. The messianic king from the Davidic line promised in Psalm 89 is called "my firstborn" (Ps. 89:27) and "faithful witness" (89:37). Paul, writing to the Colossians, likewise calls Jesus "the firstborn from among the dead" (Col. 1:18). Colosse was located only eleven miles southeast of Laodicea, and Paul's letter was known to the Christians there (4:16). The Laodicean title describing Jesus as "the ruler of God's creation" (Rev. 3:14) also parallels language found in Colossians 1:15, "the firstborn over all creation." In Revelation the kings of the earth consistently oppose God (e.g., 16:14, 16; 19:19). The question whether Christ or Caesar is sovereign is answered immediately in the book: Christ is!

To him who loves us and has freed us from our sins by his blood, and has made us to be a kingdom and priests to serve his God and Father (1:5b–6). John erupts in praise as he recalls four things that Christ has done for the people of God. Jesus loves them and has redeemed them by his blood. As Jesus expressed it, "greater love has no one than this, that he lay down his life for his friends" (John 15:13). The promise to be a kingdom and priests recalls God's promise to the Israelites on Mount Sinai, "You will be for me a kingdom of priests and a holy nation" (Ex. 19:6). Peter saw that promise fulfilled in Christ for all believers, both Jew and Gentile, "But you are a chosen people, a royal priesthood, a holy nation" (1 Peter 2:9). The kingdom of God from an earthly perspective undoubtedly looked powerless in the face of the mighty Roman empire. Exclusion from both the Jewish priesthood and the priesthood of the pagan cults likewise brought religious separation. Yet God promises a ministry to the believers that guarantees rulership in an alternative kingdom and priesthood in a superior sanctuary. In Revelation the word "Father" is always used with a possessive pronoun, emphasizing God's relationship to Jesus Christ (cf. 2:27; 3:5, 21; 14:1).

Look, he is coming with the clouds (1:7). The manner and situation of Christ's coming is now vividly portrayed. Four things will characterize his Parousia: (1) It is with the clouds; (2) every eye will see him; (3) his pierced body will be seen especially by his executors; and (4) everyone on earth will mourn because of him. The language of this verse, set as poetry in the NIV, is drawn from Daniel 7:13 and Zechariah 12:10. Whereas Zechariah limits the looking and mourning to the house of David and the inhabitants of Jerusalem, Revelation universalizes the reference to include people from every tribe on earth. This text from Zechariah is also quoted in John 19:37, but the emphasis in the Fourth Gospel is on the historical witness of the Roman soldiers to Jesus' pierced body. Matthew's version of the Synoptic apocalypse likewise mentions the universal mourning that will break forth at the appearance of the Son of Man before the gathering of the elect (Matt. 24:30–31). Do the Christians participate in the mourning, or is this restricted to only unbelievers? Since only unbelievers are depicted as mourning in Revelation (cf. 18: 9, 11, 15, 19), they are the ones who become remorseful at Jesus' coming when they recognize him whom they have rejected.

I am the Alpha and the Omega . . . the Almighty (1:8). "Alpha" (A) and "Omega" (Ω) are the first and last letters of the Greek alphabet. This title, first attributed to the Lord God (cf. 21:6), is later assumed by Jesus (22:13). Alpha and Omega, like "First and Last" (1:17) and "Beginning and End" (with which it is coupled in 21:6), is a figure of speech stating extreme opposites to emphasize all that lies in between. Here it highlights the eternal nature of God, who is now at work in human history. "Almighty" is a frequent designation for God in the Old Testament. Its Hebrew form (*šadday* or *ṣ^eba'ôt*) is translated *pantokratōr* in the Greek Old Testament (cf. 2 Cor. 6:18). Nine out of its ten occurrences in the New Testament are in Revelation, where it emphasizes his sovereignty and dominion over creation.

MODERN PATMOS
▼

Almighty is always used in Revelation to speak of God, never of Jesus.

The Vision of the Son of Man (1:9–20)

There are four numbered septads, or series of sevens, in Revelation—churches, seals, trumpets, and bowls. The beginning and end of these septads serve as major structural markers in the book. The first septad is the seven messages to the churches in Asia. But before Jesus speaks these prophetic messages to the Asian churches, he reveals himself in a dramatic vision to John.

Companion in the suffering . . . on the island of Patmos (1:9). John's banishment to Patmos was not unique in the first century. The Romans often exiled political prisoners to islands in the Aegean Sea.[13] Two primary types of exiles occurred. The first, called *deportatio in insulam*, could be pronounced only by the emperor and was often given to important citizens who fell from favor. The banishment was permanent, and these Romans subsequently lost their civil rights and their property. The second, called *relegatio ad insulam*, could be imposed by a provincial governor. The sentence could be either temporary or permanent, but normally did not require the loss of Roman citizenship or property. John's exile to Patmos probably fell into the latter category.[14]

Because of the word of God and the testimony of Jesus (1:9). John attributes the cause of his exile to his obedience and witness. The expression (or its parts)— "the word of God and the testimony of Jesus"—is an important catch phrase in Revelation and found nine times. In 1:2 it signifies the content of John's vision, which he sees and records. The testimony of Jesus is, first of all, his own words (recorded primarily in chs. 1–3) and those of his angel, which are directed to the seven churches (22:16). This is the same message that Jesus himself preached during his earthly ministry. It is also what the early church proclaimed about Jesus. The central gospel message, commonly called the kerygma, focused especially on Jesus' death, burial, and resurrection. Because of this testimony, John and the saints are persecuted (cf. 6:9; 12:11; 20:4). The word of God is his commands to obey and to endure (12:17; 14:12), even as it is Jesus' (3:8, 10).

The Roman government, beginning with the emperor Nero, no longer considered Christianity as a sect of Judaism, which was a legal religion in the empire. Instead Rome began to view it as an undesirable foreign cult that was a menace to society. John's testimony about

▶ **The Island of Patmos**
IMPORTANT FACTS:[A-1]

- Population: over 50,000
- Volcanic and barren island comprising about 14 square miles
- Harbor at Skala lay thirty-seven miles off the coast of Asia Minor
- Under the jurisdiction of the port city of Miletus and guardian of its western sea boundary from the island fortress of Castelli
- Small Greek Orthodox church surrounds sacred grotto where John traditionally received his vision
- Home of Monastery of St. John the Theologian since 1088

Jesus Christ was viewed as a political crime and hence punishable under Roman law. His suffering was the price paid for obeying a different King and testifying to a different Lord.

On the Lord's Day I was in the Spirit (1:10). This is the earliest text designating Sunday, the first day of the week (cf. Acts 20:7; 1 Cor. 16:2), as "the Lord's Day." Two later Christian texts, *Didache* 14:1 and Ignatius's *Letter to the Magnesians* 9:1, confirm this understanding of the Lord's Day as Sunday.

This is the first of four times in Revelation when John finds himself "in the Spirit." On each occasion an angel summons John to see a vision, whether of the Son of Man (Rev. 1:10), the heavenly throne (4:2), the prostitute Babylon (17:3), or the new Jerusalem (21:10). Some commentators see these "in the Spirit" experiences as a structural key to the book. The content of each vision comprises the section that follows, with the four visionary blocks framed by an introduction and conclusion.[15] The weakness of this proposal is that the seventh trumpet concludes in chapter 11, and John then sees fresh visions in chapters 12–16 that are not introduced with the "in the Spirit" formula. Also, in chapter 21 the phrase occurs in the second vision of the new Jerusalem rather than in the first, where the section clearly begins. John's prophetic experiences resemble those of the prophet Ezekiel, who was taken in the Spirit to Babylon where he received a vision of the captivity (Ezek. 11:24). Ezekiel was later brought by the Spirit to a dry plain where he saw the vision of the valley of dry bones (37:1).

The seven churches (1:11). When John wrote to the Asian Christians, there were more churches in the province than just these seven. Seven other sites are certain locations of churches in the first century: Troas (Acts 16:8–11; 20:5–12), Assos (20:13–14), Miletus (20:15, 17), Colosse (Col. 1:2), Hierapolis (4:13), Tralles (Ignatius), and Magnesia on the Meander (Ignatius).

W. M. Ramsay conjectured that the order of the seven churches represents a circular postal route that a courier would usually follow along the existing Roman roads.[16] (The modern Turkish highways largely follow the same routes.) Such a route, although not proven, might well have existed. Official Roman correspondence would be distributed from Ephesus to the district, or conventus, centers in the province. The mention of only seven churches suggests that John's use of the number seven here is representative and symbolic. Therefore Revelation was to be circulated beyond its original addressees, even as Paul's letter to the Colossians was (4:12).

"Like a son of man" (1:13). In this opening vision John uses much figurative language to describe Jesus Christ. Similar imagery is found in the visions of a "son of man" figure seen by Daniel (Dan. 7:9–14; 10:5–19). While John's inclination is to identify this figure as an angel, his hair white as wool and snow links him to Daniel's "Ancient of Days." Many of the vivid descriptions and titles of Jesus presented in chapter 1 are found again at the beginning of each of the seven messages, although in largely reverse order.

Out of his mouth came a sharp double-edged sword (1:16). The striking image of the sharp sword proceeding from his mouth is used three other times in Revelation (cf. 2:16; 19:15, 21). In each of

▶ Knowing the Future

People seem to have an innate interest in knowing "what will take place later." Today many seek to know the future through horoscopes, seances, Ouija boards, and fortune tellers. The ancient residents of Asia likewise had an interest in knowing the future. Two of the most famous oracles in antiquity were located near the seven churches.

Claros was near Ephesus and drew inquirers from as far away as the Black Sea. The Roman historian Tacitus, himself once a governor of Asia, describes how the oracle was consulted: "Here it is not a prophetess, as at Delphi, but a male priest . . . who hears the number and the names of the consultants, but no more, then descends into a cavern, swallows a draught of water from a mysterious spring, and . . . delivers his response in set verses dealing with the subject each inquirer has in mind."[A-2] The oracle, in its typical cryptic fashion, apparently fore-

told the death of Germanicus, the adopted son of Tiberius, when he visited it. Five inscriptions have been found at Claros describing the visits of delegations from Laodicea who were apparently regular visitors to the oracle.[A-3]

The other oracle was located at Didyma, near Miletus, and also dedicated to the god Apollo. Its temple was the third largest structure in the Greek world. Visitors brought their questions to the sanctuary where a prophetess, after a ritual bath, drank from a sacred spring for inspiration. Her prophecy, in hexameter verse, was transcribed and delivered to the inquirer by the prophet of Apollo.[A-4] The Asian churches were thus situated in a place where oracles and prophecy were highly valued. The spread of Christianity spelled the doom for oracles, and by the fourth century the pool of potential clients inquiring at these sacred springs had dried up.

---

these texts the sword is a metaphor for the tongue that Jesus uses to speak words of judgment against his enemies. Most of these titles have their background in the Old Testament. (For the intertextual background of the Old Testament references in Revelation, consult the cross references in your NIV Bible or UBS Greek New Testament.)

I am the First and the Last (1:17). A title such as the First and the Last, first given to the Lord Almighty in Isaiah (Isa. 44:6; 48:12), is now assumed by Jesus. Such sharing of titles emphasizes the divinity of Jesus and his equality with the Father. The Greek word translated "Last" is *eschatos*, from which is derived the the-

ological term *eschatology*. Eschatology is usually described as the teaching about last things. However, events are not at the center of eschatology; rather a person is—Jesus Christ, the Last One, the *Eschatos*.

I am the Living One. . . . And I hold the keys of death and Hades (1:18). The figure whom John is worshiping further identifies himself as the One who was dead but now lives forever. John now realizes that he is seeing another post-resurrection appearance of Jesus, who declared, "I am the resurrection and the life" (John 11:25). Following Jesus' resurrection, the angels at the tomb asked the women, "Why do you look for the living [One] among the dead?" (Luke 24:5).

"Death" and "Hades" are almost synonymous terms for the place of the dead in the Greek Old Testament (cf. Prov. 5:5), where Hades translates the Hebrew word *Sheol*. Peter quoted Psalm 16:10 as a prophetic word about Jesus' resurrection: "because you will not abandon me to the grave [*hadēs*]" (Acts 2:27).

"Keys" is a metaphor for authority in Revelation (cf. Rev. 1:18; 9:1; 20:1). The only other New Testament text to use "Hades" and "keys" together is Matthew 16:18–19. There Jesus affirmed that the powers of death cannot prevail against the church and that he has given the church, epitomized by Peter, the authority to allow or forbid entrance into the kingdom. Because of his resurrection, Jesus now has power over death and the grave.

Write, therefore, what you have seen, what is now and what will take place later (1:19). Some commentators regard this verse also as a structural key to the book. A threefold division based on this text states that chapter 1 is what has been

---

▶ The Structure of the Seven Messages

The so-called "letters" to the seven churches are probably the most familiar section of Revelation. Since the book's opening and closing (1:4; 22:21) exhibit distinctive letter forms absent in these chapters, it is preferable not to call them letters. Even a casual reading reveals a similar structure among them. These structural elements have parallels with ancient Near East covenants, imperial edicts, and rhetorical letter forms. However, given John's immersion in Old Testament literature, it seems best to describe them as prophetic messages influenced by such examples as Balaam's seven oracles (Num. 22–24), Amos's prophecies to the seven nations (Amos 1–2), and Ezekiel's oracles against the nations (Ezek. 25–32). Seven sections, or sayings, can be recognized in these prophetic messages to the seven churches:

Address—Command to write to the angel of each church
Epithet—Title of Jesus drawn largely from the opening vision in chapter 1
Praise—Commendation for each church's positive deeds
Blame—Rebuke for each church's negative deeds
Coming—Call to repent with imminent judgment for failing to do so

Hearing—Call to hear and obey what the Spirit is saying to the churches
Promise—Eschatological promises given to the victors who overcome

This structural pattern holds true except for several notable exceptions. The messages to Smyrna and Philadelphia—churches experiencing persecution from the Jews—contain no blame sayings. The final message to Laodicea—the lukewarm church—contains no praise saying. In the first three messages—to the three leading cities of Asia—the hearing saying precedes the promise saying. In the final four messages the order is reversed. Lastly, the middle letter to Thyatira is the longest—230 words in the Greek text—with the characteristic central emphasis of chiastic structure (see ch. 12). The spiritual struggle in the Thyatiran church epitomizes that faced by the other churches. The hearing sayings sound familiar because Jesus uses a similar expression in his parables, "He who has ears to hear, let him hear" (Mark 4:9, 23). Such hearing sayings serve as a wake-up call to his listeners, as he tries to grab their attention. Modified hearing sayings are found in Revelation 13:9 and 22:17, another indication that the original Asian audience is still being addressed in these later chapters.

seen, chapters 2 and 3 are what is now, and chapters 4–22 are what will take place later. However, a better translation of "what is now" is "what they are," that is, the explanation Jesus provides for the imagery. For the symbolic meaning of the stars and the lampstands is immediately given for John to write down. With the phrase "what will take place later," Jesus declares that he is Lord of the future. For the Asian Christians facing uncertain times ahead, this knowledge must have brought comfort and encouragement.

The mystery (1:20). Jesus now gives John the interpretation of two elements of the vision. He calls them a "mystery," even as God's divine plan and the identity of the prostitute/woman are likewise called mysteries (10:7; 17:5, 7). John, like Paul (cf. Eph. 1:4; 3:9; 5:32; Col. 1:26; 2:2), refers to mysteries not as hidden spiritual matters known only to a few initiates, as in ancient mystery religions, but as divine secrets now revealed to all believers.

The seven stars are the angels of the seven churches (1:20). These angels are addressed first in each of the seven messages. Actual angels rather than human pastors are the probable referent here. In the early church the presence of angels

was assumed at the assemblies (1 Cor. 11:10), and, as we saw in Revelation 1:1, angels were an integral part of worship in Asia.

The seven lampstands are the seven churches (1:20). The lampstand, or menorah, was a fixture found first in the desert tabernacle (Ex. 27:21; Lev. 24:2–4) and later in the first and second temples (2 Chron. 4:20; 1 Macc. 4:49–50). The lampstand in the temple was permanently extinguished when Titus destroyed Jerusalem in A.D. 70 and carried the lampstand to Rome as booty.[17] This lampstand is depicted on a panel on the triumphal Arch of Titus erected in Rome a decade later. A lampstand graffito on the steps of the Library of Celsus (c. A.D. 110) can still be seen in Ephesus today. It is one of the few evidences of a Jewish presence in the city. John transforms this traditional image of a single menorah with seven bowls to an image of seven individual lampstands. The Asian churches are thus depicted as holy vessels of spiritual light in their respective communities (cf. Matt. 5:14–16).

To the Church in Ephesus (2:1–7)

Holds the seven stars in his right hand and walks among the seven golden lampstands (2:1). Two attributes of deity are clearly suggested by these images—omnipotence and omnipresence. Jesus is especially present among his churches, knowing firsthand the situations in each. Similar imagery, probably traditional, was used by the emperor Domitian in A.D. 83 to celebrate the deification of his infant son following his death. Coins were issued showing the child seated on a globe surrounded by seven stars. This is

◀ *left*

LAMPSTAND GRAFFITO

This depiction of the *menorah* was inscribed on the pavement near the Library of Celsus in Ephesus.

▶

**TEMPLE OF
DOMITIAN**

Remains of the
temple in Ephesus.

▶ Ephesus

Ephesus (modern Selçuk) was the fourth largest city in the Roman empire after Rome, Syrian Antioch, and Alexandria. Its population numbered over 250,000 residents. An important port and commercial center, Ephesus was the western terminus of a road that ran eastward across Asia Minor. Inscriptions refer to the city as "First and Greatest Metropolis of Asia."

After the Romans created the province of Asia in 129 B.C., Ephesus became increasingly important as an administrative center. In the first century A.D., the city became the official residence of Roman proconsul of Asia. Although a temple for Roman residents to Dea Roma, the patron goddess of Rome, and Divus Julius, the deified Caesar, was built as early as 29 B.C., a temple for the imperial cult was not built in the city until A.D. 89/90. Some scholars who hold a late date for the book see the building of the cult temple by Domitian as the life setting for the conflict with the state depicted in Revelation 13.[A-5]

Ephesus was known throughout the ancient world as the temple keeper (*neōkoros*; cf. Acts 19:35) of the goddess Artemis. The temple of Artemis was one of the seven wonders of the ancient world and its largest religious structure, measuring 220 by 425 feet. Thousands journeyed to Ephesus each spring for the annual Artemisia festival, recalling the Jewish pilgrimages to Jerusalem for the feasts. Although the worship of Artemis is not mentioned specifically in Revelation, it remained an opponent of Christianity in the city until the temple's destruction by the Goths in about A.D. 262. At least fourteen other deities have been identified with temples in first-century Ephesus. The Ephesian Christians therefore had an ongoing struggle with the pervasive paganism in their city.[A-6]

the first of a number of motifs in Revelation that are shared with the imperial cult, suggesting that the latter is a satanic parody of divine truth.

Those who claim to be apostles but are not (2:2). The Ephesians are commended for deeds of hard work and perseverance. Deeds are important to Jesus because he mentions them either explicitly or implicitly in each message. The teaching of Revelation is thus in harmony with that of James: Faith without deeds is dead (James 2:17, 26). One good deed was their intolerance of wickedness, particularly in those who purported to be Christian leaders.

The early church, particularly at Ephesus, was plagued by false apostles and teachers. At Miletus Paul prophesied that even some of the Ephesian elders would tragically betray the cause of Christ by distorting the truth and leading away disciples (Acts 20:29–30). Timothy's primary duty at Ephesus was to command certain persons to cease teaching false doctrine (1 Tim. 1:3). Hymenaeus, Alexander, and Philetus are even named as Ephesians who wandered from the truth (1:19–20; 2 Tim. 2:17–18). When John arrived in Ephesus, this church probably examined even his message. Found to be a true apostle, John now exercised apostolic authority over the church, even as Paul did. The criteria used to examine apostles and prophets became formalized in the *Didache*, a late first-century manual summarizing early church practice. One example is: "And when the apostle leaves, he is to take nothing except bread until he finds his next night's lodging. But if he asks for money, he is a false prophet" (*Did.* 11:6).

Forsaken your first love (2:4). In spite of hardships, the Ephesians have not grown weary in resisting evil. Yet the congregation has experienced a great spiritual fall: They have forsaken their first love. Years of vigilance concerning orthodoxy (correct doctrine) have perhaps dulled their sensitivity to orthopraxy (correct practice), both of which are necessary for a spiritually healthy congregation. Jesus' remedy for the church is repentance and a return to their first work—love. The message of love characterizes the teaching of Jesus (e.g., John 13:34–35). Love

---

▶ **Local References**

Does each of the seven messages contain facts and characteristics unique to its own city? W. M. Ramsay, who is perhaps the best-known advocate for local references, identified numerous features in the messages related to each city's geography and history.[A-7] Other scholars are more skeptical of such supposed links, viewing these associated ideas simply as literary devices devoid of historical connections.[A-8] Since John probably (and Jesus certainly) had a firsthand knowledge of the seven cities and their churches, the inclusion of local references is likely. Indeed the rhetorical situation of each church—suffering, persecution, false teaching, materialism—relates to the life setting of its host city. The vivid imagery often relates to known Asian backgrounds, so it is difficult to deny all local references. Local references are either generic or familiar enough that the audiences in the other churches can understand them. However, the repetition of such images as "crown" (2:10; 3:11), "white clothes" (3:4, 18) and "new name" (2:17; 3:12) suggests that caution must be used in limiting their relevance to localized associations.

for one another expressed in good deeds is likewise reiterated in 1 John 3:11–18.

I will come to you and remove your lampstand (2:5). This is the first of Jesus' warnings to come in judgment if each church does not repent or is not found faithful. With the Ephesian church, failure to repent seemingly means that Christ will close down the church. A less harsh, and perhaps better, reading is that Christ will move the Ephesian lampstand from its leadership position as an apostolic church among the Asian churches and pass its authority along to another congregation. Ephesus remained an important ecclesiastical center until Constantinople gained preeminence in the latter fourth century A.D. The Third Ecumenical Council, which dealt with the heresies of Nestorianism and Pelagianism, was held in Ephesus in 431 in the Double Church, whose ruins remain at the site.

The practices of the Nicolaitans (2:6). The Ephesians are commended for hating the practices of this obscure sect, mentioned again in the letter to Pergamum (2:15). An early tradition names Nicolaus, one of the first seven deacons in Jerusalem, as the founder of this sect (Acts 6:5). However, there is little evidence, apart from the similar name, that this proselyte from Antioch was connected with the group. The word Nicolaitan (literally, "victor over the people") is a wordplay on Revelation's key word *nikaō*, "to be victorious, conquer" and translated "overcome" in the victor sayings. Unlike the true victors, who were to overcome by resisting the existing political, social, and religious order, the Nicolaitans apparently advocated accommodation to pagan society by eating food sacrificed to idols and engaging in sexual immorality.[18]

Eat from the tree of life, which is in the paradise of God (2:7). The imagery of the promise is drawn primarily from the account of the primeval garden in Genesis 2–3. "Paradise" is the word used in the Septuagint for Eden. After the Fall, Adam and Eve were forever barred from eating of the tree of life in the Garden of Eden. The Ephesians who overcome will experience a reversal of the Fall and the restoration of eternal access to God. This promise of eternal life in God's presence is foundational to all the other promises. A possible local reference involves the grove Ortygia outside of Ephesus, thought to be the traditional birthplace of Artemis. This sacred grove, called a *paradeisos*, still

CULT TEMPLES

(left) Ruins of the temple of Apollo at Didyma.

(right) The scant remains of the temple of Artemis at Ephesus. The Byzantine-era church of St. John is in the background.

drew pilgrims in the first century.[19] The paradise available to the worshipers of Artemis paled in comparison to the coming paradise of God.

To the Church in Smyrna (2:8–11)

I know your afflictions and your poverty (2:9). Jesus first assures the Christians in Smyrna that he knows what they are going through. Believers have apparently lost their jobs or their businesses are being boycotted, hence depriving them of material support. Such economic discrimination is well known in many parts of the world even today where Christians comprise a minority.

A synagogue of Satan (2:9). Certain Jews in Smyrna and Philadelphia (3:9) are called a synagogue of Satan. Satan, mentioned here only in passing before his formal introduction in Revelation 12:9, is opposing the church not only through false teachers but also through members of the Jewish community.

The denunciation of the Jews here is not anti-Semitic (Jesus and John were both Jews); rather it is directed at institutional Judaism of the period, which became a formidable opponent of the church. It was the rulers of the synagogue in various Roman cities who often persecuted Paul (e.g., Acts 13:50; 14:2, 19), and Jews from Asia were responsible for Paul's imprisonment in Jerusalem (Acts 21:27–36). In the Gospel of John, written to an

SYMRNA

The agora with Mount Pagus in the background.

▶ Smyrna

Smyrna (modern Izmir) was a major seaport on a gulf of the Aegean located forty miles northwest of Ephesus. It claimed to be the home of the great poet Homer. Smyrna was noted for its beauty in the ancient world. Some of its coins read "First of Asia in beauty and size"—a statement continually contested by its chief rivals, Ephesus and Pergamum. The Roman writer Cicero called Smyrna "the city of our most faithful and most ancient allies."[A-9] Her long-time alliance with Rome began in 195 B.C. when Smyrna became the first city anywhere to erect a temple to the goddess Roma.[A-10]

In A.D. 26 Tiberius chose Smyrna from eleven Asian applicants to become the keeper for the second imperial cult temple in Asia. No archaeological evidence of this temple has yet been discovered.[A-11] A disciple of John named Polycarp later served as the bishop of Smyrna. His confession shortly before his dramatic execution (c. A.D. 156) epitomizes that of martyrs throughout the centuries: "For eighty-six years I have been his servant, and he has done me no wrong. How can I blaspheme my King who saved me?" (*Mart. Poly.* 9:3).

audience around Ephesus, "the Jews" are repeatedly singled out as the enemies of Jesus (e.g., John 2:18; 5:18; 10:31). As F. F. Bruce notes, the Jews here are not the people as a whole but "the religious establishment in Jerusalem, whether the Sanhedrin or the temple authorities."[20] Later, at the martyrdom of Polycarp, the Jews played a prominent role in his execution (*Mart. Poly.* 12.2; 13.1; 17.2; 18.1). For John and the other Jewish believers, the doors of the synagogue have been closed to them, and its leaders are inciting the Roman authorities to persecute the church.

Suffer persecution for ten days (2:10). Jesus confirms that suffering is coming, but the Christians are encouraged not to be afraid. In fact, the period of persecu-

tion will be short—only ten days. Ten days is symbolic for a brief period of time. Daniel and his three Hebrew friends refused to eat the defiled Babylonian food and were tested for ten days. When the period was over, they emerged vindicated (Dan. 1:12–15), as those in Smyrna are expected to be.

The crown of life (2:10). For those who die in the persecution, a crown of life is promised. The victor's crown, or wreath, was an established eschatological image in early Christian literature. Both Paul and Peter told their Anatolian audiences that they would receive a crown at the Lord's coming (2 Tim. 4:8; 1 Peter 5:4). This imagery has an interesting local reference related to Smyrna's topography. The acropolis Mount Pagus, which

---

▶ Jews in Asia

A community of Jews probably lived in each of the seven cities. Obadiah 20 mentions some exiles of Jerusalem who had settled in Sepharad, a likely reference to Sardis. About 210 B.C. the Seleucid ruler Antiochus III relocated 2,000 Jewish families from Mesopotamia to Phrygia and Lydia. Since Sardis was the capital of Lydia and Laodicea was an important city in Phrygia, both cities probably received Jewish settlers at this time.

As citizens in the Asian cities, these Jews could maintain civic associations and were allowed to practice their own laws. When the local civic administrators prevented the Jews from sending money to the temple in Jerusalem, the Jews appealed to Augustus, who confirmed their right.[A-12]

Sardis is the only city in Asia Minor where an ancient synagogue has been discovered. A synagogue, part of a Roman bath and gymnasium complex, has been excavated and restored by American archaeologists in recent years. Although the synagogue dates from the early third century A.D., its

remarkable size and central location indicate the wealth and strength of a long-standing Jewish community.[A-13]

The presence of Jews in Ephesus is richly documented, particularly by the Jewish historian Josephus who makes ten references to that fact.[A-14] However, the synagogue mentioned in Acts 19:8 has never been located by archaeologists.

Similarly, little archaeological or literary evidence exists for the synagogues mentioned at Smyrna and Philadelphia. The small amount of gold confiscated from the Jews of Pergamum in 62 B.C. suggests the presence of only a small community there.[A-15] Lydia probably became a God-fearer through the influence of Jews in her native city of Thyatira (Acts 16:14). Twenty pounds of gold bound for Jerusalem was confiscated in Laodicea by the proconsul Flaccus (62 B.C.). This amount suggests a Jewish population of over 7,500 male adults plus women and children in the city at the time.[A-16]

▶ Nike Christians

Nike, the namesake of the well-known athletic company, was the Greek goddess of victory. She is usually represented as a winged maiden, alighting from flight, holding in each hand her most frequent attributes—a palm branch and a wreath. Numerous coin types that circulated in Asia depict Nike in this way. The Roman Senate installed Nike's statue in its chambers in 29 B.C. to commemorate the beginning of Augustus's rule and opened its sessions each morning with a sacrifice to her.[A-17]

Athletics in the Greco-Roman world were as popular as they are today. The *koinon,* or league, of Asia sponsored games in each of the seven cities except Thyatira. The larger festivals were held every five years in Ephesus, Pergamum, and Smyrna. The leader of the League of Asia, who also served as chief priest of the emperor cult, often presided as the judge of the festival. Major events at such games included running and boxing (cf. 1 Cor. 9:24–27). The winners usually received symbolic crowns, or wreaths (*stephanoi*), made out of olive, pine, wild celery, or bay leaves. Palm branches (cf. Rev. 7:9) were also symbols of victory given to those victorious in the games. The Greek verb *nikaō* is found repeatedly on a well-known Greek inscription dating from 400–350 B.C., which lists the amphorae to be given to the victors at the Panathenaic games in Greece.[A-18]

Jesus exhorts the Asian believers to triumph spiritually over the internal and external enemies confronting them. Victory is assured because Jesus himself has been victorious (cf. 3:21; 5:5). For the Christians who overcome, participation in the future blessings of the new heaven and new earth is promised. These same blessings are promised to us today if we too will become Nike Christians.

loomed over the city, was described by ancient writers as its crown.[21]

The second death (2:11). A connection between death and Smyrna existed in the ancient world. Its name was identical to the Greek word for the sweet-smelling spice in which dead bodies were wrapped for embalming (e.g., that of Jesus; John 19:39). A number of mourning myths became associated with the city, particularly that of Niobe, the Greek mythological figure whose tear-stained face was thought to be etched in the marble of nearby Mount Sipylus.[22] A city associated with suffering produced a church known for its suffering. Second death is not further defined until chapter 20.

To the Church in Pergamum (2:12–17)

Him who has the sharp, double-edged sword (2:12). Two types of swords are mentioned in Revelation—the long *rhomphaia* here, which was used for piercing and cutting (cf. 1:16; 2:16; 19:15, 21), and the short dagger-like *machaira,* which measured less than sixteen inches (6:4; 13:10, 14). The Roman governor of Asia exercised the *ius gladii,* or right of the sword, from his bench of judgment in Pergamum. In the province

▶

PERGAMUM

(top left) A tunnel to the sacred pools in the Asklepion at Pergamum.

(top right) A view of the acropolis of Pergamum from the walkway at the Asklepion.

(bottom) The theater on the side of the acropolis of Pergamum.

▶ Pergamum

Pergamum (modern Bergama) was situated fifteen miles inland from the Aegean coast about seventy miles north of Smyrna. It was the capital of the Attalid empire for over a century (263–133 B.C.). When Attalus III bequeathed his kingdom to the Romans in 133 B.C., the city became the first seat of the new province of Asia. Pliny the Elder calls the city "the most famous place of Asia."[A-19] Its four patron deities were Zeus, Athena, Dionysus, and Asclepius, all of whom appear on the city's coinage. The temple to Athena Nikephoros ("Victory-Bearer") was the most important in the city. These temples were situated on a spectacular acropolis that towered a thousand feet over the lower city. Also located on the acropolis was the city's famous library, which totaled over 200,000 volumes, the second largest in antiquity after Alexandria. After the Alexandrian library was partially destroyed by Julius Caesar in 47 B.C., Pergamum's library was plundered in 41 B.C. by Mark Antony, who presented it to his lover Cleopatra. Nevertheless, the city remained a center for learning. Population projections for Pergamum in the first century estimate over 150,000 residents.[A-20]

he represented the authority of the emperor, who himself carried a sword or dagger as a symbol of his office.[23] The governor's power to render capital punishment gave him the right of life and death in his jurisdiction. As Pilate, the governor of Judea, said to Jesus at his trial, "Don't you realize I have power either to free you or to crucify you?" (John 19:10). By using this epithet in the message to Pergamum, Jesus establishes his preeminence, even over the Roman governor. This image echoes his response to Pilate, "You would have no power over me if it were not given to you from above" (John 19:11).

Where Satan has his throne (2:13). The throne of Satan has been variously identified as the altar of Zeus, the temple of Asclepius, or the shape of the acropolis. However, the church's most pernicious enemy was Rome, who had its tentacles both in Asia's political and religious affairs. The first temple in Asia to be dedicated to the emperor cult was built in Pergamum in 29 B.C. by Augustus. A similar temple was also built then in Nicomedia (moder Izmit), the capital of the province of Bithynia. By the time Revelation was written, emperor worship had been established in Pergamum for over a century. Unfortunately, no archaeological evidence for this imperial cult temple, which is believed to have been built in the lower city, has been found yet. Because Satan was the underlying force in Rome's hostility to the church, Pergamum could be described as his throne.

Antipas, my faithful witness (2:13). Antipas is the only believer named in Revelation who had died for the faith. He was probably a leader of the church in Pergamum. The word "martyr" is derived from the Greek word *martys*, here translated as "witness." Jesus is the first faithful witness (1:5), who is also called the "true witness" in Revelation 3:14. James, the brother of Jesus and leader of the early Jerusalem church, is likewise called a true witness. He was executed in A.D. 62 during the high priesthood of Ananus II by being thrown down from the pinnacle of the temple, stoned, and beaten with a fuller's club.[24] Because the early Christian witnesses were sometimes put to death, "martyr" came to have the connotation of one who died for the faith. The theme of martyrdom is prominent in Revelation (cf. 6:9; 11:3; 12:11; 17:6).[25]

The teaching of Balaam (2:14). The seven prophecies of Balaam are among the most eloquent in the Old Testament (Num. 23–24). Because of his greed, however, Balaam disobeyed God and counseled the Moabite king Balak to seduce the Israelites away from God through sexual immorality and idolatry (25:1–3). In the New Testament, Balaam is portrayed as the prototypical false prophet (see 2 Peter 2:15; Jude 11). The teaching of Balaam was, in practice, probably the same as that of the Nicolaitans (see comments on Rev. 2:6).

Eating food sacrificed to idols (2:14). The issue of eating idol meat is mentioned explicitly in this message and in the one to Thyatira (2:20). Ramsay describes the situation: "In both Pergamum and Thyatira some of the Christians still clung to their membership of the pagan associations and shared in the fellowship of the ritual meal."[26] Eating food sacrificed to idols is one of the four practices from which the Jerusalem council asks Gentile believers to abstain

(Acts 15:29; 21:25). Paul addresses this issue from Ephesus in his first letter to Corinth (1 Cor. 8:1–13; 10:19–33). The raging conflict that tore apart congregations in the early decades of the Gentile churches later appears resolved. Around A.D. 100 the command, probably based on the teachings of Paul and John, is simply "keep strictly away from meat sacrificed to idols, for it involves the worship of dead gods" (*Did.* 6:3).

The hidden manna (2:17). The promise of hidden manna is very obscure. Manna, of course, is the supernatural sustenance provided by God during Israel's forty years in the desert (Num. 11:6–9; Deut. 8:3; Josh. 5:12). Aaron sets aside a golden jar of manna to be placed in the ark as a testimony for future generations (Ex. 16:32–34; cf. Heb. 9:4). When the temple is destroyed by the Babylonians in 586 B.C., its sacred objects are lost. One Jewish tradition claims that Jeremiah rescued the ark with its pot of manna and hid them in a cave on Mount Nebo until God should regather his people (2 Macc. 2:4–8). Another states that an angel hid these sacred temple objects in the earth and is to guard them until the end times (2 Bar. 6:8). Jesus uses the manna imagery in his teaching: He himself is the true bread of God and whoever eats of him will live forever in the age to come (John 6:30–58). During his earthly ministry, Jesus' teaching is largely hidden from the Jews (Matt. 13:34–35) and from his disciples (Luke 18:34). Another idea that was apparently current in the late first century is that the messianic age would be inaugurated by restoring the gift of manna (cf. 2 Bar. 29:8). Jesus now promises to give some of his manna, an image never used again in Revelation, to the victor. Apparently, manna is the spir-

itual sustenance of the future life and suggests eternal fellowship with Jesus himself, the bread of life.

A white stone with a new name written on it (2:17). A white stone had various uses in antiquity: a token of admission, a voting piece, a symbol of victory, a Christian amulet, or something used in an initiation into the service of Asclepius. White stones were also the writing surface for official edicts. One such relevant decree was issued in 9 B.C. by Paulus Fabius Maximus, the governor of Asia. This edict, confirmed by the provincial league, decreed that Augustus's birthday should be made an official holiday in Asia as well as to mark the beginning of the municipal new year. It was inscribed in Latin and Greek on a white stone and set up in the imperial cult temple in Pergamum. The decree was apparently distributed throughout the province because copies have been found in five Asian cities.[27] This was the best white stone that the province could give to its citizens; Jesus has an alternative stone to give to his overcomers.

To the Church in Thyatira (2:18–29)

The Son of God (2:18). This phrase is found nowhere else in Revelation. It anticipates the quotation in 2:27 of Psalm 2:9, a psalm in which the messianic Anointed One is twice called the "Son" (Ps. 2:7, 12). Son of God is the most important Christological title in the New Testament because it describes Jesus' relationship to God in terms of divine sonship. Although each of the Gospel writers uses the title, John gives it a distinctive emphasis in his Gospel and first letter (cf. John 20:31; 1 John 5:20).

Whose eyes are like blazing fire and whose feet are like burnished bronze (2:18). This portrayal of Jesus is apparently a polemic against the local deity Helius Pythius Tyrimnaeus Apollo, who was primarily a sun god syncretized from Lydian, Macedonian, and Greek deities.[28] Jesus is portrayed here as barefoot. Roman statuary occasionally depicted emperors and their families barefoot, an indication that the individual had entered the realm of the divine. Only here and in Revelation 1:15 is the Greek word *chalkolibanos* found in Greek literature. The term was certainly understood in Thyatira, perhaps as the product of a local metal trade guild. Although the KJV translates it as "brass" (an alloy of copper with zinc), it is better understood as "bronze" (an alloy of copper with tin).

That woman Jezebel, who calls herself a prophetess (2:20). Jezebel was the queen of Israel whose idolatrous worship of Baal was condemned by the prophet Elijah (1 Kings 16:31–21:25). Her spiritual counterpart in Thyatira is nicknamed after this notorious queen. Jesus rebukes her because of her message, not because of her gender or prophetic ministry. The daughters of Philip were well-known prophetesses (Acts 21:8–9) who had relocated to Asian Hierapolis with their father.[29]

To ease social and economic tension, Jezebel, like the Nicolaitans, advocates moral compromise with pagan neighbors by eating food sacrificed to idols and committing sexual immorality. Jesus promises to bring spiritual, maybe even physical, death upon her and her followers unless they repent. Some of the Corinthian Christians who had indulged in the same sins had also experienced premature deaths (1 Cor. 11:30). Unlike the Christians in Smyrna and Philadelphia, the suffering of the Thyatirans would not be *for* Christ but *because* of Christ.

So I will cast her on a bed of suffering (2:22). "To cast someone on a sickbed" is a Hebrew idiom meaning to punish a person with different kinds of illnesses (cf. Ex. 21:18; 1 Macc. 1:5; Judith 8:3). "Bed" (Gk. *klinē*) can also be translated as "couch." It is thus used ironically to describe Jezebel and her followers, who reclined on marble couches while dining in the banqueting hall of the pagan temples. Such couches were also used for sexual immorality, as

---

▶ Thyatira

Thyatira (modern Akhisar) was a major inland Asian city in the first century. Standing midway between Pergamum and Sardis on a broad fertile plain, its location made it an ideal commercial center. Many trade guilds were formed that grew to have an influential role in civic life. The city was particularly noted for its local purple dye derived from the madder root. As a result there was a prosperous guild of dyers. Lydia, the businesswoman Paul met in Philippi, was a purple dye seller from the city (Acts 16:14). Syncretism characterized the city's religious life. Outside the city in a sacred precinct of the Chaldeans, there was a shrine of the oriental Sibyl Sambathe. Sometime before 2 B.C. a locally organized civic cult of Rome and Augustus was dedicated.[A-21]

depicted in Greek vase paintings and described in Greek literature. Because Jezebel had used her freedom to lie on a couch of pleasure in the temples, God would instead make it a bed of sickness unless she repented.

All the churches (2:23). Apart from each hearing saying, this is the only direct mention of the other churches in the seven messages. Jezebel's message of accommodation must have appealed to believers throughout Asia, hence her correction served as an object lesson both to the church in Thyatira and to all the other Asian churches.

Satan's so-called deep secrets (2:24). Jezebel and her followers are involved in esoteric teachings that emphasize acquiring knowledge of divine mysteries, but whose source is Satan rather than God. Like their Corinthian counterparts, they believe that everything is permissible and that no sin committed in the body would harm them spiritually (cf. 1 Cor. 6:12–18). Such teaching has parallels among several second-century Gnostic groups, which likewise advocated eating meat sacrificed to idols and attending festivals in honor of the gods. Another early heresy believed that Jesus was not born the Christ, but became so when the Christ descended upon the human Jesus at his baptism (cf. 1 John 2:22; 5:1). Cerinthus was a prominent advocate of this teaching. When the apostle John spotted Cerinthus sitting in a bathhouse in Ephesus, he rushed back out without taking a bath and cried, "Let us get out of here, for fear the place falls in, now that Cerinthus, the enemy of truth, is inside!"[30] The opponents of Jezebel are to turn their focus instead on the deep things of God (cf. 1 Cor. 2:10).

Authority over the nations (2:26). This is the only letter to have a double promise to the victors who are to do his will to the end. Jesus first promises the same authority over the nations as he himself received from the Father. The nature of that rule is quoted from Psalm 2:9, the only certain quotation from the Old Testament in Revelation. It says of the Messiah, "You will rule them with an iron scepter; you will dash them to pieces like pottery." That rule is finally established when the rider on the white horse strikes down the nations with his iron scepter (Rev. 19:15). The victors, seen as the armies of heaven riding on white horses (19:14), will begin to exercise their rule during the thousand years (20:4).

The morning star (2:28). This striking metaphor is a probable allusion to Balaam's third oracle, "A star will come out of Jacob" (Num. 24:17). The next line, "a scepter will rise out of Israel," repeats the scepter imagery found in Psalm 2:9. The faithful in Thyatira are promised both rule and relationship with the Morning Star! The image of a star from Jacob became a stock messianic expression in intertestamental Judaism.[31] The messianic leader of the Jewish revolt in A.D. 132 was given the name Bar Kokhba, which is translated "son of the star." Second Peter 1:19 is another New Testament text that links Jesus with this metaphor: "And the morning star rises in your hearts." In antiquity, the planet Venus was linked to the morning star. From Babylonian times, it was a symbol of rule. The Roman legions carried Venus's zodiac sign, the bull, on their standards. Therefore, the church and the empire had conflicting notions about what the morning star heralded for the world.

To the Church in Sardis (3:1–6)

A reputation of being alive, but you are dead (3:1). The Greek historian Herodotus records that Croesus consulted the oracle at Delphi about his course of action regarding Cyrus and the Persians, who threatened from the east. The oracle counseled that Croesus would destroy a great empire if he crossed the Halys River into Persian territory. Thinking that the destruction of Cyrus's empire was prophesied, Croesus attacked. After an inconclusive campaign, Croesus retreated to Sardis whereupon Cyrus launched a surprise attack. The seemingly impregnable acropolis was taken through a security lapse, and Croesus and Sardis were captured by Cyrus in 547 B.C. The Lydian king had destroyed his own great empire.[32] Sardis had an illustrious history, but by the first century it was on the decline. The church likewise had a better past than present. Instead of moving forward, it was resting on its reputation, and for this reason Jesus calls it a dead church.

I will come like a thief (3:3). The metaphor of the thief, with its elements of surprise and unpreparedness, is a familiar one in New Testament eschatology. Jesus likens his return to that of a thief in one of his parables (Matt. 24:42–44). Both Paul (1 Thess. 5:2) and Peter (2 Peter 3:10) compare the day of the Lord to the unexpected coming of a thief. In this context, however, Jesus' promise refers not to his coming at the Parousia, but to an imminent coming in judgment. Unless the Christians in Sardis repent and demonstrate their faith through deeds

SARDIS

The temple of Artemis near the acropolis of Sardis.

▶ Sardis

Sardis (modern Sart) is located in the fertile Hermus River valley approximately thirty-five miles southeast of Thyatira and sixty miles east of Smyrna. It was the capital of the Lydian empire (c. 680–547 B.C.) The wealth of the legendary King Croesus (c. 560–547 B.C.) came from the gold found in the Pactolus River, which flowed through the city. As the westernmost point on the Royal Road, the city also prospered greatly from trade. Following Alexander the Great's capture of the city from the Persians (334 B.C.), it served as the capital of the Seleucid empire (281–190 B.C.).

The Romans assumed control of Sardis following a period of rule by Pergamum (190–133 B.C.). In A.D.

17, Sardis was devastated by an earthquake. The emperor Tiberius promised ten million sesterces for rebuilding Sardis and remitted taxes for five years. Nine years later, the city lost its bid to become the home of the second imperial cult temple in Asia.[A-22]

A large Ionic temple to Artemis was built in Sardis, although it was never finished. The population during the Roman period numbered between 60,000 and 100,000 residents.[A-23] Melito was a prominent bishop of Sardis in the second century. He is remembered for his *Homily on the Passion* and for the letter he preserved from Antoninus Pius forbidding the league of Asia from continuing the persecution of Christians (A.D. 161).[A-24]

consistent with the gospel, Jesus will come at a time unknown to them.

Dressed in white (3:4, 5). White clothing is used in Revelation to depict moral and ritual purity. The metaphor is frequently used in other biblical and intertestamental literature. God on his throne is depicted as wearing white (Dan. 7:9), angels wear white clothing (e.g., Dan. 10:5; 2 Macc. 11:8; Acts 1:10), and Jesus appears in white garments at his transfiguration (Matt. 17:2). Those seated at the messianic feast are dressed in white (*4 Ezra* 2:38–40). In the *Shepherd of Hermas*, Hermas in his vision sees the faithful rewarded with white clothing (*Herm.* 68.3). On the other hand, soiled clothing indicates defilement. When Zechariah sees a vision of Satan accusing the high priest Joshua, the priest's sin is represented as dirty garments (Zech. 3:1–3). A minority of the believers in Sardis have remained faithful, and Jesus promises that they will be dressed in white as victors. The Laodiceans are later told by Jesus to buy white clothing to cover the shame of their spiritual nakedness (Rev. 3:18). The victorious martyrs who have been slain because of their faithful witness are also depicted in heaven wearing white robes (6:11; 7:9, 13–14).

The book of life (3:5). In the Old Testament, the book of life represents a register of God's covenant people (Ex. 32:32–33; Isa. 4:3; Dan. 12:1). To be blotted out of his book meant to forfeit the privileges of covenant status. This perspective is likewise seen in *1 Enoch*: "the names of (the sinners) shall be blotted out from the Book of Life" (*1 Enoch* 108:3). Jesus tells the seventy-two to rejoice because their names are written in heaven (Luke 10:20). Likewise, Paul tells the Philippians to rejoice always because their names are written in the book of life (Phil. 4:3; cf. Heb. 12:23). Greek cities in the ancient world maintained a list of citizens in a public register. When someone committed a criminal action and was condemned, he lost his citizenship and his name was then erased from the register. This action, using the same Greek verb *exaleiphō*, is attested by

THE SYNAGOGUE AT SARDIS

The interior remains of the fourth-century A.D. synagogue; the Torah table is in the foreground.

▼ ▶

several ancient authors and inscriptions.[33] Those who overcome are promised that they will never lose their citizenship in the heavenly city.

Acknowledge his name before my Father and his angels (3:5). This promise closely resembles Jesus' statement to the twelve disciples in Matthew 10:32: "Whoever acknowledges me before men, I will also acknowledge him before my Father in heaven." The parallel in Luke 12:8 substitutes "the angels of God" for "my Father in heaven." The text in Revelation conflates, or combines, this word of Jesus, but it does not mention the aspect of denial found in both Synoptic sayings. Since a public forensic context is indicated in the earthly acknowledgment, some kind of heavenly courtroom scene is undoubtedly envisioned for the divine acknowledgment. The Christians in Sardis are thus warned that a relationship exists between their conduct on earth and their final sentence rendered before the heavenly Judge.

To the Church in Philadelphia (3:7–13)

Holds the key of David (3:7). In Revelation 1:18, Jesus declares that he holds "the keys of death and Hades." Jesus here describes his spiritual authority using language drawn from Isaiah. God had vowed to depose Shebna, the steward of the king's palace (and probable vizier over the land), for hewing a grave for himself in a place of prominence among the tombs of the kings (Isa. 22:15–19). God instead promises to give his authority to another named Eliakim (22:20–21). "The key of David"—a symbol of that authority—would be placed upon his shoulder. In Old Testament times, keys were often large and therefore carried over the shoulder. What Eliakim opened throughout Judah "no one can shut, and what he shuts no one can open" (22:22). As a type of the Messiah, Eliakim is to function as the godly administrator of the Old Testament theocratic kingdom ruled by the Davidic dynasty. Peter and the church likewise are appointed earthly stewards of the keys of the kingdom (Matt. 16:19). This same key of authority is to be exercised particularly in the areas of excommunication (18:18) and the forgiveness of sin (John 20:23). Jesus, who now reigns "on David's throne and over his kingdom," is

REFLECTIONS

WHAT WOULD JESUS SAY TO YOUR church today? His message would likely follow the pattern found in the seven letters. After greeting your church in _____, he would introduce himself with one of his divine names. Since most churches have positive features, he would first commend your church for the things it has done right. But most churches also have areas of weakness where improvement is needed. Jesus would lovingly, yet firmly, point out where repentance is required. For those churches living under persecution, Jesus' message would be singular—persevere through the testing and endure. Jesus is still speaking to every congregation today through the Holy Spirit. Each church must hear what the Spirit is saying to maintain an effective witness in its community. And each Christian must likewise obey Jesus' message to overcome in order to receive the same great promises of eternal life in the new heaven and new earth.

▶Philadelphia

Philadelphia (modern Alascehir) is located about thirty miles southeast of Sardis. Its acropolis rests on a spur of the Tmolus range, with the basin of the Cogamus River stretching below. The newest of the seven cities, Philadelphia was founded by the king of Pergamum, Eumenes II (197–159 B.C.), or perhaps by his brother, Attalus II (159–138 B.C.). When the Romans attempted to turn Attalus against his brother, he remained loyal and earned the nickname "Philadelphus."[A-25] The name of the city reflects the love between these brothers. The city was strategically situated at the junction of several major roads and became the gateway to Phrygia and points eastward.

Because of its newness, the city had few religious traditions. An inscription from around 100 B.C. documents the presence of cultic altars for at least ten gods and goddesses in the city.[A-26] The frequency of earthquakes caused the region around Philadelphia to be called the Catacecaumene, "the burnt land." Like its neighbor Sardis, Philadelphia was devastated by an earthquake in A.D. 17. The daily aftershocks forced the residents to abandon the city and live temporarily in the surrounding country-side.[A-27] The only crop that would produce in the volcanic soil was grapes, and vineyards dotted the countryside, even as they still do today.[A-28]

▲

PHILADELPHIA

The ruins of the ancient stadium.

the master Keyholder, carrying the government on his shoulders (cf. Isa. 9:6).

An open door that no one can shut (3:8). The Philadelphians have little strength to exercise their God-given key of authority, undoubtedly because of the opposition of the "synagogue of Satan." Therefore, Jesus intervenes and opens a

door for them that their opponents cannot shut. The shut door has been understood to refer to the excommunication of Christians from the synagogue according to the Twelfth Benediction issued by the Jews at the Council of Jamnia in A.D. 90. However, this benediction only formalizes the earlier practice of local synagogues, which excommunicated those who professed Jesus (cf. John 9:22; 12:42; 16:2).[34] The "open door" metaphor in the New Testament usually refers to an opportunity to evangelize. Paul wrote to the nearby church at Colosse, "And pray for us, too, that God may open a door for our message" (Col. 4:3). Evangelization, however, does not appear to be in mind here since Jesus admonishes the Philadelphians only to "hold on to what you have" (Rev. 3:11), which is not an encouragement for active outreach. Rather, the phrase looks forward to the open door to heaven, which

John is given in 4:1. This same open door to fellowship with God is likewise available to the Philadelphians, in spite of their exclusion from the synagogue.

Fall down at your feet and acknowledge that I have loved you (3:9). While the door of the synagogue may be closed to the Christians, the door to the church will soon be opened by the Jews in a surprising turnabout. Isaiah prophesied that the Gentiles would worship at the feet of Israel (Isa. 49:23; 60:14). In an ironic twist, the unbelieving Jews will worship at the feet of the true Israel (cf. Gal. 6:16). This dramatic acknowledgment that God's covenant love now rests on Jewish and Gentile believers is Jesus' sign to the Philadelphians that he holds the key.

The hour of trial (3:10). Because the Philadelphians have heeded the command to endure patiently, Jesus pledges to exempt them from the universal trial to come soon upon "those who live on the earth" (or "earth dwellers"; *katoikountes*). This distinctive participle is found here and in ten other texts. The earth dwellers consistently oppose God and his will on earth (13:8; 12, 14 [2x]; 17:2, 8). Within Revelation, this hour of trial unfolds through the seal, trumpet, and bowl judgments. Exemption from the hour of trial is not deliverance from persecution in the great tribulation, because those later depicted as slain are martyred at the hands of the earth dwellers (6:9–11; cf. 11:10 [2x]). The trial is God's wrath poured out on the rebellious earth dwellers (8:13), and only the Christians are spared divine judgment.

A pillar in the temple of my God (3:12). Every Greco-Roman city had temples that were supported by pillars capped with exquisite capitals of the Doric, Ionic, or Corinthian orders. Coins from the Asian cities often featured pictures of their civic temples. For example, the temple of Artemis appears on many coins of Ephesus, some showing the correct number of eight pillars that fronted the temple while other types are miniaturized, showing only four pillars. Asian temples were built to withstand earthquake damage. Their foundations were laid on beds of charcoal covered with fleeces, which caused the structure to "float" on the soil like a raft. Each block was joined to another by metal cramps, so the platform was a unity. The temples would be among the most secure structures in the city.[35] This promise of eternal security and safety would certainly comfort the Philadelphians always living with the threat of imminent destruction by an earthquake.

I will write on him the name of my God (3:12). Pillars with names inscribed on them are commonly seen at sites throughout western Turkey today. Two

A PILLAR WITH NAMES

This pillar in the Ephesian city council building is inscribed with the names of the priests of Artemis.

inscribed Doric pillars found at the Prytaneion in the upper agora at Ephesus are of particular interest. In this important building burned the eternal flame of the city's hearth dedicated to the goddess Hestia. Some of the inscriptions found on these pillars list the names of the members of the League of Curetes, a class of priests affiliated with the temple of Artemis. During the reign of Augustus, these priests began to perform both religious and civic duties. Their main responsibility, however, was to oversee the celebration of the birth of Artemis in the Ortygian grove every year. So the imagery of pillars inscribed with names was familiar to the Asian believers. Upon the pillar/believer will be written three names—that of God, the heavenly new Jerusalem, and the new name of Jesus. The significance of these names is further developed in Revelation 19–22.

To the Church in Laodicea (3:14–22)

Lukewarm—neither hot nor cold (3:16). This statement probably refers to the city's water supply. The white travertine cliffs at Hierapolis, in view six miles north of Laodicea, were formed because of the nearby mineral hot springs. Colosse, about eleven miles to the east, was known for its cold pure waters. Laodicea, on the other hand, received its water supply through an aqueduct built by the Romans. Its source was an abundant spring five miles to the south. This water, which had a high mineral content, apparently arrived in the city lukewarm. Calcified pipes from the water system can still be seen near the city's water tower.[36] "Lukewarm" does not refer to believers who lack zeal or are half-hearted, but rather to those whose works

are barren and ineffective. Even as Jesus would spit out lukewarm water, he promises to spit out such Christians.

You say, "I am rich . . . ." But . . . you are wretched, pitiful, poor, blind, and naked (3:17). In A.D. 60, an earthquake devastated the Asian cities of the Catacecaumene, including Philadelphia and Laodicea. Laodicea had accepted aid from Rome following earlier earthquakes. However, after the earthquake in 60, only Laodicea among the Asian cities refused to accept Roman financial assistance and recovered using its own resources.[37] This indicates Laodicea's wealth and civic independence. The key word in the Laodicean letter is "rich" (3:17, 18), which reappears in chapter 18 (18:3, 15, 19). The Laodiceans prided themselves on their self-accomplishments and financial independence. This attitude seems to be reflected in the church, for the congregation apparently participated in the wealth of its host community. The socioeconomic situation of Laodicea was a microcosm of Rome's excessive materialism depicted in chapter 18.

Cover your shameful nakedness (3:18). The city was noted in antiquity for a breed of sheep that produced soft, raven-black wool.[38] This local wool presumably was the raw material for the textile factories that the Romans established here to manufacture the sleeved tunic and the hooded cloak.[39] This industry was another factor in the city's prosperity. A certain irony is found in this figure: Jesus finds his people naked despite the local looms that produced their own version of "designer" clothing. Nakedness is a symbol of shame in the Old Testament and results from God's judgment. Isaiah, speaking of the Virgin Daughter of Babylon, cries, "Your nakedness will be exposed; and your shame uncovered" (Isa. 47:3; cf. Nahum 3:5). Only the white garments of purity and righteousness given by Jesus can cover their spiritual nakedness (see also comments on Rev. 16:15).

▶Laodicea

Laodicea (three miles north of modern Denizli) was situated forty miles southeast of Philadelphia along the Lycus River valley. It was one of several cities founded around 260 B.C. by the Seleucid ruler Antiochus II, which he named after his wife Laodice. Its location at the junction of the main road that ran westward one hundred miles through the Meander River valley to Ephesus and eastward across Anatolia to Syrian Antioch caused the city to thrive as a commercial and banking center.[A-29] Laodicea was the capital of the conventus of Cibyra, and in 50 B.C. Cicero resided in the city ten weeks conducting judicial business.[A-30] Paul's letter to the Colossians was to be read to the church in Laodicea (Col. 4:16). It is possible that the Laodicean letter mentioned in the same verse is the present letter of Ephesians. Although Paul lived in Ephesus for about two and a half years, the readers addressed in Ephesians 1:15 had never personally met him (cf. Col. 2:1). There is no evidence that Paul ever visited the Laodicean or Colossian churches.

LAODICEA

The ruins of the ancient city.

Salve to put on your eyes, so you can see (3:18). Laodicea was the home of a medical school in the first century.[40] One of its graduates was Demosthenes Philalethes, a renowned ophthalmologist who wrote an influential textbook on the eye. An ancient healing formula called Phrygian powder was also linked with the city. Zinc and alum were common in the area and formed the active elements in the popular eyesalves marketed by the city's merchants.[41] Thus, this image is also rich in irony: The Laodiceans live in a place noted for its treatment of the eye, yet they are spiritually blind.

I stand at the door and knock (3:20). Holman Hunt's famous painting, *The Light of the World*, shows Jesus standing at a door and knocking to enter. Who is to receive Jesus, according to his announcement here, is not unbelievers but Christians. The imagery is reminiscent of Jesus' parable of watchfulness (Luke 12:35–40). The master's servants are to be prepared for his knock on the door at any hour. In the ancient world, eating together was a sign of intimate friendship. Perhaps this is a reference to the Eucharist where a celebration of the bread and wine occurred. More likely, it is a general meal, much like the love feast celebrated in the early church (Jude 12).

The right to sit with me on my throne (3:21). Laodicea was a "throne city" because Zeno, one of its citizens, was elevated by the Romans to the kingship of Cilicia in 39 B.C. and of Pontus in 36. This was the city's reward for resisting the invader Labienus Parthicus.[42] Zeno's family continued to rule in some measure in Anatolia over the next century. The Zenoid family figures prominently on the city's coinage. The throne was the most visible symbol of the power of an earthly king. In ancient Israel, the king could share his throne with his son (2 Kings 21:1) or his mother (1 Kings 2:19), and such co-regencies were a common feature of the Davidic dynasty in Judah. Jesus thus promises to share his reign in the eternal kingdom with those who overcome.

The Throne in Heaven (4:1–11)

A door standing open in heaven (4:1). Doors play a prominent role in the final two messages to the churches. While

▶ Interpreting the Seven Prophetic Messages

How should these seven messages be interpreted for the church today? One popular approach has been to identify each church with a particular period in church history. Many Christians, particularly in the West, would see the present age as epitomized by the Laodicean church. The weakness of such a typological approach has been its subjectivity. Depending on the creativity of the interpreter, the churches could be linked to a variety of epochs and individuals. Although the seven messages were addressed to particular churches and life settings, each letter was meant to be read by the other churches. The seven churches were representative of all the Asian churches, with their strengths and weaknesses. Such a representative view is preferred for interpreting the letters today. Within the universal church, at all times and in all places, there are churches matching each of the seven churches. In the body of Christ today, churches still struggle with the issues of apathy, materialism, persecution, false teaching, and formalism.

Jesus himself provides the open door for the church in Philadelphia (3:8), the Laodiceans are required to open the door to fellowship with him (3:20). This image provides a thematic transition to the next section of the book. John's next vision shares many elements with Ezekiel's initial vision, which also begins with heaven being opened (Ezek. 1:1).

Come up here, and I will show you what must take place after this (4:1). John hears a familiar voice whose piercing timbre reminds him of a trumpet. This same voice, which earlier instructs him to write to the seven churches (1:10–11), now invites him to leave earth and enter into the heavenly realm. What John sees next is "what will take place later" (1:19). John's heavenly experience is a highly sensory one, filled with colorful sights, loud sounds, and exotic smells, which continue through the rest of the vision. Much of the imagery is drawn from God's appearance to Moses on Mount Sinai (Ex. 19) and the visions of Ezekiel.

A throne in heaven with someone sitting on it (4:2). While "in the Spirit" for the second time (cf. 1:10), John sees a heavenly throne occupied by an otherworldly figure. At his commission, Isaiah likewise "saw the Lord seated on a throne, high and exalted" (Isa. 6:1). Enoch, in his heavenly vision, also saw a throne with the Great Glory sitting on it (*1 Enoch* 14:18–25). John, like other Jewish authors, never describes him, because God declared, "You cannot see my face, for no one may see me and live" (Ex. 33:20).

The appearance of jasper and carnelian. A rainbow, resembling an emerald, encircled the throne (4:3). The divine figure reminds John of two precious stones—jasper and carnelian. Jasper is usually an opaque red, brown, or yellow color, while carnelian is translucent red or yellowish-red. The Greeks and Romans highly valued carnelian, especially in jewelry-making. The rainbow encircling the throne is compared to a green emerald. The three stones are later used to describe the new Jerusalem (21:11, 19). In his heavenly vision, Ezekiel similarly compared the heavenly throne to a precious stone—in his case, a sapphire—and likened the radiance of the figure on it to "a rainbow in the clouds on a rainy day" (Ezek. 1:28). Jasper and emerald were two of the stones in the high priest's breastpiece (Ex. 28:18, 20).

Twenty–four elders (4:4). The appearance of these elders is striking: Their white garments, crowns, and thrones are eschatological rewards already promised to the victors (2:10; 3:5, 21). In Revelation 7:11, they are clearly distinguished from the angels. These elders with their golden incense bowls later serve as representative priests of the saints (5:8). They are also among the heavenly chorus giving thanks for the saints' vindication (11:16–18; 19:4). Twenty-four is a significant number in the temple ministry. Twenty–four divisions of priests rotate

through their ministry (1 Chron. 24:3–19), and twenty-four groups of singers prophesy with harps, lyres, and cymbals (25:1–31). Revelation uses the number twelve and its multiples symbolically; in the heavenly city are the names of the twelve tribes and the twelve apostles (Rev. 21:12, 14). These twenty-four elders are probably to be understood as the heavenly representatives of the Old Testament and New Testament saints.

From the throne came flashes of lightning, rumblings and peals of thunder (4:5). Throughout Revelation, lightning and thunder accompany every heavenly proclamation as a kind of divine emphasis. These phenomena, accompanied by an earthquake, signal the conclusion of each sevenfold judgment—the seals (8:5), the trumpets (11:19), and the bowls (16:18). Thunder and lightning typically accompany divine theophanies, such as God's giving of the law on Mount Sinai (Ex. 19:16; 20:18). And when God spoke to Jesus on one occasion, the crowd nearby believed it had thundered (John 12:29). It is through the sevenfold Spirit around the throne that God executes his will on earth.

A sea of glass, clear as crystal (4:6). Before the throne John sees a transparent expanse that reminds him of a body of water so clear, one can see through it. He likens its clarity to crystal. When Moses, Aaron, and Israel's elders saw the Lord on Mount Sinai, "under his feet was something like a pavement made of sapphire, clear as the sky itself" (Ex. 24:10). Ezekiel likewise saw an expanse that sparkled like ice above the four living creatures (Ezek. 1:22). The Greek belief that crystals were formed like clear ice clearly underlies the Septuagint's translation of

crystal here in Ezekiel. In fact, crystals are an almost transparent quartz rock. Asia Minor was an important source for crystal. The Romans considered crystal a luxury, and a crystal drinking bowl reportedly sold for the exorbitant sum of 150,000 sesterces (approx. $1,800,000). Pliny the Elder recorded that the largest crystal he ever saw—weighing fifty pounds—was dedicated in the Capitol by Livia, wife of the emperor Augustus. When Nero smashed two crystal cups upon realizing that his political situation was lost, his anger was vented in a costly manner.[43] Heaven is presented, both here and in chapter 21, as a place of splendor and extravagance.

Four living creatures . . . covered with eyes, in front and in back (4:6). John now sees around the throne some otherworldly beings. Each has a different appearance—like a lion, an ox, a man, and a flying eagle. These four creatures, clearly patterned after the cherubim that Ezekiel had seen, are, as usual, transformed in Revelation. Such symbolic winged creatures figure prominently in the mythology and architecture of the ancient Near East. Winged creatures dating from 1200–800 B.C. have been discovered by archaeologists at such diverse sites as Carchemish, Aleppo, and Nimrud. At the Phoenician city of Gebal (Byblos), a carved representation of two cherubim supporting the throne of King Hiram (c. 1000 B.C.) have been found.[44] While Ezekiel's cherubim all have the same four faces—of a man, a lion, an ox (or cherub), and an eagle (Ezek. 1:10; 10:14)—each of John's visionary creatures has a single face. These creatures represent God's created order in a unique way. Humankind is the head of all creation and noted for his intelligence, the lion is the chief of the wild animals and noted for his ferocity, the ox is the chief of the domesticated animals and noted for his strength, and the eagle is the chief of the birds of the air and noted for his freedom. Another difference between the visionary figures is that Ezekiel's have four wings (1:6; 10:21) while John's have six. John's creatures resemble the six-winged seraphim that Isaiah saw around the throne (Isa. 6:2). Two of the wings are used for covering their face, two for covering their feet (perhaps a euphemism for genitals), and two for flying. Eyes cover the entire bodies of the cherubim seen both by Ezekiel (Ezek. 1:18; 10:12) and John. These eyes symbolize God's omniscience and probably function like the eyes of the sevenfold Spirit (Rev. 5:6).

Holy, holy, holy is the Lord God Almighty (4:8). Around the clock the living creatures lift up worship to the One who sits on the throne. Their expression of exaltation echoes the triasagion—holy, holy, holy—proclaimed by the seraphim in Isaiah 6:1. The use of this liturgical formula must have been common in the

early church because Clement, in his letter to the Corinthians (c. A.D. 95), encourages them to cry out to God using the same words (*1 Clem.* 34:6). "Lord God Almighty" is declared by Amos (Amos 4:13 LXX) to be the name of the Creator of the natural world. While Almighty (*pantokratōr;* see comments on Rev. 1:8) suggests God's activity in creation, it speaks primarily of his supremacy over all things. Added is his unique name in Revelation: "who is, and who was, and who is to come" (cf. 1:4, 8), which in effect declares that he "lives forever and ever" (4:9). The living creatures begin the euphony of worship around the throne by celebrating God as the eternal One of all time.

The twenty-four elders fall down before him ... and worship him (4:10). The perpetual heavenly adoration inaugurated by the living creatures elicits a similar response from the elders. On three other occasions the elders are seen falling down and worshiping God (5:14; 7:11; 11:16). Worship in the ancient world was more than just vocal expression; it also involved physical action. One gesture

▶ The Living Creatures in Church History

The four living creatures have often been depicted in Christian paintings, drawings, and church decorations. This stems from a popular interpretation that associates them with the four Gospels. Which creature symbolizes a particular Gospel has varied among interpreters. Irenaeus linked the lion with John, the ox with Luke, the human face with Matthew, and the flying eagle with Mark.[A-31] Victorinus in his *Commentary on the Apocalypse,* the first known commentary on Revelation (4th century), made a different association—the lion with Mark, the man with Matthew, the ox with Luke, and the

eagle with John. Augustine connected the lion with Matthew, the man with Mark, the ox with Luke, and the eagle with John. Augustine's interpretation has been adopted by many subsequent interpreters because the inner character of each Gospel seems to accord best with its related creature. Matthew presents Jesus as the messiah from the tribe of Judah, Mark as the servant, Luke as the Son of Man, and John as the Son of God. While such a symbolic interpretation has produced interesting Christian art, it is doubtful that the Asian audience understood the living creatures in such a symbolic way.

▸ Worship in Revelation

A key activity in Revelation is worship. Verbal expressions of praise in Revelation are presented in the NIV in poetic form. In fact, there is more poetry in Revelation than in any other New Testament book. The two poetic hymns in this chapter are the first of nineteen hymns and antiphonal responses found throughout the book.[A-32] Revelation's hymns incorporate many traditional Jewish and Christian liturgical elements: the language of hallelujah (19:1, 3), amen (5:14; 19:4), and holy (4:8); doxology (5:13; 7:12); thanksgiving (11:17–18); and acclamation (12:10–12; 19:1–2).

The heavenly worship portrayed in Revelation sharply contrasts with the reality faced by the Asian believers. At Pergamum, the emperor Augustus had organized an imperial choir to celebrate his birthday annually, with lesser birthday celebrations conducted monthly. Thirty-six members constituted the choir, which performed in the imperial cult temple. They were the cheerleaders, so to speak, for promoting imperial festivals. As one edict of the league of Asia decreed, "One should each year make clear display of one's piety and of all holy, fitting intentions towards the imperial house."[A-33]

The Christians were thus confronted with the ultimate choice: Do we worship God or Caesar? The frequent portrayal of true heavenly worship in Revelation reiterated to the believers caught in this epic struggle that God was the only true object of veneration.

was to bow down by kneeling. The psalmist invites Israel, "Come, let us bow down in worship, let us kneel before the LORD our Maker" (Ps. 95:6). Another action was to prostrate oneself. In the Old Testament this posture is described in relationship to human authorities as well as to pagan deities and the true God Yahweh. Once, after David addressed the assembly of Israel, "they bowed low and fell prostrate before the LORD and the king" (1 Chron. 29:20). The Jewish writer Philo describes how the barbaric custom of falling down in adoration before the emperor was introduced into Italy, which was contrary to native feelings of Roman liberty. When Philo led a Jewish delegation from Alexandria to Rome in A.D. 39/40, the Jews refused to prostrate themselves in worship before Gaius Caligula and thus offended the emperor.[45]

They lay their crowns before the throne (4:10). Crowns presented by a subject to a ruler was a typical act of subservience in antiquity. When Mark Antony visited Ephesus in 41 B.C., the Judean Jews sent an embassy to petition him regarding the injustice to their people. This delegation brought him a golden crown, the reception of which Antony acknowledged in his reply. Such a gift was common practice, for Josephus records the presentation of a crown from nearly every Jewish embassy to the Romans.[46] In A.D. 63 the Parthian royal prince Tiridates laid his crown before the effigy of Nero, signifying his submission to the emperor. In 65 Tiridates traveled to Rome to regain his crown, visiting the cities of Asia on his return to Parthia.[47]

You are worthy, our Lord and God, to receive glory and honor and power (4:11).

The elders now express their worship to God who is worthy to receive three things: glory, honor, and power. Two reasons are given for his worthiness. First, he has created everything. God is first introduced in Scripture as the Creator of the universe (Gen. 1–2). Second, not only did he bring the world into existence, but he also sustains his creation "by his powerful word," according to the author of Hebrews (Heb. 1:3). God's foundational witness to the world is through creation (cf. Acts 14:15–17). Early Christians acutely felt the tension when they were asked to acclaim the emperor as Lord and God (Lat. *dominus et deus*). Gaius Caligula was the first living emperor to claim divinity, calling himself "best and greatest," a title traditionally reserved for the chief Roman deity Jupiter. Nero accepted acclaim as *dominus*. However, it was Domitian who specifically adopted the twin titles Lord and God. Not only did he send out letters under these names, but also demanded that he be addressed by them.[48]

The Scroll and the Lamb (5:1–14)

A scroll with writing on both sides and sealed with seven seals (5:1). In the first century there were primarily two types of written documents—parchments (2 Tim. 4:13) and scrolls. Parchment was made from the skins of sheep and goats, and its name is derived from the Latin word *pergamena*. This refers to Pergamum, which was a center of parchment production and traditionally believed to be the place of its invention.[49] Parchment was more expensive than papyrus, but its greater durability and erasability caused it to become the predominant book material by the fourth century A.D.

Scrolls were made of papyrus from the Nile delta in Egypt and usually written on one side. This was the side on which the fibers ran horizontally, which made it easier to write on with a pointed reed pen dipped in black ink made from charcoal, gum, and water.[50] The scroll that John sees in God's hand is called an opisthograph because it has writing on both sides. In his initial vision Ezekiel also sees a two-sided scroll containing words of lament and mourning and woe (Ezek. 2:9–10). Prophets often recorded their visions on a scroll (cf. Jer. 36:1–32). However, when a scroll was sealed, its contents could not be read by unauthorized readers (cf. Isa. 29:11; Dan. 12:9). Thus, a scroll with its seals intact indicated that

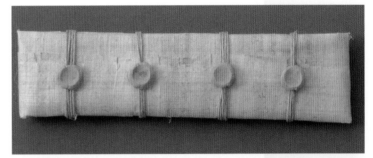

R E F L E C T I O N S

REVELATION'S PORTRAYAL OF HEAVENLY WORSHIP suggests that worship should be an integral part of the Christian life. It is to be more than a weekly experience done as part of a "worship service." Rather, it is an ongoing activity based on our relationship with the living God. Revelation provides a vocabulary for our worship whether expressed through singing, crying out, or shouting. It also suggests various postures such as standing or falling prostrate. Jesus overcame the devil's temptation with this declaration, "Worship the Lord your God and serve him only" (Luke 4:5–8; cf. Deut. 6:13). By worshiping God and the Lamb, we as Christians, in essence, deny worship to the devil's "beasts," who arise in each generation.

▶Archaeologists Find a Scroll With Seven Seals

In 1962, Ta'âmireh Bedouin tribesmen discovered a number of papyri in caves north of Jericho. The American School of Oriental Research purchased these papyri, which included parts of sealed scrolls. The least damaged among these was a papyrus roll sealed with seven seals. After these seals were cut, the papyrus was moistened carefully and the folds flattened. Much of the left side of the document was missing because it was unprotected by the sealings or by the tough fiber strings that bound the rolled papyrus in its sealings. Six turns of the roll revealed only a blank, so the archaeologists began to suspect a fraud. However, on the seventh turn twelve lines of Aramaic script appeared. The scroll was a legal document recording the sale of a slave named Yehohanan and was dated March 18, 335 B.C. All the papyri turned out to be legal or adminis-trative documents.A-34 When John saw a similar scroll with seven seals, he would immediately recognize that its contents were important heavenly business.

a document had not been tampered with and its contents were secure.

Who is worthy to break the seals and open the scrolls? (5:2). A mighty angel rhetorically asks who has the requisite spiritual authority to discover the scroll's contents. God himself is worthy as the Creator (4:11), but no created beings in heaven or earth have the rank or status to do so. The importance of such a document is indicated by who has the clearance to open and read it. John's reaction is profound weeping because he is distressed that the contents of this heavenly scroll may not be revealed.

The Lion of the tribe of Judah, the Root of David, has triumphed (5:5). Finally, an elder announces that someone qualified has been found to open the scroll. His identity is indicated by two messianic titles. "The Lion of the tribe of Judah" refers back to Jacob's prophetic blessing over his son: "You are a lion's cub, O Judah" (Gen. 49:9).[51] In the apocalyptic vision of Ezra, contemporaneous with

Revelation, the lion is interpreted as the Messiah "who will arise from the off-spring of David" (2 Esdras [*4 Ezra*] 12:31–32, NRSV). The second title is drawn from the Septuagint reading of Isaiah 11:1, "A scepter will come out from the root of Jesse." Paul interprets the parallel verse in Isaiah 11:10 in a messianic sense as well: "The root of Jesse will spring up, one who will arise to rule over the nations" (Rom. 15:12). The One who is the Lion and the Root is able to open the sealed scroll because of his triumph. Before his death, Jesus announces his triumph to the disciples, "But take heart! I have overcome the world" (John 16:33). In both sentences the word *nikaō* is used. The victory that Jesus has promised the Asian believers is predicated on his triumph as the Messiah, the basis of which is next depicted.

A Lamb, looking as if it had been slain (5:6). When John looks to see this heavenly Victor, he sees not a Lion but a Lamb in the center of the throne. How-ever, the Lamb is not dead but standing alive in the midst of the living creatures and elders. This is a superb example of John's use of irony. Before God delivered the Israelites from Egyptian bondage, he commanded them, "Go at once . . . and slaughter the Passover lamb" (Ex. 12:21). Israel was to celebrate this festival each Passover to commemorate their deliverance (12:1–14). The unblemished lambs set apart for the Passover sacrifice were ritually slaughtered with their throats cut between the collarbones. This ritual slaughter mark on the neck allows John to identify the peculiar nature of this Lamb.[52] Lamb is the most common title for Jesus in Revelation and is used twenty-eight times.

He had seven horns and seven eyes (5:6). Juxtaposed on the Lamb in surreal fashion are seven horns and seven eyes. Horns are a biblical metaphor for power. Asaph exclaims, "I will cut off the horns of all the wicked, but the horns of the righteous will be lifted up" (Ps. 75:10). Seven, the biblical number of complete-ness or perfection, describes the absolute power and authority of the Lamb. The equality of the One on the throne (Rev. 4:5) and the Lamb is suggested because both possess the sevenfold Spirit.

Each one had a harp and they were holding golden bowls full of incense, which are the prayers of the saints (5:8). After the Lamb takes the scroll from the One who is sitting on the throne, the living creatures and the elders fall down in worship before him. In the left hand of each elder is a harp. The ancient harp was a stringed instrument apparently invented by Jubal (Gen. 4:21). Its portability and rich sound combined to make it Israel's favorite instrument. David was proficient on the harp (1 Sam. 16:15–23), and many of his psalms were to be sung to its accompaniment (e.g., Pss. 4, 6, 54, 55). The Levites prophesied and offered praise to God in the temple accompanied by harps, lyres, and cymbals (1 Chron. 25:1–8; 2 Chron. 5:11–13). As part of their worship, Paul encourages the Asian

---

▸ Sacrifices in the Ancient World

Animal sacrifice not only characterized the worship of the Jews, but also that of the Greeks and Romans. The Jews could only offer sacrifices at the temple in Jerusalem. Therefore, Jews from Asia and other parts of the Diaspora would travel to the Holy City for the annual feasts (e.g., Acts 2:1–11). Sacrifices to the pagan gods occurred in every Greco-Roman city with a temple. The Greek religious calendar (several of which still survive today) included a list of sacrifices, indicating which god or hero was to receive the offering on a given day. Most commonly, the thighbones of slaughtered animals, wrapped in fat, were burned on a raised altar for the gods. The meat was then cooked and eaten by the priests and priestesses and those sacrificing.[A-35]

Often the remainder of the carcass was sold at the public meat market, the macellum. This issue of meat sacrificed to idols was a problem in the churches at Ephesus, Pergamum, and Thyatira. Pliny the Younger reported in the early second century that Christianity had become so successful in Bithynia and Pontus that the sacred rites at temples had lapsed and no one would buy the flesh of the sacrificial victims. He pointed out to the emperor Trajan, however, that his policies had successfully reversed this trend and sacrifices were again being offered.[A-36]

Christians to "sing psalms, hymns and spiritual songs" (Col. 3:16). This singing was probably accompanied by a harp.

The elders hold golden bowls of incense in their right hands. These censers are designed to fit in the palm of the hand. Bowls similar to these have been found at archaeological sites throughout the Near East. Twelve golden censers, each weighing ten shekels (4 oz.), were given by the tribal leaders of Israel for worship in the tabernacle (Num. 7:14, 20). Solomon later made similar bowls for use in the temple (2 Chron. 4:22), and these were among the items taken by the Babylonians when they pillaged the temple (2 Kings 25:15). While the harps represent the praise of the saints, the golden incense bowls represent their prayers (cf. Rev. 8:3). David expressed their liturgical relationship, stating: "May my prayer be set before you like incense" (Ps. 141:2).

They sang a new song (5:9). New songs are sung before the throne three times in Revelation: here by the elders, in 14:3 by the 144,000, and in 15:3 by all the victors. This singing fulfills the prophecy in Isaiah 42:10 where the nations are exhorted to sing a new song because the Lord will make his servant "a covenant for the people and a light for the Gentiles" (42:6). Isaiah's servant songs (chaps. 42–53) provide a rich prophetic background for John's imagery.

You were slain, and with your blood you purchased men for God (5:9). "You are worthy," the same words addressed in Revelation 4:11 to the Lord God, are now sung to the Lamb by the elders. His death fulfills Isaiah's prophecy of the servant who "was led like a lamb to the slaughter" (Isa. 53:7). Jesus the Lamb was slain willingly and purchased people with his blood. The Greek word *agorazō*, translated "purchased," is a term of the public marketplace. Every Greco-Roman city had a marketplace called the agora, or forum, where slaves would be bought and sold. Here the metaphor of the slave auction is used to describe Christ's spiritual purchase of individuals for God (cf. Rev. 14:4). Peter used similar language when he addressed the Asian church, "It was not with perishable things such as silver or gold that you were redeemed . . . but with the precious blood of Christ, a lamb without blemish or defect" (1 Peter 1:18–19).

From every tribe and language and people and nation (5:9). In Revelation salvation is always portrayed as a gift for both Jews and Gentiles. The ethnocentrism of Judaism was superceded by the universal nature of the gospel. As Jesus commanded, "Therefore go and make disciples of all nations" (Matt. 28:19). Such universalism is marked with this inclusive terminology—tribe, language, people, and nation—used six other times in Revelation but always with variations (cf. 7:9; 10:11; 11:9; 13:7; 14:6; 17:15). Such language certainly has a background in Daniel who saw in his vision the Ancient of Days worshiped by "all peoples, nations and men of every language" (Dan. 7:14). The Table of Nations found in Genesis 10 documents the dispersion of the descendants of Noah according to clans, languages, territories, and nations (10:5, 20, 31). From the total of this list, the Jews deduced that there were seventy nations in the world.

You have made them to be a kingdom and priests (5:10). Christ's redemption made all believers "a kingdom and priests" (cf. 1:5–6). His people will reign on the earth as kings. Whether this reign is to be physical or spiritual, to be on the present earth or the new earth, is left unstated at this time. However, the priestly duties are now spiritual and to be performed through the ministry of praise and prayer. Because the early church had no temple or formal priesthood, the pagans regarded Christians as atheists. At his trial in Smyrna, Polycarp was asked by the Roman proconsul to repent by saying, "Away with the atheists!" meaning the Christians. Rather than renounce his congregation and his Lord, Polycarp instead looked at the lawless heathen gathered in the stadium and exclaimed, "Away with the atheists!" (*Mart. Poly.* 9.2–3). Shortly after he was burned at the stake.

The voice of many angels, numbering thousands upon thousands and ten thousand times ten thousand (5:11). John now gives his attention to a spectacle around the throne so extravagant that the number of its participants is incalculable. Similar descriptions of angels in heaven in Daniel 7:10 and Hebrews 12:22 suggest it is impossible to count them. Enoch in his vision of heaven saw tens of millions of angels around the throne (*1 Enoch* 14:22). The angels form a part of the ever-widening circle of worshipers around the throne beyond that of the living creatures and elders. Their song echoes that of the elders: The Lamb who is slain is worthy. Seven attributes are now named, which the Lamb is to receive: power, wealth, wisdom, strength, honor, glory, and praise. David lavished similar praise upon the God of Israel: "Yours, O LORD, is the greatness and the power and the glory and the majesty and the splendor, for everything in heaven and earth is yours" (1 Chron. 29:11).

Every creature in heaven and on earth and under the earth and on the sea . . . singing (5:13). In the Old Testament, the natural order is often depicted as participating in the praise of God (cf. Isa. 55:12). In Psalm 96 the psalmist exhorts, "Sing to the LORD a new song; sing to the LORD, all the earth." Here the created order is singing such a new song. Paul wrote that creation groans as it awaits its total freedom in the new created order (Rom. 8:19–22). Nevertheless, all creation is now seen rejoicing over its Creator who has made such final liberation possible. Their praise is directed both to God on the throne and to the Lamb. For the first time in Revelation, the two together become the focus of praise. Glory, honor, and power—prerogatives attributed to the Lord God in Revelation 4:11 and to the Lamb in 5:12—are now shared by both.

REFLECTIONS

CHRISTIANITY'S PRESENTATION OF a religious priesthood with no animal sacrifices must have been truly radical in the first century. The sacrificial demands of the new covenant are quite different. Our financial offerings are to be cheerful and heartfelt sacrifices, moving beyond a mandated tithe (2 Cor. 9:7; Phil. 4:18). Our ongoing prayer and praise is now to rise heavenward as spiritual offerings (Heb. 13:15; Rev. 5:8). Finally, our own bodies are to be offered sacrificially as a regular spiritual act of worship (Rom. 12:1–2). Through such spiritual sacrifices, our lives become acceptable, pleasing, and holy to God.

The four living creatures said, "Amen" (5:14). The living creatures and the twenty-four elders reappear one last time to close this great heavenly scene. The living creatures, caught up in worship, close with a simple "Amen," while the elders silently prostrate themselves again before the throne.

The First Six Seals (6:1–17)

The Lamb opened the first of the seven seals (6:1). Only one person is authorized to open the heavenly scroll, and the victorious Lamb now breaks each of its seals, one by one. The living creatures take turns inviting John to look at four horsemen who are released at the unfastening of the first four seals. The prophet Zechariah likewise saw riders on colored horses who were sent forth into the earth (Zech. 1:8–11). The color of each horse symbolizes the reality it represents: white for victory, red for blood, black for famine, and pale (gray) for death. While the scroll itself represents the broader destiny of humanity, the seals appear to represent a specific historical period, from the ascension of Jesus to the fall of Jerusalem (A.D. 30–70). This is suggested by the close correlation between the first six seals and Jesus' prediction of events to be fulfilled within a generation (see "False Christs"). By opening the first seal, Jesus precipitates the apocalyptic situation prophesied in the Synoptics and whose fulfillment is now seen in Revelation. The "birth pains" have indeed begun (Matt. 24:8).

right ▶

SEAL

Jasper seal bearing the inscription "Amos the Scribe" (seventh century B.C.).

▶ False Christs

False Christs have appeared periodically throughout history. Numerous false prophets appeared during the Jewish revolt. One named Jesus prophesied for seven and a half years in Jerusalem, crying, "Woe to Jerusalem!"[A-37] In recent years, Jerusalem has been the focal point for a "messiah syndrome." The Israeli police have a special unit to deal with individuals who appear claiming to be the Messiah. One of the most unusual incidents in the history of Messianism relates to Smyrna. Sabbatai Zevi was born there in 1626 to a prosperous Jewish broker. Sabbatai was a manic-depressive visionary who was expelled from the city by the other rabbis in the 1650s. He wandered around the east for a decade, but in the summer of 1665 returned to Smyrna where he became the center of a messianic frenzy. Hysterical scenes of mass repentance, which began in Smyrna's streets, soon spread throughout the entire Jewish world. When news of Sabbatai's messianic claims reached England, it heightened the expectations of Christians there that the year 1666 was to be apocalyptic. However, Sabbatai was arrested by the Turks and in September 1666 brought before the Sultan. Faced with the choice of death or conversion, Sabbatai became a Muslim. Many of his disciples followed him into Islam, while others refused to believe his apostasy.[A-38] The fact that Christians became involved in his movement shows the church's susceptibility to date-setting and to messianic claims, particularly Jewish ones.

There before me was a white horse! Its rider held a bow, and he was given a crown, and he rode out as a conqueror bent on conquest (6:2). Several interpretations for this seal have been proposed. Some identify the first rider with the Parthians, who were Rome's bitter rivals along its eastern frontier. However, Nero secured the peace with the Parthians in A.D. 63 and the Romans had no further trouble with the Parthians during the rest of the first century. If the rider cannot be identified with them, whom does he represent? His description as a crowned conqueror riding a white horse certainly has messianic overtones. In fact, Jesus is depicted similarly at his return (19:11–12). Some interpret the rider as Jesus himself, or closely related, as the spread of the gospel throughout the world. Given the judgment brought by the next three riders, it is problematic to view the first rider's mission as redemptive. What of the rider's bow? In Greek mythology, Apollo was the god who inspired prophecy, and he is often depicted carrying a bow. The bow probably represents false prophecy, whose effect has already been felt in the Asian churches. A comparison of the seven seals with the Synoptic apocalypses (see "The Seven Seals and the Synoptic Apocalypses") validates the interpretation that the rider is a false prophet, the first of many antichrists to come.

Then another horse came out, a fiery red one. Its rider was given power to take peace from the earth. . . . To him was given a large sword (6:4). The sword represents war that was to fall upon the earth, taking away the peace. Ezekiel 21 celebrates the sword as God's instrument of judgment, "I will draw my sword from its scabbard. . . . I have stationed the sword for slaughter" (Ezek. 21:3, 15). The troika of seals 2 through 4—war, famine, and death—is often portrayed together as instruments of divine judgment in the Prophets. For example, in Jeremiah 14:12 the Lord says, "I will destroy them with the sword, famine and plague" (cf. Ezek. 6:11–12; 12:16).

There before me was a black horse! Its rider was holding a pair of scales in his hand (6:5). The balance held by the third rider symbolizes divine judgment. Daniel declared to King Belshazzar, "You have been weighed on the scales and found wanting" (Dan. 5:27). Leviticus 26:26 describes the distribution of bread during times of famine: "They will dole out the bread by weight. You will eat, but you will not be satisfied" (cf. Ezek. 4:16). In the Old Testament period, the balance consisted of an equiarmed beam with two pans; however, in the Roman period the common balance was the steelyard type, which used only one pan and a counterpoise. Balances were normally used by merchants to weigh large quantities of coins, metal, and items such as spices (cf. John 19:39).

A quart of wheat . . . and three quarts of barley for a day's wages (6:6). Products

SCALE

A reconstruction of a Roman scale utilizing the the original parts.

such as grain were measured according to various dry measures. A quart (*choinix*, 1.081 of a quart) of wheat and three quarts of barley were being sold at the inflated price of a denarius—a day's wages. This price was eleven to sixteen times the price of wheat in Sicily during this period. Such overpricing of grain in a famine occurred during the latter years of Nero's reign.[53] A man normally consumed a quart of wheat each day. Because a family could no longer afford wheat, they were forced to survive by eating barley. Hence the famine indicated is only moderate and not life-threatening. Rome received most of her grain supply from Egypt; and when the giant grain ships failed to deliver their precious commodity, bread and circuses were put on hold. In A.D. 51, the emperor Claudius barely escaped a hostile crowd during a grain shortage and resulting famine that left Rome with only a fifteen-day supply of grain.[54] During their revolt, the Jews in Jerusalem experienced great famine. Thousands died as relatives fought over the smallest morsel of food. The most horrific example involved a young mother named Mary of Bethezuba who, because of her hunger, tore her baby from her breast and roasted it, devouring half the corpse. This abomination of infant cannibalism horrified both the Jewish rebels and the Romans.[55] Although this act was extreme, it illustrates how the ravages of hunger can overrule even the most basic instinct of mother to child.

Do not damage the oil and the wine! (6:6). In A.D. 92 Domitian issued an edict that half of the vineyards in the provinces should be cut down. The previous harvest had produced an abundance of wine but a lack of wheat, so the order was issued to correct a perceived imbalance in production. The order provoked outrage in Asia, and a delegation headed by the Smyrnean orator Scopelianus was sent to Rome to

---

▶ The Seven Seals and the Synoptic Apocalypses

The seven seals show a close correlation with the synoptic apocalypses found in Jesus' Olivet Discourse in Matthew 24, Mark 13, and Luke 21. They correspond not only in prophetic subject but also in order and in detail. The following chart compares the seals with Matthew's version. There are several minor differences between the accounts: Earthquakes are distinctively emphasized in the Synoptics, and, among the Synoptics, pestilence is mentioned only in Luke's account (Luke 21:11).

Seals–Revelation 6	Matthew 24
1. False Christ (2)	False Christs (4–5)
2. Wars (3–4)	Wars (6–7)
3. Famine (5–6)	Famines (7)
4. Pestilence (7–8)	Earthquakes (7)
5. Persecutions (9–11)	Persecutions (9–10)
6. Earthquake, solar eclipse, ensanguinal (blood-stained) moon, stars falling (12–13)	Solar & lunar eclipse, stars falling, heavenly bodies shaken (29)
7. Heavenly silence (8:1)	Son of Man appears (30)

The Synoptic apocalypses all conclude with the appearance of the Son of Man. With the fulfillment of these signs and the soon passing away of the forty-year generation (Matt. 24:34), it is no wonder that many Christians expected Jesus to return soon. However, the seventh seal is silent about such a coming, and this difference was perhaps intended to signal the churches that the Parousia was delayed and that any expectation of an imminent return needed to be adjusted.

protest the action. The order remained moot because the emperor failed to implement it. Some commentators see Domitian's edict behind this reference, and, in fact, it is one of the few pieces of internal evidence pointing to a late date. However, famines were frequent in the East (cf. Acts 11:28), and many of the cities in Asia Minor never could produce enough corn for their populace.[56]

And there before me was a pale horse! Its rider was named Death, and Hades was following close behind him (6:8). The pale-colored horse of the fourth seal suggests the appearance of sick persons and corpses. Its rider comes as a pair whose identity is personified. Death is the deadly agent while Hades becomes the domain for his victims. Although the two are here depicted as vital forces on earth, Jesus has already declared his spiritual authority over them (1:18). Death and Hades are authorized to kill a fourth of the earth using sword, famine, pestilence, and wild beasts. These same four dreadful judgments, once promised to idolatrous Jerusalem (Ezek. 14:21), are now coming upon the whole world. Wild beasts, although not mentioned before, are the carnivorous scavengers who now move in to terrorize the decimated populace and to gorge themselves on the scattered corpses.

In the Septuagint, death is the frequent translation of the Hebrew word *debner* meaning "pestilence" (cf. Jer. 15:2–3). Pestilence was sent as divine judgment upon Israel when the covenant was broken. However, if his people repented, God promised to forgive their sins and heal the land of its pestilence (2 Chron. 7:13–14). Pestilence is the probable means of death promised to the followers of Jezebel (Rev. 2:23). The NIV reading, "I will strike her children dead," fails to specify how death will occur. This is explicit in the Greek text: "with death," that is, "with pestilence" (REB). Often pestilence accompanied the siege of cities. Poor sanitation in overcrowded conditions and contaminated water supplies provided the breeding ground for such diseases as typhoid and cholera. (These diseases threatened the survivors of the devastating earthquake in Turkey in 1999.) A plague and its effects on an ancient city were vividly described by the Greek historian Thucydides when Athens was devastated during the Peloponessian War in 430 B.C.: "Indeed the character of the disease proved such that it baffles description, the violence of the attack being in each case too great for human nature to endure."[57] During the summer of 65 when Nero was persecuting the church, a plague broke out in Rome killing 30,000 residents. Pestilence also broke out in Jerusalem due to overcrowding during the Roman siege in A.D. 70.[58]

I saw under the altar the souls of those who had been slain (6:9). With the opening of the fifth seal the perspective changes from earth to heaven. Beneath

◀ *left*

ROMAN RIDER

A coin depicting a Roman soldier on a horse.

the altar John sees a group of individuals who have been slain, even as the Lamb was (cf. 5:9). Because these saints are dead, they do not have bodies; yet they maintain an individual identity as eternal souls. Like John, they were persecuted because of the word of God and the testimony of Jesus Christ (cf. 1:9). Their loud petition echoes that of the psalmist who also asked, "How long, O Lord?" He then cried, "Before our eyes, make known among the nations that you avenge the outpoured blood of your servants" (Ps. 79:5, 10). The song of Moses declared God's willingness to "avenge the blood of his servants; he will take vengeance on his enemies" (Deut. 32:43). Because of God's promise to avenge his people, Paul counseled Christians never to seek revenge themselves (Rom. 12:19).

Each of them was given a white robe, and they were told to wait a little longer (6:11). Here the faithful are depicted in white robes, just as the victors are promised that they would be dressed in white (3:5). These white robes indicate the group's blessedness as they patiently await the time when God will avenge his enemies. The robes perhaps are individual honors of victory given in anticipation of the general rewards to be given at the Parousia. The seal closes with an ominous prediction: More martyrs still remain to be killed to complete the heavenly assembly. A famous early martyr was Ignatius, the bishop of Antioch. In A.D. 110, Ignatius was taken to Rome to be thrown to the beasts in the Colisseum. While passing through Asia, he wrote letters to five churches in the province—to Ephesus, Magnesia on the Meander, Tralles, Philadelphia, and Smyrna—as well as to Polycarp, the bishop of Smyrna. Ignatius

expressed his attitude toward martyrdom: "May I have the pleasure of the wild beasts that have been prepared for me.... Fire and cross and battles with wild beasts, mutilation, mangling, wrenching of bones, the hacking of limbs, the crushing of my whole body, cruel tortures of the devil—let these come upon me, only let me reach Jesus Christ!" (*Rom.* 5:2–3).

There was a great earthquake. The sun turned black like sackcloth made of goat hair (6:12). Various cosmological phenomena characterize the sixth seal. These are stock expressions commonly associated with divine judgment in the Old Testament. Isaiah predicted that before the day of the Lord, "The stars of heaven and their constellations will not show their light. The rising sun will be darkened and the moon will not give its light" (Isa. 13:10; cf. Joel 2:10–11). These Old Testament passages were cited by Jesus in his Olivet Discourse to describe the heavenly signs that would accompany his return (Matt. 24:29). Premature darkness and an earthquake were signs that accompanied Jesus' crucifixion (27:45, 51). The evangelists recognize in these cosmic occurrences a fulfillment of divine judgment upon Israel. Such prodigies (Lat. *prodigia*) were likewise understood by the Romans to be portents warning of divine wrath. Roman historians often listed the prodigies that were observed annually or those seen accompanying important historical events. During the reigns of Tiberius (A.D. 14–37) and Claudius (A.D. 41–54), Tacitus noted that few prodigies occurred; however, during Nero's reign (A.D. 54–68) prodigies multiplied. At the end of the tumultuous year A.D. 69, he observes that "there were prodigies in the sky and on the earth, warnings given by thunderbolts, and prophecies of the future, both joyful and gloomy, uncertain and clear."[59] The Jewish historian Josephus writing for a Roman audience, mentioned numerous prodigies that were seen around Jerusalem before its fall. A star resembling a sword hung over the city as well as a comet that lasted a year. One night in the temple a light illuminated the sanctuary and the altar for half an hour. Josephus concluded that the Jews imprudently ignored these warnings from God and hence were conquered.[60]

The whole moon turned blood red (6:12). This vivid image echoes Joel who declared that God would turn "the moon to blood before the coming of the great and dreadful day of the LORD" (Joel 2:31). This lunar phenomenon is called an ensanguinal moon and depicts the deep copper color that the moon assumes during a total eclipse. Such an eclipse occurred on October 18, 69. The historian K. Wellesley gives this vivid description of the prodigy: "The moon itself was turned to blood. Its eclipse, which entered its maximum phase of near totality at 9.50 p.m., four hours after dusk, gives it a sinister copper-coloured appearance as the light of the sun, drained of its blue component, was refracted round the earth by the latter's atmosphere, and fell dimly upon the almost full orb of the moon. This must surely be a portent of disaster and death."[61] Seven days later Vitellius' army

▶ Roman Society

Ancient Roman society was highly stratified and divided into legal groups. The seven groups mentioned in 6:15 approximately parallel the Roman social order. At the top was the emperor (*imperator* or *princeps*) and his household (*familia Caesaris*). Allied client kings, like Herod, ruled the frontiers of the empire not yet incorporated as provinces. The "princes" were the ruling elite of Roman society who filled the principal civic magistracies by serving as quaestors, praetors, and consuls. Highest were the senators (*senatores*) who numbered approximately six hundred and held property worth at least one million sesterces. During the first century wealthy individuals from provinces like Asia were gradually admitted into the Senate.

Next were the equestrians (*equites*) who numbered several thousand members. Membership came through birth or appointment by the emperor and property holdings of 400,000 sesterces. From these ranks came the generals (*tribuni militum*), who commanded Rome's twenty-eight legions stationed along the empire's frontier.[A-39] These generals had great influence over their troops, and it was four generals and governors—Galba, Otho, Vitellius, and Vespasian—who used their legions to vie for the principate following Nero's suicide.

In each city of the empire was a group of the one hundred most "mighty" men called *decuriones*. Some *decuriones* in the Roman cities were also citizens. Roman citizenship was a further important social distinction. In the first century, a minority of individuals outside of Italy were Roman citizens. Paul's status as a citizen (Acts 16:37; 22:25–29) was therefore unique, particularly in the eastern provinces. Following these groups were the freeborn urban plebs and the rural peasantry. The rest of the population was divided between the free persons and the slaves. Slaves were common throughout the empire because its economy was based on slave labor. At least one third of the residents of a major urban center like Ephesus would be slaves, suggesting around 100,000 slaves among its populace. The early church, reflecting the society at large, had great social diversity among its members—rich and poor, free and slave. [A-40]

was completely routed at the second Battle of Cremona, ensuring the accession of Vespasian as emperor.

Fall on us and hide us from the face of him who sits on the throne and from the wrath of the Lamb! (6:16). This is the desperate cry of the inhabitants of the earth, whom John classifies in a sevenfold manner (see "Roman Society"). Their retreat to caves is again a stock reaction to God's judgment: "Men will flee to caves in the rocks and to holes in the ground from dread of the LORD" (Isa. 2:19, cf. 2:10, 21). At last the earth dwellers recognize the source of their woes—the One on the throne and the Lamb. The day of divine wrath has finally arrived, and no one can resist God's purposes any longer. The Lamb who loved and shed his blood for the sins of his people (Rev. 1:5) is here described as the same Lamb whose wrath is so great that the wicked cannot stand against it.

The Sealing of the 144,000 (7:1–8)

Four angels standing at the four corners of the earth, holding back the four winds (7:1). The successive opening of the seals has fulfilled all the necessary earthly and heavenly signs. Yet the destructive winds that will initiate the day of the Lord are held back. In Jewish thought, four winds stood at each corner of the compass. These winds could either destroy a nation (Jer. 49:36) or bring new life (Ezek. 37:9). In Zechariah these winds are personified as chariots pulled by different colored teams of horses, which go out from the presence of the Lord throughout the earth (Zech. 6:5–7). At his second coming, Jesus taught that the angels "will gather his elect from the four

winds, from one end of the heavens to the other" (Matt. 24:31). Although that time is near, a divine pause is introduced in the tension.

A seal on the foreheads (7:3). Another angel commands the angels holding the four winds not to harm the earth until the seal of the living God is dispensed. A seal, which was used to authenticate the heavenly scroll, is now placed on the foreheads of God's servants. The Old Testament background for this sealing is found in Ezekiel 9, although its specific nature will not be discussed until Revelation 14:1. The seal functions similarly in Revelation, separating God's servants from the faithless earth dwellers and marking those who are to be exempted from the coming divine judgments. Because of such marking, a Jewish author who wrote after Pompey desolated the temple in Jerusalem (63 B.C.) declared that famine and sword and death "will retreat from the devout like those pursued by famine. But they shall pursue sinners and overtake them" (*Pss. Sol.* 15:7–8). In antiquity, foreheads were often marked to designate slaves or devotees of a deity (*3 Macc.* 2:29).

Sealing assumed a more symbolic interpretation in early Christian theology. Paul taught the Asian churches that "you were marked in him with a seal, the promised Holy Spirit" (Eph. 1:13; cf. 4:30). However, this seal of ownership is placed in the heart (2 Cor. 1:22). Paul spoke of another kind of seal that God places on the faithful in Ephesus to distinguish them from the false teachers and their wicked acts (2 Tim. 2:19).

Those who were sealed: 144,000 from all the tribes of Israel (7:4). The sealing that was announced is now described as a completed task. The number and identity of the sealed are given next: 12,000 (12 times 1,000) are sealed from each tribe of Israel. The twelve tribes of Israel are listed numerous times in the Bible (e.g., Gen. 35:23–26; 49:3–27; Deut. 33:6–25), and Reuben as the firstborn usually heads these lists. Revelation's list has several notable differences. Judah is listed first because from this tribe came the Lion of Judah, the firstborn from the dead (cf. Rev. 1:5; 5:5). John also includes Manasseh, the firstborn of Joseph, while omitting his younger brother Ephraim. Dan is also omitted, and it has been suggested that this omission occurred because of Dan's role as an apostate worship center in northern Israel (1 Kings 12:29–30). The church father Irenaeus postulated that Dan was omitted because the antichrist was to come from this tribe, a belief based on the Septuagint reading of Jeremiah 8:16: "From Dan we will hear the sound of swift horses."[62] Both are dubious suggestions since Dan is mentioned first among the tribes to receive land in the restored Israel (Ezek. 48:1). No satisfactory explanation arises from the text to account for these changes.

Although the 144,000 are spared the divine wrath poured out in seals 1–4, they are not spared the persecution of the earth dwellers. This leads to the conclusion that they are probably the martyrs under the altar seen in Revelation 6:9–11. This group representing all the tribes of Israel is most likely comprised of Jewish believers. "Twelve tribes" is used as a figure of speech for Jewish Christians in James 1:1. For over a decade (A.D. 30–45) the early church was predominantly Jewish. Acts 1–9 describes the expansion of the gospel among the Jews. Stephen was the church's first martyr (Acts 7:60), and following his death a great persecution broke out against believers (8:1). The church in Jerusalem experienced great hardship until it left the city before its destruction in A.D. 70.

Sectarian groups such as the Jehovah's Witnesses often interpret this number literally to define the number of "true believers." The expanded number of God's people that John sees in his next vision suggests that any attempt to restrict the number to be saved is misguided.

The Great Multitude in White Robes (7:9–17)

A great multitude that no one could count, from every nation, tribe, people and language, standing before the throne and in front of the Lamb (7:9). In this vision John's temporal perspective is fast forwarded to the time of the Parousia. There are several visions like this in Revelation that are proleptic, that is, they present a future event as if it has already happened. Many elements of this vision represent the heavenly perspective following Christ's coming elaborated in chapters 19–22. A dramatic transformation occurs in Revelation 5:6 when John turns to see a lion and instead sees a

NIKE HOLDING A PALM BRANCH

A relief of Nike in Ephesus along Curetes Street.

slaughtered lamb. Here the exclusive tribes of 144,000 Jews are similarly transformed into an inclusive multitude encompassing every race, ethnic group, and nation on earth. From this group Christ purchased individuals with his blood (5:9).

While a metropolis like Ephesus might have many ethnic groups among its population, only in Rome could the total ethnic population represented in the empire and beyond be found. Juvenal's tongue-in-cheek comment bears this out: "Long ago the Orontes has overflowed into the Tiber."[63] (The Orontes was the river flowing through Syrian Antioch, while the Tiber flowed through Rome.) Such ethnic diversity likewise characterized the early church. This picture fulfills numerous Old Testament prophecies that speak of the gospel going forth to all nations. These prophecies are all based on God's foundational covenant promise with Abraham: "All peoples on earth will be blessed through you" (Gen. 12:3).

The phrase "great multitude" has an interesting historical tie. Both the Roman historian Tacitus and the Roman presbyter Clement spoke of "great multitudes" of Christians who lost their lives under Nero.[64]

They were wearing white robes and were holding palm branches in their hands (7:9). Like the twenty-four elders, this multitude around the throne is also dressed in white robes, which identifies the group as victors (cf. 3:4, 18; 4:4). They are also holding palm branches (cf. 2 Esd. 2:45–46). The palm tree is indigenous to the warm Mediterranean climate, and to the ancient Greeks and Romans the palm served as a symbol of victory. The Greek author, Pausanius, provides the background: "But

at most games they use a wreath of palm, and everywhere the winner has a palm branch put in his right hand. The reason for the tradition is this: they say when Theseus came home from Crete he held games at Delos for Apollo, and crowned the winners with palm."[65] In the third century B.C., the Romans began to award palm branches to the winners at the games, a custom taken over from the Greeks. Palm branches are depicted on many coin types from Asia, and a particular favorite was a standing Nike with a wreath and palm.[66] The palm branch also became a symbol of victory for the Jews. After Simon captured Gaza in 141 B.C., he and his men entered the city rejoicing and carrying palm branches "because a great enemy had been crushed and removed from Israel" (1 Macc. 13:51 NRSV). When Jesus made his triumphal entry into Jerusalem shortly before his passion, the crowds heralded his arrival by waving palm branches (John 12:13). Understanding these Jewish and Greco-Roman backgrounds, the palm branches in the hands of the martyrs make a powerful statement of their triumph over the forces of evil. This multi-ethnic multitude now celebrates God and the Lamb for one primary benefit they have received—salvation.

All the angels . . . fell down on their faces before the throne and worshiped God (7:11). Space in heaven is obviously of a different dimension than on earth. For this great multitude is now joined around the throne by a myriad of angels. These angels again raise their voices in worship, this time to God and not the Lamb. As in Revelation 5:12, they ascribe seven attributes to him, which are the same except "thanks" is substituted for "wealth."

▶The Church and the Tribulation

Revelation provides a mixed portrait regarding the subject of Christians and tribulation. John himself was suffering on Patmos, while Antipas had already been martyred in Pergamum. The believers in Smyrna and Philadelphia had been persecuted, and those in Smyrna were about to endure even more trials. The picture here in Revelation 7 shows many who had shed blood for their faith. However, the four other churches in Asia had yet to experience significant tribulation.

In the modern church three main views of the tribulation are currently taught. Pretribulationists believe that the rapture of the church will occur before the great tribulation. The catching up of John to heaven in Revelation 4:1 is seen as a type of the rapture. Because the church is not mentioned between chapters 4–18, it must there-

fore be absent when the seal, trumpet, and bowl judgments fall upon the earth.

Midtribulationalists hold that the church will be on earth during the first half of the great tribulation, but at its midpoint after three and a half years the church will be raptured. Thus, the church is spared the more severe judgments of divine wrath that will come upon the earth.

Posttribulationists believe that the rapture will not occur until the great tribulation is over. Christians will be on earth during the judgments described in Revelation but will be protected, even as Israel was during the plagues that came upon Egypt. Regardless of one's perspective, we must all heed the warning with which Jesus prepared his church: "In the world you have tribulation, but take courage; I have overcome the world" (John 16:33 NASB).[A-41]

These are they who have come out of the great tribulation (7:14). One of the elders engages in a question-and-answer exchange with John, who is asked to identify this group in white robes. Rather than guess, John defers to the elder who identifies the multitude as those who have come out of the great tribulation. This is the last explicit mention of tribulation in the book, although its reality continues to be described. Daniel spoke of a great tribulation to be endured by the saints when the end came (Dan. 12:1). Jesus also warned his disciples about those days, "For then there will be a great distress, unequaled from the beginning of the world until now" (Matt. 24:21). In his third vision, Hermas, an early Christian, was refused permission

to sit at the right hand of the angel because this special place was reserved for those who had endured "scourgings, imprisonments, great tribulations, crosses, and wild beasts for the sake of the Name" (*Vis.* 3.2.1). The scale of such suffering described in this postapostolic document (ca. A.D. 95–100) accords with the historical facts of Nero's persecution. Finally, the Christian reviser of the *Ascension of Isaiah* (early 2d cent.) recalled that it was the king of iniquity, Nero, who persecuted the plant (i.e., the church), which the twelve apostles of the Beloved had planted (*Mart. Ascen. Isa.* 4:3).

They have washed their robes and made them white in the blood of the Lamb (7:14). This imagery related to the action of the tribulation saints seems paradoxical—clothing is reddened, not whitened, when dipped in blood. The symbolism is obviously spiritual and not literal. After the Exodus from Egypt when the law was given at Mount Sinai, the Israelites consecrated themselves by washing their clothes and abstaining from sexual relations (Ex. 19:14–15). While the victors in Sardis were commended for not defiling their garments (Rev. 3:4), here the commendation is for cleansing them. This portrait shows the victors as active, not passive, participants in their salvation. For this action, they are qualified to receive the benefits of heaven described in the following three verses.

Therefore, "they are before the throne of God and serve him day and night in his temple; and he who sits on the throne will spread his tent over them" (7:15). Serving God in his temple fulfills the promise to the victors in Philadelphia: That they would be pillars "in the temple of my God" (3:12). This temple in which they serve is not to be understood in any material sense like the temple in Jerusalem. Its spiritual reality is expressed well by the author of Hebrews: "For Christ did not enter a man-made sanctuary that was only a copy of the true one; he entered heaven itself" (Heb. 9:24). The promise that God would spread his tent over his people resonates throughout the Bible. In the desert his Shekinah presence manifested itself through the cloud by day and the fire by night (Ex. 13:21). Solomon built the temple as a place for God to tabernacle forever (1 Kings 8:12–13). Isaiah prophesied that a day will come when "the LORD will create over all of Mount Zion and over those who assemble there a cloud of smoke by day and a glow of flaming fire by night; over all the glory will be a canopy" (Isa. 4:5). This promise that God would dwell with his people was initially fulfilled with the coming of Jesus, who made his dwelling (literally, "tabernacled") among us (John 1:14). Here is a proleptic announcement that a day is coming when the tabernacle of God is with his people forever.

Never again will they hunger; never again will they thirst (7:16). The language of the heavenly benefits for those who endured the tribulation is drawn directly out of Isaiah 49:10. There the servant of the Lord promised to restore his people to the land, where he will care for them. The provisions for God's people in both passages include no hunger or thirst, no sun or scorching heat beating down, and springs of water. In Revelation the servant of Isaiah is identified as the Lamb who will shepherd his people. This same Lord, who was David's shepherd (Ps. 23:1), declared, "I am the good shepherd" (John 10:11, 14). Instead of a literal fulfillment of this Servant Song back to the physical land of Israel, John importantly sees a spiritual fulfillment of Isaiah's prophecy in heaven.

And God will wipe away every tear from their eyes (7:17). This final benefit is especially fitting for those who have shed so many tears in behalf of the kingdom of God because of their tribulation. It fulfills a promise that, at the time of the final messianic banquet, "the Sovereign LORD will wipe away the tears from all faces" (Isa. 25:8). This personal act of divine comfort will finally occur for all in the new Jerusalem after the old order of things, including death, has passed away (Rev. 21:4).

The Seventh Seal and the Golden Censer (8:1–5)

When he opened the seventh seal, there was silence in heaven for about half an hour (8:1). The Lamb's opening of the seventh seal does not bring the anticipated Parousia, but instead heavenly silence. Heaven has been full of sound up to this point with uninterrupted praise around the throne. In the Old Testament silence is frequently a precursor of judgment (cf. Isa. 41:1; Amos 8:3). During the final plague of the firstborn, the Israelites and their animals were commanded to remain silent (Ex. 11:7). After Babylon's judgment was determined by the Lord from his heavenly temple, "let all the earth be silent before him" (Hab. 2:20; cf. Zech. 2:13). With the opening of the last seal, the scroll is finally opened and its contents fully seen. The fury of the coming judgments has now moved even heaven to silence. Half an hour symbolizes a brief time and is the shortest period mentioned in Revelation.

The seven angels who stand before God . . . were given seven trumpets (8:2). The content of the seventh seal is another vision of seven angels who are given seven trumpets of judgment. This is the first mention of seven specific angels before the throne, who are probably not the angels of the seven churches. Jewish tradition identifies seven holy angels who offer up the prayers of the saints as they enter before the glory of the Holy One (Tobit 12:15). Seven other angels are responsible later for pouring out the seven bowls of God's wrath (Rev. 15:1).

Another angel, who had a golden censer, came and stood at the altar (8:3). A familiar sight in the ancient world was animal and incense sacrifices offered from altars dedicated to various deities. Such altars would be typically made of stone. Israel's worship at the tabernacle and temple required both an altar of burnt offering and an altar of incense. The altar of incense was made of acacia wood overlaid with pure gold. At each corner were four projections called horns (see 9:13). The priests of Israel were commanded in the law to burn incense on the altar every morning and evening. Zechariah the priest burnt incense in the temple for the evening offering (Luke 1:10–11). Once a year on the Day of Atonement, the high priest was to rub blood from the sin offering on its horns (Ex. 30:7–8). A glass bottle, probably used at the synagogue, has been discovered in Ephesus. It is inscribed with the Greek word for altar of incense and also depicts a seven-branched menorah.[67]

The Greeks originally worshiped before an altar and only later did these altars come to be associated with temples. The largest and most spectacular Greek altar was the altar of Zeus at Pergamum. Built during the reign of Eumenes II (197–159 B.C.), the altar sat in a horseshoe-shaped sanctuary that rose forty feet from a base measuring 112 by 120 feet. Its situation on the acropolis rising a thousand feet above the lower city has suggested to some interpreters that this altar is "the throne of Satan" mentioned in Revelation 2:13. The regular columns of dense smoke that billowed up from this altar would certainly suggest to an observer below what a heavenly incense offering might look like. Augustus built a monumental altar called the Ara Pacis in Rome in 13 B.C. and modeled it after the altar of Zeus. John sees only an altar of incense in heaven because the sacrifice of the Lamb made unnecessary any further sacrifices on the altar of burnt offering (cf. Heb. 7:27).

He was given much incense to offer, with the prayers of all the saints (8:3). The golden bowls full of incense in 5:8 represent the prayers of the saints. The heavy smoke from the incense suggests that many prayers are offered to God. The saints' prayer in part surely echoes the martyrs' cry in 6:10: "How long . . . until you judge the inhabitants of the earth and avenge our blood?" That moment of judgment has finally begun, for the angel now takes the censer filled with coals from the altar and hurls its contents to the earth (8:5). Incense was an integral part of worship in Israel's tabernacle and temple. It was prepared according to an exact formula given by God: "Take fragrant spices—gum resin, onycha and galbanum—and pure frankincense, all in

equal amounts, and make a fragrant blend of incense" (Ex. 30:34–35). Incense was one of the gifts presented to the infant Jesus by the Magi from the east (Matt. 2:11). Spices like frankincense and myrrh came from southern Arabia along trade routes established as early as the mid-second millennium B.C. These were among the luxury trade goods imported by Roman merchants (Rev. 18:13). In the Roman world, incense was commonly used with animals as sacrifices to the gods and to the emperor. Coins from Ephesus (3d cent. A.D.) show worshipers standing before an imperial temple with their arms raised in acclamation. A garlanded altar topped by a burning flame stands in their midst with a bull standing ready for sacrifice. In the temple's pediment is the Greek transcription of the Latin word *vota* (vows). Such vows were made annually to the gods to protect the emperors in the coming year.[68] Pliny the Younger asked Christians to deny Christ by making offerings of wine and incense to the emperor Trajan's statue.[69]

Peals of thunder, rumblings, flashes of lightning and an earthquake (8:5). Each of the judgment cycles of seals, trumpets (11:19), and bowls (16:18) ends with these same cosmological phenomena. This similar language would alert early hearers of the book that a section had ended and a new one was beginning. The literary term for such recurring phrases that indicate sectional openings and closings is *inclusio*.

The First Six Trumpets (8:6–9:21)

The seven angels who had the seven trumpets (8:6). The trumpet used in ancient Israel was of two basic types—a

◀ *left*

SHOFAR

The ceremonial Jewish trumpet made of a ram's horn.

shofar made from a ram's horn and a metal trumpet made of bronze or silver. Because the Greek word *salpigx* is used for both types in the Septuagint, it is impossible to determine which is meant in Revelation. Trumpets played a role in Israel's religious calendar. The Jewish new year began with the Feast of Trumpets (Lev. 23:23–25), and the year of Jubilee was inaugurated by the shofar being blown throughout Israel (25:9). Trumpets played a major role in warfare as signaling instruments (Num. 10:8–9). The use of seven trumpets to defeat God's enemies is seen in the destruction of Jericho when seven priests blew seven trumpets for seven days before its walls collapsed (Josh. 6:4–20). Detailed instructions on the military use of trumpets can be found in one of the Dead Sea Scrolls, *The War of the Sons of Light against the Sons of Darkness* (1QM 3:1–11; 7:12–9:8). Trumpets are often depicted on Roman reliefs in association with civic ceremonies and military triumphs. Josephus mentions the importance of the trumpet to the Roman army: "The hours for sleep, sentinel-duty, and rising, are announced by the sound of the trumpet; nothing is done without a word of command."[70]

The trumpet call, which signaled judgment, came to have a special escha-tological association with the Day of the Lord (Joel 2:1; Zeph. 1:16). Both Jesus (Matt. 24:31) and Paul (1 Thess. 4:16) declared that a trumpet will sound at the Second Coming. The seven trumpets in Revelation 8–11 should not be confused with that last trumpet because they are preparatory and not final. Interestingly, trumpet imagery is not used in Revelation 19 to announce Christ's return. While only a fourth of the earth was affected by the seal judgments (Rev. 6:8), a third of the earth is now devastated by the trumpet judgments. A progression is thus seen in the intensity of the judg-ments. These judgments have many sim-ilarities with the plagues of Egypt (see "The Trumpet and Bowl Judgments and the Egyptian Plagues" at 15:6).

There came hail and fire mixed with blood, and it was hurled down upon the earth (8:7). The first trumpet brings an environmental disaster. Hail and light-ning, perhaps triggering wildfires, con-sume whatever plants, trees, and grass are in their path. Such losses affect food sup-plies, fuel and building materials, as well as forage for livestock. Joel described the Day of the Lord similarly: "For fire has devoured the open pastures and flames have burned up all the trees of the field" (Joel 2:19). Famine would be the inevitable result of such a catastrophe.

Something like a huge mountain, all ablaze, was thrown into the sea (8:8). Whereas the first trumpet affects the land, the second wreaks havoc on the sea. The picture seems to describe the erup-tion of a volcano near the coastline. The fiery ash lights the sky. The seismic activ-ity produces a tidal wave that destroys sea creatures and capsizes vessels caught in its path. The eruption of Mount

Vesuvius in A.D. 79 provides an interesting parallel. On August 24 the mountain exploded, burying the coastal cities of Pompeii and Stabiae under lava and ashes and Herculaneum under mud. The Roman naturalist Pliny the Elder, who also commanded the fleet at nearby Misenum, set sail across the Bay of Naples to rescue a friend at Stabiae. He became trapped by the rough surf once ashore and could not escape by sea. He choked to death through inhalation of the dense fumes. His nephew Pliny the Younger described his uncle's death and his own escape in two remarkable letters to the historian Tacitus. His description of the volcano's destructive effects provides an eerie parallel to our text: "We also saw the sea sucked away and apparently forced back by the earthquake: at any rate it receded from the shore so that quantities of sea creatures were left stranded on dry sand. On the landward side a fearful black cloud was rent by forked and quivering bursts of flame, and parted to reveal great tongues of fire, like flashes of lightning magnified in size."[71]

A great star, blazing like a torch, fell from the sky (8:10). The third trumpet brings forth a star resembling a meteor or comet that contaminates the earth's freshwater sources. Falling stars are an apocalyptic motif heralding disaster and death, and are mentioned four times in Revelation. Here and in 6:13 the stars represent cosmic phenomena; in 9:1 and 12:4 they are personified as angelic beings. At God's judgment of Edom "all the starry host will fall" (Isa. 34:4). Jesus alluded to this text in the Synoptic Apocalypse when he declared that, following the distress of the last days, "the stars will fall from the sky" (Matt. 24:9; Mark 13:25). The single destructive star mentioned here has a parallel in *Sibylline Oracle* 5.158–59: "a great star will come from heaven to the wondrous sea and will burn the deep sea and Babylon itself." However, the star seen by the Sibyl fell on saltwater, destroyed rather than poisoned, and was angelic rather than cosmic.

The name of the star is Wormwood (8:10). The star that poisons these drinking supplies is called Wormwood, or "Bitterwood" (*apsinthos*). The plant *Artemesia absinthium* is a perennial herb that produces small, yellow flowers and grows throughout the eastern Mediterranean. Dioscorides Pedanius, a military doctor and pharmacologist during the reigns of Claudius and Nero (A.D. 41–68), described three types of *absinthium* known to the Romans. The most bitter type grew in the Anatolian provinces of Pontus and Cappadocia. Because it harmed the stomach and caused headaches, it was administered primarily for external purposes.[72] A toxic agent found in wormwood is thujone, which causes intoxication, hallucinations, convulsions, and damage to the central nervous system. However, it is usually not lethal. In the Old Testament bitter water came to symbolize disobedience, and wormwood was linked with judgment. After the Exodus, the Israelites came to the spring of Marah and tried to drink its bitter water. Although the people grumbled against Moses, God provided a piece of wood to sweeten the water before testing them to see if they would keep his commands (Ex. 15:23–25). Twice in Jeremiah God made this declaration regarding Israel and its prophets: "I am feeding this people with wormwood, and giving them poisonous water to drink" (Jer. 9:15; 23:15 NRSV). Although one third of the drinking supply is affected, only a vague "many" die from these contaminated waters.

A third of the sun was struck, a third of the moon, and a third of the stars, so that a third of them turned dark (8:12). The final judgment on the natural world affects the heavens. Darkness on the sun, moon, and stars produces a blackout even during the daytime. Such darkness could be caused by smoke, dust, or volcanic ash—all products of the previous judgments. Solar or lunar eclipses could also cause such heavenly darkness. In Joel's day, a plague of locusts was sent as divine judgment. Their numbers were so great that at their approach the skies became darkened (Joel 2:10). Such darkness also characterized God's judgment of Pharaoh: "When I snuff you out, I will cover the heavens and darken their stars" (Ezek. 32:7). Like the other three trumpet judgments, the effect of the fourth is also just partial.

An eagle that was flying in midair call out in a loud voice, "Woe! Woe! Woe to the inhabitants of the earth" (8:13). Like the seal sequence, a break occurs between the fourth and fifth trumpets where three "Woes" are announced. Woe is typical prophetic language used to announce impending judgment: "Look! An eagle is swooping down, spreading its wings over Moab . . . Woe to you, O Moab! The people of Chemosh are destroyed" (Jer. 48:40, 46). Jesus issued seven Woes to the scribes and Pharisees (Matt. 23:13–32). The ominous tone of the eagle's declaration suggests that the final three trumpets will be even more devastating. This messenger is flying in midair, or middle heaven. Revelation portrays a typical Jewish cosmology with three heavens (cf. 2 Cor. 12:2). The upper heaven is revealed in Revelation 4:1 when John begins to see a series of visions around the divine throne. The celestial middle heaven is the home of the sun, moon, planets, and stars (cf. Rev. 14:6; 19:17). The lowest atmospheric heaven is mentioned as clouds in 1:7.

I saw a star that had fallen from the sky to the earth. The star was given the key to the shaft of the Abyss (9:1). The fifth trumpet shifts the divine wrath to a new region—that beneath the earth. This woe and the next are the lengthiest and most complex of the judgments seen in Revelation. The "star" that John sees is an angel, as in 20:1, who is given the key (i.e., authority; cf. 3:7) to open the Abyss.

The consequences are a plague unlike anything yet experienced on earth. The Abyss was believed to be the underworld prison of evil spirits. When the demons were cast out of the demoniac by Jesus, they pleaded with him not to send them to the Abyss (Luke 8:30–31). The Abyss was also considered the realm of the dead. Jesus, after his death, descended into the Abyss ("deep" NIV; Rom. 10:7 quoting Deut. 30:13 LXX). However, in Revelation the name Hades is used for the realm of the dead (cf. Rev. 1:18; 6:8; 20:13, 14), reflecting the Septuagint in which the Hebrew *Sheol* is translated by "Hades" rather than "Abyss."

Smoke rose from it like the smoke from a gigantic furnace (9:2). Large furnaces were used in antiquity to burn limestone into lime. Limestone was stacked in concentric layers to form a dome. At the bottom was an opening to supply fuel for the fire, while the top contained a hole for air and smoke to escape. Another type of furnace was used for smelting ore, mainly iron. Such furnaces required great and prolonged heat, and the fires produced

▶ The Plutonium: An Asian Abyss

An epitaph from Diogenes Laertius (3d cent. A.D.), which describes the underworld as "the black abyss of Pluto," suggests a possible local reference.[A-42] Just north of Laodicea was the city of Hierapolis (cf. Col. 4:13). The city was noted for its shaft to the underworld. The Sibyl—an ecstatic prophetess depicted as an aged woman—wrote from Egypt: "Hierapolis also, the only land that has mingled with Pluton."[A-43] The patron deity of Hierapolis was Apollo and beneath his temple was the Plutonium, the dwelling place of Pluto, the god of the dead in Greek mythology. Strabo described the Plutonium's entrance as "an opening of only moderate size,

large enough to admit a man, but it reaches a considerable depth."[A-44] Spewing from the shaft was a dense mist that brought immediate death to any living creature, such as livestock or birds, that happened into the opening. Only the local eunuch priests of Cybele were immune, but they survived only by holding their breath. In 1962, Italian archaeologists uncovered the entrance to the Plutonium during their excavations. Because a strong smelling gas continues to be emitted, a sign at the entrance of the shaft warns would-be explorers: DANGER POISONOUS GAS.

thick, dark columns of smoke. The destructive judgment of Sodom and Gomorrah produced a similar effect: "and he [Abraham] saw dense smoke rising from the land, like smoke from a furnace" (Gen. 19:28). Jesus' use of "fiery furnace" in his parables suggests that the image is synonymous with hell (Matt. 13:42, 50).

And out of the smoke locusts came down upon the earth (9:3). Locusts were a common plague in the ancient world, and total devastation was usually left in their wake. These insects were the eighth plague that God sent against Egypt: "Nothing green remained on tree or plant in all the land of Egypt" (Ex. 10:15). In Revelation, however, these locusts do not devour their usual fodder but instead attack humans. These locust/scorpions are empowered to sting anyone missing the seal of God on their foreheads (cf. Rev. 7:3). Thus, all the earth dwellers, not just a third, are affected.

And the agony they suffered was like that of the sting of a scorpion when it strikes a man (9:5). Numerous species of arachnids are found throughout the eastern Mediterranean region. Their poisonous venom kills the insects and spiders upon which they feed but, while painful to humans, rarely kills them. Sirach names scorpions as one of God's instruments of vengeance (Sir. 39:30). The venom of these locusts is sufficiently toxic to torture the victims for five months. This period of time again indicates incompleteness: God is not yet ready for his judgment to be terminal. The pain, however, is so great that everyone seeks death but cannot find it (cf. Job 3:21). There is no assisted suicide for these earth dwellers under divine judgment.

◄

ROMAN CHARIOT AND HORSES

The locusts looked like horses prepared for battle (9:7). The uncanny resemblance of locusts to horses was proverbial in antiquity: "They have the appearance of horses; they gallop along like cavalry" (Joel 2:4). Hence their arrival was likened to that of an enemy army (Rev. 9:5). Joel is a key source for John's description of the locusts. An army of locusts "has the teeth of a lion" (Joel 1:6), and they make a noise "like that of chariots" (2:5).

The angel of the Abyss, whose name in Hebrew is Abaddōn, and in Greek, Apollyōn (9:11). The two names given the ruler here suggest that John and part of his audience were bilingual. In Old Testament Wisdom literature, *Abaddōn* ("Destruction") is closely linked with *Sheol* ("Death"; cf. Job 26:6; Prov. 15:11). In the LXX, *Abaddōn* is usually translated by the Greek word *apōleia*, with *Apollyōn* being its personal form. *Apollyōn* has also been understood to be a word play on the god Apollo in his role as destroyer. *Apollyōn* may also be another clue to identify Nero as the church's persecutor because Nero's patron deity was Apollo. This identification is likely, given John's only other use of *apōleian* in 17:8, 11, when the beast—the eighth emperor, Nero *redivivus*—is ready to go to his destruction. Nero's voice and appearance were compared to those of Apollo, and he was hailed as "our Apollo."[73] Nero also had a coin struck depicting himself in the guise of Apollo playing a lyre, while other coins from his reign show him with a hairstyle identical to Apollo's. It has been suggested that the reference is an indirect attack on Domitian, who apparently liked to be regarded as Apollo incarnate. However, no Roman sources link Domitian with Apollo, but instead record that Domitian revered the goddess Minerva the most.[74] This devotion was expressed by the consistent issuance of four coin types annually, the erection of temples, and the sponsorship of an annual festival in Minerva's honor. If the allusion in Revelation 9:11 is to Apollo, and it probably is, the reference is to Nero and not to Domitian.

Release the four angels who are bound at the great river Euphrates (9:13). A voice from the heavenly altar commands the sixth angel to issue the release order. Four angels were introduced in 7:1, who were to hold back the destructive four winds until God's servants were sealed. In contrast, four other angels, poised on the Euphrates River for their moment of divine judgment, are released to destroy a third of humanity. In Revelation the east is the direction from which both redemption (7:2) and destruction (9:14; 16:12) come. In the Old Testament Israel's eschatological enemy likewise came from the east (Isa. 41:2; 46:11) or from the north (Jer. 6:1, 22; Ezek. 38:6).

The Euphrates and the Tigris were the two great rivers of Mesopotamia. Both were headwaters into which the river in the garden of Eden flowed (Gen. 2:14). Today the source of the Euphrates is in eastern Turkey. The river drains a course of 1,780 miles before emptying into the Persian Gulf. In the Old Testament, the Euphrates is also called "the great river" (Deut. 1:7; Josh. 1:4), and it formed the northeastern boundary of the Promised Land (Gen. 15:18; Deut. 1:7). In the first century the Euphrates River marked the eastern frontier of the Roman empire. The river, because of its limited number of fords, served as an effective barrier to the Parthians and Armenians to the east. The southernmost ford was at Zeugma ("bridge"; near Birecik, Turkey), where the Romans stationed a legion during the 60s. Here was the most likely place where an army from the east would be mobilized to cross.

The number of mounted troops was two hundred million (9:16). The size of this demonic army is literally a double myriad of myriads, 2 x 10,000 x 10,000. The numerical background for this huge number is Daniel 7:10: "ten thousand times ten thousand stood before him (God)." The number is probably to be understood figuratively as an innumerable host. The troops released at the Euphrates are compared to a deadly mounted cavalry. Armored cavalry developed in the Middle East in the 9th or 10th centuries B.C. The Parthians favored armored horses and riders (*kataphraktoi*) in warfare, and used them in 53 B.C. to defeat decisively the Romans near the Euphrates at Carrhae (Haran [Gen. 12:4–5]; Harran, Turkey). By the first century A.D., the Romans had their own mounted cavalry, and such troops were used in Judea during the Jewish revolt. The armored breastplates of the cataphracts consisted of either mail or scale shirts.[75]

The heads of the horses resembled the heads of lions, and out of their mouths

came fire, smoke and sulfur (9:17). The second woe brings death to a third of humanity. The horselike creatures are the instruments of death, and they accomplish their mission in a twofold way—with their mouths and their tails. The use of the snake simile in 9:19 suggests that the "horses" are demonic beings, whose purposes are to make life a hell on earth for the earth dwellers.

The rest of mankind ... still did not repent of the works of their hands (9:20). This is the first of three vice lists found in Revelation (cf. 21:8; 22:15). Paul presents similar catalogs of sins in his writings (cf. Rom. 1:29–31; 1 Cor. 6:9–10). Such lists, developed by Hellenistic Jews to describe the sins of the pagan world, often regarded idolatry as the root sin (cf. Wisd. Sol. 14:22–29). The earth dwellers who survive the second woe still fail to acknowledge God. They persist in violating the first two of the Ten Commandments (Ex. 20:3–4) and in worshiping the demons who energize the idols (cf. Deut. 32:17; 1 Cor. 10:19–20). The prophets often chastised Israel for worshiping idols: "All who make idols are nothing, and the things they treasure are worthless. Those who speak up for them are blind; they are ignorant, to their own shame" (Isa. 44:9; cf. Jer. 10:3–9). Unlike the living God, these idols cannot see, hear, or walk (Dan. 5:23).

In Ephesus at least twenty-six other gods and goddesses besides Artemis were worshiped (cf. Athens; Acts 17:16). Gold statues of Artemis were carried in processions through Ephesus. The Greeks associated gold with divinity, equating its near indestructibility with the gods' immortality. During this period solid gold was used only for the statues of emperors and gods.[76] Smaller statuettes of bronze have also been discovered. Most of the cult statues, including three of Artemis found by excavators in the city, were made of quality marble. The gods are also represented in mosaics and frescos found in the upper-class homes in Ephesus. Such idolatry was found throughout the other cities of Asia.

The earth dwellers are likewise cited for continual disobedience of commandments 6–8: murder, adultery, and theft (Ex. 20:13–15). Here in Revelation is the first mention of repentance since chapters 2–3. The judgment on those who fail to repent is an explicit reminder both to the Nicolaitans and to Jezebel and her followers of their potential destiny. For idolatry and sexual immorality are the primary sins that Jesus identified in the Asian churches.

Their magic arts (9:21). Magical arts comes from the Greek word *pharmakon*, from which the English word pharmacy is derived. Except for Paul's inclusion of it among the works of the flesh ("witchcraft," NIV; Gal. 5:20), the *pharm-* word group is used exclusively in Revelation (cf. 18:23; 21:8; 22:15). To alter one's fate and to protect oneself against evil spirits, the Greeks and Romans employed magical practices. Ephesus was known for its magical arts and for its "Ephesian letters"—written magical spells believed to provide power to ward off evil spirits. Some in the Ephesian church had probably once practiced the magical arts and, following their conversion, were among those who had burned their occult scrolls publicly (Acts 19:19).

Although magic was officially disapproved in the Roman empire, it was still widely practiced. For example, a consul named Marcus Servilius Nonianus wore a piece of papyrus around his neck inscribed with the Greek letters *rho* and *alpha* to ward off eye inflammation. People would often curse their enemies by writing the victim's name on a lead tablet, consecrate him or her to the spirits of the underworld, and then stick a long nail through the name. In one such inscription, a chariot driver cursed his opponents, asking that both the horses and the drivers be killed.[77] Lovers used special charms to attract the object of their affection. Two popular forms of divination were augury, which is the interpretation of a divine message given by the flight pattern or eating habits of birds, and extispicium, which is the interpretation of signs found in the entrails of sacrificial animals. Divination was employed to undertake every activity of life, from getting married to going to war. This common practice, however, is repeatedly denounced in Revelation.[78]

The Angel and the Little Scroll (10:1–11)

Then I saw another mighty angel coming down from heaven . . . his face was like the sun, and his legs were like fiery pillars (10:1). The seventh trumpet and final two woes are delayed while John sees another vision of a mighty angel. His appearance with a cloud and a rainbow indicate that he is a special messenger from the heavenly throne (cf. 4:3). Like the son of man (1:16), this angel also has a face beaming like the sun. The remarkable appearance of this angel has suggested comparison with the Colossus of Rhodes, one of the seven wonders of the ancient world. Chares of Lindos cast this 110-foot statue from bronze around 282 B.C. It depicted the sun god Helios, whose rayed head is also seen on Rhodian coins of this period. In 227, fifty-six years after it was dedicated, an earthquake toppled the Colossus breaking it at its knees. An oracle advised the citizens not to rebuild the statue, so it was left lying next to its base for hundreds of years. The fame of the Colossus was still widely recognized in the first century A.D., as both Pliny the Elder and Strabo comment on its extraordinary size.[79] The exact appearance of the statue is unknown, but it certainly stood erect with perhaps a right hand extended upward. However, the medieval image of his legs spanning the entrance to the harbor is incorrect. Wherever this statue stood in Rhodes, its gleaming bronze legs, resembling fiery pillars, stood visible to land and sea.

He was holding a little scroll, which lay open in his hand (10:2). When the first mighty angel appears in 5:2, he asks John who is worthy to open the sealed scroll in God's right hand. Once the seventh seal is opened (8:1), that scroll is not mentioned again until now. A second mighty angel holds an opened "little" scroll in his right hand. Because the Greek form is a diminutive here, some scholars have suggested a second scroll is now revealed. However, the scroll's small size is only in relation to the angel's large hand, and "scroll" and "little scroll" are used inter-

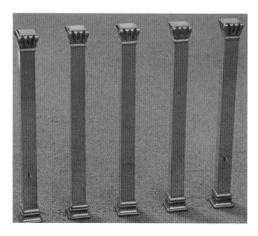

▶

PILLARS

Reconstruction of the five golden pillars of the tabernacle.

changeably in the chapter (10:8, 9, 10). Thus, it is likely that only one scroll is seen throughout these visions.

He planted his right foot on the sea and his left foot on the land (10:2). The land and the sea are the primary foci of the first two trumpet judgments (8:7–9). The stance of this mighty angel suggests that he represents the Creator of the earth and the sea and that further judgment still awaits them both. His shout like a lion's roar suggests a possible link with the lion of Judah (5:5), but the simile is for comparison of sound, not for identification purposes.

Seal up what the seven thunders have said (10:4). To this point John is allowed to record the contents of his visions. However, an unknown voice from heaven now forbids him to write down the mysterious utterance of the seven thunders, who appear only here in Revelation. Perhaps their message concerns the final seven bowls of judgment, whose disclosure is premature at this time. Daniel was told to seal up his visions (Dan. 8:26; 12:4, 9). And Paul, after being taken up into the third heaven, was likewise forbidden to describe his revelation (2 Cor. 12:4). Following the final vision, John is commanded by the angel not to seal up the words of this prophecy (Rev. 22:10).

Then the angel . . . raised his right hand to heaven. And he swore by him who lives forever and ever (10:5–6). The angel takes an oath to add credence to his statements that follow. Such a practice is mentioned several times in the Old Testament. At the close of his visions, Daniel saw an angelic figure hovering above the water who "lifted his right hand and his left hand toward heaven, and I heard him swear by him who lives forever" (Dan. 12:7). The Song of Moses describes the oath of vengeance God takes against his adversaries: "I will lift up my hand to heaven, and I will swear with my right hand" (Deut. 32:40 LXX). Today witnesses in court likewise raise their right hand to swear that they will tell the truth.

There will be no more delay! (10:6). The angel literally declares to John that "time (*chronos*) will be no longer." This time reference links back to the fifth seal where the martyred servants are told to wait "a little longer" (literally, "a short time"; 6:11) for the rest of their brothers and sisters to be killed. Daniel praised God because "he changes times and seasons" (Dan. 2:21). Here in Revelation, God has now determined that the short time has run out.

The mystery of God will be accomplished, just as he announced to his servants the prophets (10:7). The angel next dramatically announces: When the seventh trumpet is sounded, God's purposes will be completed. God has always used his prophets to reveal his plans: "Surely the Sovereign LORD does nothing without revealing his plan to his servants the prophets" (Amos 3:7). As a New Testament prophet, John is commanded to prophesy later in verse 11. The mystery of God relates to his divine purposes in redemption and judgment on earth. Paul was also a prophet (Acts 13:1) who frequently declared the mysteries of God, particularly those related to the Parousia (1 Cor. 15:51; 2 Thess. 2:7). The angelic announcement here is again proleptic because John's prophecy does not immediately bring the consummation, but instead concerns the final period of tribulation and judgment on earth. Thus, John's new prophetic assignment is to warn his audience of its approach.

Take it and eat it. It will turn your stomach sour, but in your mouth it will be as sweet as honey (10:9). The command to take the open scroll from the right hand of the mighty angel and to eat it signals the beginning of a new period of ministry. At Ezekiel's prophetic commissioning, he was also commanded to eat a scroll (Ezek. 2:8; 3:1). Like Ezekiel's scroll (Ezek. 3:3), John's tasted sweet as honey in his mouth. However, it became sour after John swallowed it. The bitterness of the coming judgments apparently gives John an upset stomach.

You must prophesy again about many peoples, nations, languages and kings (10:11). The event is John's recommissioning as a prophet, and he is told the subject of his future prophecy. The mention of kings is a departure from John's

fourfold formula, which usually mentions tribes (cf. 5:9; 7:9). As it relates to the Roman empire, the word "kings" is better translated as "emperors." This is particularly true in chapter 17 where seven emperors are mentioned in the context of the great prostitute Rome.

The Two Witnesses and the Seventh Trumpet (11:1–19)

I was given a reed like a measuring rod and was told, "Go and measure the temple of God and the altar, and count the worshipers there" (11:1). The 144,000 and the great multitude are introduced after the sixth seal (ch. 7) as God's servants and martyrs on earth. Now, after the sixth trumpet, these servants are presented as two new figures—worshipers and witnesses. John, like Ezekiel (Ezek. 8:1–11:25), receives a vision of worshipers in the temple in the "holy city" (cf. Isa. 52:1). While Ezekiel's worshipers are marked for destruction because of

MOUNT OF OLIVES IN JERUSALEM

their idolatry, John's are preserved because they measure up to the divine standard. Reeds were commonly used as measuring rods in biblical times. They grew along rivers and in marshy areas in Palestine and Egypt, often to heights of twenty feet with a stem up to three inches in diameter. For regular construction purposes, reeds were either three or six long cubits (approximately five or ten feet). Ezekiel used a rod six cubits long to measure the new temple that he saw in his vision (Ezek. 40:3, 5). John is now instructed to perform a similar prophetic act, but unlike Ezekiel's vision, few details are given.

The New Testament speaks of the temple in three dimensions—heavenly, physical, and spiritual—and in Revelation John refers to the temple similarly. The heavenly temple, first mentioned in Revelation 7:15 and again in 11:19, is the heavenly reality of which the earthly temple was only a copy (cf. Heb. 9:1–25). Paul, writing from Ephesus, addressed the subject of the church as the spiritual temple, "Don't you know that you yourselves are God's temple" (1 Cor. 3:16; cf. 6:19). Although the temple here in Revelation 11:1 is primarily a figure for the church, there appears to be a secondary reference to the temple still standing in Jerusalem. Historically, the only group eligible to worship at the temple in Jerusalem were Jewish believers, and these are numbered earlier as part of the 144,000 (Rev. 7:4–8).

But exclude the outer court; do not measure it, because it has been given to the Gentiles. They will trample on the holy city for 42 months (11:2). The outer court was the only area of the temple that Gentiles could enter. They were barred from the inner courts by a

WARNING INSCRIPTION

A first-century inscription from the balustrade around the Jerusalem temple warning Gentiles not to enter on the pain of death.

balustrade that contained thirteen inscribed stones that read in Greek and Latin: "No intruder is allowed in the courtyard and within the wall surrounding the temple. Those who enter will invite death for themselves." Two of these warning inscriptions are on display in the Istanbul Archaeological Museum and the Rockefeller Museum in Jerusalem. The trampling of the holy place by Israel's enemies was a common theme in Old

REEDS

Papyrus reeds growing along the bank of the Nile River in Egypt.

Testament apocalyptic texts (cf. Isa. 63:18; Dan. 8:13). Before the end, the Gentiles would lay siege to Jerusalem and trample it (Zech. 12:3 LXX). In his Olivet Discourse, Jesus prophesied using similar words: "Jerusalem will be trampled on by the Gentiles until the times of the Gentiles are fulfilled" (Luke 21:24). The Roman siege and destruction of Jerusalem in A.D. 70 is a fulfillment of these prophecies. The Jewish revolt began in the fall of 66 and concluded on September 26, 70 when Titus entered the city, a period of approximately forty-eight months. (Masada did not fall until May 73, however.) The time mentioned for the trampling in Revelation is forty-two months. While this period approximates the length of the Jewish revolt, its prophetic fulfillment lies in the time of the persecution of the spiritual temple—the church.

And I will give power to my two witnesses, and they will prophesy for 1,260 days, clothed in sackcloth (11:3). Nowhere does John identify the two witnesses who are divinely empowered. However, their prophetic activities mirror those of Moses and Elijah, whose spirit they clearly embody (cf. Mal. 4:4–5). At Jesus' transfiguration Moses and Elijah were the two witnesses, representing the Law and the Prophets respectively (Matt. 17:3–4). Their period of prophesying is given as 1,260 days, which equals forty-two months in the Jewish lunar calendar of thirty days each. It is also equivalent to three and a half years, the period of judgment that Elijah pronounced against Ahab and Israel (Luke 4:25; James 5:17). Whereas God's people in heaven are dressed in white clothing (Rev. 7:9, 14), the two witnesses wear sackcloth during their ministry on earth.

This sackcloth is black and made from goat's hair (cf. 6:12). The Israelites put on sackcloth on the day of judgment as a sign of lament while seeking to avert God's wrath (Isa. 3:24; Jer. 4:8; Ezek. 7:18). Conversely, Daniel expressed his true repentance by fasting and covering himself with sackcloth and ashes (Dan. 9:3). The sackcloth on the two witnesses symbolizes the message of judgment that they will proclaim to the earth dwellers.

The two olive trees and the two lampstands that stand before the Lord of the earth (11:4). Olive trees produced the oil used as fuel in ancient lamps (Matt. 25:3, 8). Olive oil was also a core ingredient for the special anointing oil used by the priests in worship (Ex. 30:22–33). The lampstand, or menorah, was not a typical household item, but rather was used ceremonially in Israel's worship (see comments on Rev. 1:20). Zechariah saw similar imagery in a vision and asked what the olive trees represented (Zech. 4:3, 11). An angel explained, "These are the two who are anointed to serve the Lord

of all the earth" (4:14). The two anointed men in Zechariah's day were Zerubbabel and Joshua, who represented Israel's kingship and priesthood respectively. This suggests that the two witnesses, while also being patterned after actual individuals, are likewise representative of New Testament spiritual realities.

Fire comes from their mouths and devours their enemies (11:5). Fire destroying a third of humanity comes from the mouths of the demonic horses in the sixth trumpet (9:17–18). Now a similar destructive fire is emitted from the mouths of the two witnesses against those attempting to harm them. However, such temporal judgment is not the final divine judgment of fire to be given to God's foes (cf. 20:10, 15). Fire from heaven played an important role in the ministries of Moses and Elijah. When the Israelites complained about their hardships, God sent fire among them that was only abated through Moses' prayers (Num. 11:1–3). And when Korah rebelled against Moses' authority, God sent fire that consumed 250 elders (16:35). The famous confrontation on Mount Carmel between Elijah and the prophets of Baal was resolved when God sent fire to consume the sacrifice and the altar (1 Kings 18:38). At Elijah's word fire twice fell from heaven to consume a captain and his fifty men sent by King Ahaziah (2 Kings 1:9–12). On one occasion the disciples sought to demonstrate their power by asking Jesus if they should call down fire on a village of inhospitable Samaritans (Luke 9:54). The prophetic activity of Moses and Elijah serves as a model for the ministry of the two witnesses.

These men have power to shut up the sky so that it will not rain ... and they have power to turn the waters into blood (11:6). The two witnesses are empowered to perform miracles in the natural world like their prophetic forerunners. Elijah declared that it would not rain in Israel for a time; and when the drought was over, his prayer brought rain again (1 Kings 17:1; 18:41–42). Moses was given power to turn the Nile River into blood (Ex. 7:14–24). This was the first of ten plagues that God brought against Egypt through Moses.

The beast that comes up from the Abyss will attack them, and overpower and kill them (11:7). The beast is now introduced for the first time. His place of origin is the Abyss, where the demonic locusts of the fifth trumpet also originate (9:2–3). The beast is a malevolent character whose ultimate mission is to kill the two witnesses. By implication, he is the power behind the death of Antipas, the faithful witness in Pergamum (2:13).

REFLECTIONS

THE MARTYRDOM DESCRIBED IN REVELATION IS being repeated around the world today at an alarming rate. In fact, the 100 million martyrs who have died for their faith in the twentieth century are more than those martyred in the previous nineteen centuries of the church combined. This number is greater than the total of all those killed in war during the twentieth century. Researcher David C. Barrett estimates that 160,000 believers were martyred in 1996 alone. Persecution is common particularly in Africa, Asia, and the Middle East. However, shootings in schools and churches have recently produced young martyrs in the United States. Western Christians have a responsibility to be intercessors and public advocates on behalf of their brothers and sisters who are being persecuted and killed. Current information on the persecuted church can be found on the Internet at www.persecution.com.

Their bodies will lie in the street of the great city (11:8). A second type of city is now mentioned in this chapter. Whereas the holy city is the sacred domain of God's people (11:2), the great city is the dwelling place of the ungodly. This distinction is maintained throughout the rest of Revelation. Rome certainly represents the historical "great city" of the first century. During the Neronian persecution in 65, the Christians were martyred publicly. When Clement wrote to the Corinthian church several years later, he recalled two noble examples of his own generation, Peter and Paul, who "were persecuted and fought to the death" (*1 Clem.* 5:2).[80] The Christian addition of the *Ascension of Isaiah* mentions that "some of the twelve will be given into his hand," that is, Nero's, the one who murdered his mother Agrippina (*Mart. Ascen. Isa.* 4:3). Eusebius recorded an early tradition from the bishop of Corinth, Dionysius (A.D. 110–80), that Peter and Paul were martyred at the same time. However, it is more likely that Peter was martyred before Paul during the period 65–67. Eusebius also pointed out that the burial monuments of the two could be seen at the Vatican and on the Ostian Way.[81] The recent ministry and deaths of these two key apostolic witnesses, Peter to the Jews and Paul to the Gentiles, provides a compelling background for the imagery John uses here.

Which is figuratively called Sodom and Egypt, where also their Lord was crucified (11:8). Sodom was the city of wickedness that God destroyed with burning sulfur (Gen. 19:24), while Egypt was the country of Israel's oppression (Ex. 3:7–9). Ezekiel names both as places of godlessness which seduced Israel from following God (Ezek. 16:26, 46–56). The great city is thus a place of wickedness, oppression, and seduction. The reference to Jesus' crucifixion seems to identify Jerusalem as this city. However, several things suggest otherwise. First, Jerusalem is never called the great city in Revelation, although it is called such elsewhere (e.g., Jer. 22:8). Second, John employs language that is figurative and spiritual, not literal, to describe the city. Third, the use of "also" points to somewhere else besides the historical Jerusalem.

An intriguing story related to Peter—the so-called "Quo Vadis?" tradition—dates to the late second century. When the Roman church learned of a conspiracy to kill Peter, they sent the apostle out of the city. As Peter was leaving Rome, he had a vision of Jesus entering the city. Peter asked him, "'Lord, where are you going [*Quo vadis*]?' And the Lord said to him, 'I go to Rome to be crucified.' And Peter said to him, 'Lord, are you being crucified again?' And he said to him, 'Yes, Peter, again I shall be crucified.'" Peter soon came to himself and watched Jesus return to heaven. He then returned to Rome where he was arrested and later crucified (*Acts of Peter* 35). Although Jesus was crucified in Jerusalem at the behest of the Jews, the Romans bore equal culpability because it was their duly appointed governor Pilate who authorized the crucifixion. In that sense, Rome also played a role in crucifying Jesus.

For three and a half days men . . . will gaze on their bodies and refuse them burial (11:9). In the ancient world, the failure to receive a proper burial was the greatest insult at death (cf. Ps. 79:3–4; Jer. 22:18–19). When Pompey was assassinated in Egypt following his defeat by Julius Caesar, his body was abandoned and left unburied.[82] Roman funerary law normally forbade such care of corpses: "Whoever strips or exposes to the rays of the sun a body entrusted to permanent burial or left for a short period of time in some place, commits sacrilege."[83] Josephus called the Zealots barbarous and an outrage to humanity because they forbade the burial of the dead during the siege of Jerusalem and in fact killed those who attempted to bury their relatives.[84] The great anger of the earth dwellers against the two witnesses is expressed by this ultimate indignity. The deaths of the witnesses provoke a great celebration in which the residents from every nation rejoice over their release from torment (Rev. 11:10). A gift exchange often accompanied public festivals in the Greco-Roman world, and such an exchange now ensues.

But after the three and a half days a breath of life from God entered them (11:11). Even as the two witnesses prophesied for three and a half years (= 1260 days; cf. 11:3), their death lasted only three and a half days. At the conclusion of this brief period, the two witnesses come back to life. At creation the divine breath gave life to all humanity (Gen. 2:7). And when Ezekiel saw the valley of dry bones, God told him to prophesy to the bones: "I will put breath in you, and you will come to life" (Ezek. 37:6). The unexpected resurrection of the witnesses strikes terror in the onlookers, even as Jesus' resurrection brought great fear to the Roman guards at the tomb (Matt. 28:4).

Then they heard a loud voice from heaven saying to them, "Come up here" (11:12). The mighty angel, whose descent from heaven begins this vision

(10:1–3), now invites the two witnesses to join him. His invitation is the same as that extended to John, although John's heavenly ascent is only visionary (4:1). The witnesses return to heaven in a cloud, even as Jesus did at his ascension (Acts 1:9).

Some midtribulationalists interpret the ascension of the two witnesses as representing the rapture of the church. (Other midtribulationists see the rapture occurring at Rev. 14:14.) Because their return to heaven occurs at the end of 1,260 days, it stands at the midpoint of the seven–year tribulation, but before the final outpouring of wrath in the final forty-two months. Two things in Revelation argue against this interpretation. First, this event concludes the sixth trumpet and the second woe, and, therefore, it is not midway in Revelation's sevenfold cycle. Rather, it occurs just before the final judgment announced in the seventh trumpet. Second, the translation of Enoch (Gen. 5:24) and Elijah (2 Kings 2:11) to heaven without experiencing death is a type of the New Testament rapture. But the two witnesses have died; and when they go up to heaven, it is as resurrected, not raptured, saints. The event seems to symbolize the resurrection of the dead saints, not the rapture of the living ones.

The survivors were terrified and gave glory to the God of heaven (11:13). The severe judgment that follows the resurrection of the two witnesses is still partial, as only a fraction of the city and its residents are affected. The survivors give the same response that the angel later calls for when he announces the eternal gospel: "Fear God and give him glory" (14:5). Since other earth dwellers later fail to glorify God (16:9), the response of the earthquake survivors suggests that they at last repent and acknowledge his lordship. Whether such repentance is voluntary is questionable. Nebuchadnezzar likewise glorified God, but only after he was judged for his pride and arrogance (Dan. 4:29–37). The continued worship of idols in the palace suggests that the king's conversion was temporary (5:4). This is the only passage in Revelation that *may* suggest a large-scale conversion before the Parousia. Every other text is pessimistic regarding the willingness of the earth dwellers to repent in the face of divine judgment (Rev. 9:21). The second woe, begun in 9:13, is at last over.

The seventh angel sounded his trumpet (11:15). Unidentified voices in heaven make an announcement following the seventh and final trumpet. God has at last established his rule on earth. The answer to the prayer of Jesus and the saints throughout church history—"your kingdom come, your will be done on earth as it is in heaven" (Matt. 6:10)—is now finally answered. This eternal kingdom is ruled by both the Lord and his Christ, who ascended to the throne following his victory over death (Rev. 3:21; 5:5).

And the twenty four elders . . . fell on their faces and worshiped God (11:16). The elders, last seen in 7:13–17, are again heard in heaven thanking God that his reign on earth has begun. The familiar description of God as past, present, and future (1:8; 4:8) here assumes a new dimension. He is now acclaimed as the God only of the present and past. He is no longer the One who is to come because the future has now arrived forever.

The nations were angry; and your wrath has come (11:18). The language of the song echoes the messianic Psalm 2. There the angry nations are also described as God's enemies upon whom he pours his wrath (Ps. 2:1–5). The elders also announce proleptically the final judgment, which has two parts—rewarding the prophets and saints for their faithfulness, which Jesus does at his coming (Rev. 22:12), and destroying those who have opposed God's purposes on earth (20:11–15).

Then God's temple in heaven was opened, and within his temple was seen the ark of his covenant (11:19). The trumpet cycle ends with the characteristic eschatological earthquake that concludes each judgment cycle. This must complete the third woe; however, there is no explicit mention in this chapter of its completion. Although John sees the heavenly temple in several of his visions, this is the only occasion where he sees the ark of the covenant. The ark was the central fixture in the desert tabernacle as well as in Solomon's temple. After the destruction of the temple by the Babylonians in 586 B.C., the ark and its contents, including the jar of manna, were lost. One tradition states that Jeremiah rescued the ark and hid them in a cave on Mount Nebo until God should regather

▶ Chiasmus in Revelation

Chiasmus (or chiasm) is a structural device found in many types of ancient literature including the Bible. Its name is derived from a likeness to the Greek letter *chi* (X). Chiasmus provided a way to organize documents internally because ancient writings did not use paragraphs, punctuation, or capitalization. Because most people in the ancient world were illiterate, they got their information from oral performances. For such listeners, chiastic structure provided verbal clues to introduce and close sections of text, to signal emphasis, and to define argumentation. Chiasmus was used to organize a sequence of words or ideas in a sentence, a paragraph, or even a book. Two critical elements are involved— inversion and balance. A simple chiasmus is found in Jesus' saying in Mark 2:27: "The Sabbath was made for man, not man for the Sabbath." When the inversion has a middle element, the climax often occurs at the central crossing point. Chapter 12 is uniformly placed at this crossing point in all proposed chiastic structural models of Revelation.[A-45] Even the noted British novelist D. H. Lawrence, despite his unusual approach to the book, declared chapter 12 to be "the centre–piece of the Apocalypse" because it portrays the birth of the Messiah.[A-46] Although chapter 12 falls chronologically at the middle of Revelation, its content is a flashback to the beginning of the gospel story.

his people (cf. 2 Macc. 2:4–8). Another believed that an angel hid these sacred temple objects in the earth and is to guard them until the last days (*2 Bar.* 6:8). During the second temple period, it is probable that the ark was not in the Most Holy Place. John could never have seen it anyway since only the high priest was allowed to enter the Holy of Holies once a year. Yet John now recognizes the ark, to which he has access in the heavenly temple.

The Woman, the Male Child, and the Dragon (12:1–17)

A great and wondrous sign appeared in heaven (12:1). The ancients believed that heavenly signs signaled changes on earth. The magi followed a star a great distance to see the new king of the Jews. Because Herod knew the importance of such an omen, he gathered information about the star in order to kill his potential rival to the throne (Matt. 2:1–8). During Nero's reign a comet appeared, and its appearance was generally believed to foretell a change of emperor.[85] John's audience now awaits an explanation of the meaning of this astral sign.

A woman clothed with the sun, with the moon under her feet and a crown of twelve stars on her head. She was pregnant and cried out in pain (12:1–2). The incarnation of Jesus is now described using apocalyptic and mythological symbols. The woman, whose clothing depicts her character as with the other figures in Revelation (e.g., 4:4; 17:4), wears the sun, which symbolizes her heavenly nature (cf. 1:16; 10:1). The phrase "under her feet" signifies dominion and authority over creation (cf. Ps. 8:6; Mal. 4:3). She wears the victor's crown covered with twelve stars. In Revelation 1:20, seven stars represented the seven churches; here twelve stars represent the twelve tribes of Israel. This imagery was seen by Joseph in his dream of ruling his brothers (Gen. 37:9). Isaiah depicted eschatological Zion as pregnant and giving birth: "Before she goes into labor, she gives birth; before the pains come upon her, she delivers a son" (Isa. 66:7). Therefore, Israel is prophesied as the source of the promised Messiah, and the nation is personalized in a virgin daughter of Judah named Mary who gives birth to Jesus Christ (Luke 1:27).

An enormous red dragon with seven heads and ten horns and seven crowns on his heads (12:3). The other heavenly sign that John sees is a menacing one. The imagery is borrowed from Daniel's vision of the fourth beast (Dan. 7:7). As the fourth and final one, this beast is commonly understood as the Roman empire, which is how it is interpreted in *4 Ezra* 4:10 (ca. A.D. 100). Unlike the Lamb who has seven horns (Rev. 5:6), the dragon has ten horns. His earthly representatives (to be introduced shortly)—the beast out of the sea (13:1) and the great prostitute (17:3, 7)—likewise have ten horns, which represent great satanic power. In Revelation, the number ten is used only regarding the opponents of God and their activities.

The dragon stood in front of the woman who was about to give birth, so that he might devour her child (12:4). Using tra-

HOUSE OF MARY AT EPHESUS
▼

▶ The House of Mary

In the hills above Ephesus stands a shrine called the House of Mary (Meryemana), which is visited by thousands of pilgrims each year. Here, according to one tradition, Mary lived until her death, after accompanying John to Ephesus. At his crucifixion, Jesus told John to care for his mother (John 19:25–27). Epiphanius (ca. A.D. 315–403) wrote that the Scriptures were silent, however, about John bringing Mary with him to Asia.[A-47] Later evidence from the fifth to the sixth centuries—church buildings dedicated to Mary, the *transitus Mariae* legends, and the *Euthymiac History*—located Mary's life and death specifically in Jerusalem.[A-48]

The modern claim of Mary's presence in Ephesus began with a German nun and mystic named Catherine Emmerich. In a vision received between 1818–24, Emmerich saw a house in the mountains south of Ephesus in which the virgin mother Mary had lived. In 1890 the book containing this vision was read by some Roman Catholics in Smyrna, and the local priest journeyed to Ephesus to prove that such a house did not exist. However, on his third day of exploration, July 29, 1891, he discovered the house exactly as described in the vision. Roman Catholics gather there annually every August 15 to celebrate the Feast of the Assumption of the Virgin, and both Pope Paul VI in 1967 and Pope John Paul II in 1979 have celebrated mass at the sacred spot. Nevertheless, the better historical tradition locates Mary's death in Jerusalem.

ditional Jewish imagery from the Old Testament, Revelation appears to parody a familiar Hellenistic combat myth. The dragon Python pursued the goddess Leto, who was pregnant with Apollo. Leto fled to a distant island where she eventually gave birth to Apollo who, though just four days old, killed Python.[86] The converts from paganism in Asia would surely be familiar with this mythological account of cosmic struggle. To this myth is added features of the story of Artemis, who was the daughter of Leto and twin sister of Apollo. Artemis was traditionally born just outside Ephesus in the sacred grove Ortygia. She too was a virgin who protected women giving birth. A second century A.D. statue, now on display in the Ephesus Museum, portrays her as a queen of heaven, with the moon in the background of her three-tiered crown. This symbolism stems from her common identification as the moon goddess. Two other statues of the goddess in the museum show her wearing an extravagant necklace decorated with the twelve

signs of the zodiac, which some interpreters link to the twelve stars on the woman's head. Jews were forbidden to worship the stars (Deut. 4:19), yet later the zodiac was used decoratively in the mosaic floors of a number of synagogues (e.g., Hammath at Tiberias in Galilee; 4th–7th century A.D.). Although astral imagery figures prominently in Revelation, John does not use such images to promote astrological determinism, but rather to affirm God's sovereignty over his created order.

She gave birth to a son, a male child, who will rule all nations with an iron scepter. And her child was snatched up to God and to his throne (12:5). The language echoes the messianic promise in Isaiah 7:14 that a virgin would bear a son named Immanuel. Psalm 2:7–9 speaks of the anointed Son who would one day rule the

◀ *left*

ARTEMIS OF EPHESUS

This cultic statue depicts her with her three-tiered crown.

◀

ZODIAC ON THE FLOOR OF A SYNAGOGUE

The mosaic floor of the fourth-century synagogue in Tiberius (Galilee).

nations with an iron scepter. The male child is clearly Jesus the Messiah. The earthly life of Jesus is passed over in this apocalyptic description. Only his ascension is mentioned, an event described in Acts 1:9. Though the woman's flight is announced here, it is not described until verse 14. The reason for her flight is given next.

Michael and his angels fought against the dragon (12:7). Heaven, a place of worship and divine activity to this point, suddenly becomes a battlefield. Michael leads the other angels in expelling the dragon and his angels from heaven. Michael is the archangel who helps Daniel's heavenly messenger to prevail over the prince of Persia (Dan. 10:13, 21). He is also called the prince over the Jewish people who would protect those written in the book of life during a final time of distress (12:1–2). Jude 9, alluding to a lost document called the *Assumption of Moses,* identifies Michael as the archangel who disputed with the devil over the body of Moses. Michael is listed as one of the seven archangels in *1 Enoch* 20:1–7.

The great dragon was hurled down— that ancient serpent called the devil, or

▶ Snake Imagery in Asian Religions

Pergamum was home to the renowned healing sanctuary of Asclepius, the god of healing. Known to the Romans as Aesculapius, he was also called "Savior." After Epidaurus in Greece, Pergamum was the most famous sanctuary of Asclepius in the ancient world. Sick and infirmed people seeking to be healed daily filled the roads to the city. The noted second-century A.D. orator Aelius Aristides spent thirteen years as a patient at the Asclepium. Galen (c. A.D. 130–200), antiquity's most famous physician after Hippocrates, was a native of Pergamum and received his training at the Asclepium. Asclepius was always depicted with a serpent, usually holding a staff around which a serpent was coiled. Snakes associated with the god were a popular image on coins issued not only in Pergamum, but also in Laodicea, Thyatira, and Philadelphia. A column engraved with multiple snake images greeted visitors to the sanctuary. Real snakes were a part of the healing cure in an Asclepium:

A man had his toe healed by a serpent. He, suffering dreadfully from a malignant sore in his toe, during the daytime was taken outside by the servants of the Temple and set upon a seat. When sleep came upon him, then a snake issued from the Abaton and healed the toe with its tongue, and thereafter went back again to the Abaton. When the patient woke up and was healed he said that he had seen a vision: it seemed to him that a youth with a beautiful appearance had put a drug upon his toe.[A-49]

Other deities like Dionysus, Cybele, Zeus, and the Phrygian Sabazios likewise used snakes as part of their religious rites. Snakes were thus a popular image linked with pagan deities in Asia. However, John's association of the snake with Satan certainly positioned these cults as adversaries of Christ and the church. Today the snake encircling a staff—the symbol of Asclepius and healing—continues to serve as a symbol for medical associations.

Satan (12:9). The identity of the great dragon is now fully revealed. Although the names "devil" and "Satan" were mentioned in three of the messages to the churches (2:9, 10, 24; 3:9), his formal introduction is made here. In the Septuagint, the Greek word *diabolos* ("devil") is the usual translation of the Hebrew word *satan*. In the New Testament, both terms are frequently used—*diabolos*, 37 times and *satanas*, 36 times. The serpent imagery is derived primarily from the story of the Fall in Genesis 3. There the offspring of the woman was predicted to crush the serpent's head, while the serpent would only strike his heel (Gen. 3:15). During his earthly ministry Jesus saw a similar prophetic vision of Satan's fall after the seventy–two disciples told of their victory over demons (Luke 10:17–19; cf. John 12:31). These are the only two biblical texts that speak specifically of a fall of Satan. Early church commentators such as Tertullian and Gregory the Great saw in Isaiah's description of the "son of the dawn" (Lucifer) a prophetic description of the primeval fall of Satan (Isa. 14:12). However, this text describes the historical downfall and removal of the king of Babylon because he assumes the role of a god. (Ezekiel 28 likewise describes the fall of the king of Tyre.) In the Old Testament, there is no explicit mention of a fall of Satan, only a fall of humanity. The dragon's primary mission is now also disclosed—to deceive the whole world. Even as deception motivated the teaching of Jezebel (Rev. 2:20), it becomes the dragon's key tool to manipulate his human agents throughout the rest of the book.

Now have come the salvation and the power and the kingdom of our God, and the authority of his Christ (12:10). The successful expulsion of Satan and his angels from heaven elicits a hymn of triumph from a heavenly voice: Christ's incarnation has initiated a new kingdom on earth. The message of the kingdom characterized Jesus' earthly teaching: "The kingdom of God is near. Repent and believe the good news" (Mark 1:15). This was the same message the apostles announced: "Boldly and without hindrance he [Paul] preached the kingdom of God and taught about the Lord Jesus Christ" (Acts 28:31). This heavenly hymn continues through verse 12.

The accuser of our brothers ... has been hurled down (12:10). In the Old Testament, Satan (meaning "adversary") is portrayed as the prosecuting attorney in several heavenly courtroom scenes. Satan came before the Lord and accused Job of serving God only for his blessings (Job 1:6–12). He likewise stood at the right side of Joshua the high priest, accusing him of unforgiven sin (Zech. 3:1–3). In both scenes Satan had access to God in heaven. A fundamental shift is described in Revelation. Since Satan has been cast from heaven forever, he can no longer accuse God's people. Paul captures this theological truth when he declares there is now no longer any condemnation to those in Christ Jesus (Rom. 8:1).

They overcame him by the blood of the Lamb and by the word of their testimony (12:11). Because Satan can no longer accuse God's people in heaven, he begins a campaign of terror against them on earth. The extent of his persecutions have already been shown proleptically in the visions of the martyrs (7:14) and the two witnesses (11:7). The formula for victory is now given: the blood of the Lamb coupled with their testimony

about him. However, the testimony that overcomes Satan is the same action that provokes his rage and causes him to declare war on the church (11:17). Even as Jesus was ready to lay down his life (John 10:17), the saints are now prepared to lay down theirs. They do this in obedience to Jesus' command given in the context of his Parousia: "But whoever loses his life for me and for the gospel will save it" (Mark 8:35).

Therefore rejoice, you heavens .... But woe to the earth and the sea, because the devil has gone down to you! (12:12). Satan's expulsion produces two opposite reactions: joy in heaven and grief on earth. Rejoicing has characterized the scenes of heaven up to this point; however, the seal and trumpet judgments, especially the last three trumpets, have produced great woe upon the earth. Satan's reaction to his new spiritual situation is one of fury because he realizes the kingdom of darkness has only a short time left to exist. This is the short time of God's prophetic calendar that coincides with the forty-two months or 1260 days of the church's witness.

The woman ... might fly to the place prepared for her in the desert (12:14). Verse 13, which describes the dragon's pursuit of the birth mother, resumes the narrative interrupted in 12:6. The escape to the desert recalls an earlier work of divine deliverance—Israel's exodus from Egypt. God recalls this event to Moses on Mount Sinai: "You yourselves have seen what I did to Egypt, and how I carried you on eagles' wings and brought you to myself" (Ex. 19:4). A parallel likewise exists in the early history of the Jerusalem church. In his warning about the forthcoming destruction of Jeru-

salem, Jesus admonished the disciples to flee from the city to the mountains (Matt. 24:15–22). Church tradition recalls such a flight of the Jerusalem church in A.D. 66 to Pella (modern Tabaqat Fahil), a city in the Decapolis.[87] Although Pella was not in the Transjordanian mountains, it was situated in their foothills approximately twenty miles south of the Sea of Galilee. The dragon's attempt to destroy the Jewish Christians, first in the Zealot/Roman conflict and then while crossing the Jordan in the winter floods (cf. Mark 13:18), came to nothing. Instead, the Gentile churches of the Decapolis rescued and cared for the Jewish Christian refugees. Around this time John led a community from Palestine to Ephesus. Although the Jerusalem church was now safe, the dragon was making war against the saints in Rome and the province of Asia.

Where she would be taken care of for a time, times and half a time, out of the serpent's reach (12:14). When Daniel asked how long it would be before the astonishing things seen in his vision would be fulfilled, the angel replied, "It will be for a time, times and half a time" (Dan. 12:7). John adopts this prophetic time designation to encompass the period of the woman's protection. This is identical to the 1260 days mentioned earlier in 12:6, the same period that the two witnesses prophesy (Rev. 11:3). This period delineates a time for God's people involving both protection and witness in Revelation.

But the earth helped the woman by opening its mouth and swallowing the river that the dragon spewed out of his mouth (12:16). The woman is saved by the earth from the dragon's attempt to drown her. One of Israel's ancient myths concerned God's victory over a sea monster named Leviathan. Leviathan is often translated "dragon" in the Septuagint, particularly in Job 41:1–34, which gives the fullest description of this primeval beast. Asaph also exalted before God, "It was you who crushed the heads of Leviathan [dragon, LXX] and gave him as food to the creatures of the desert" (Ps. 74:14). Rahab is another probable name for this dragon. Isaiah compared God's destruction of Rahab to the deliverance of Israel from Egypt: "Was it not you who cut Rahab to pieces, who pierced that monster through? Was it not you who dried up the sea, the water of the great deep[?]" (Isa. 51:9–10). The victory that God has previously accomplished over Leviathan is the pattern for the woman's triumph over the dragon.

Then the dragon . . . went off to make war against the rest of her offspring— those who obey God's commandments (12:17). The use of the term "offspring" links directly back to the first messianic promise in Genesis 3:15: "And I will put enmity between you and the woman, and between your offspring and hers." While offspring, or seed, can be interpreted in the singular as a specific reference to the

Messiah Jesus, John uses it as a collective noun. Obeying (literally, keeping) God's commandments was a key theme in three of the messages to the churches (Rev. 2:26; 3:3, 8, 10). The relationship between obedience to Jesus and discipleship is likewise a theme in John 14:21: "Whoever has my commands and obeys them, he is the one who loves me." Reciprocally, whoever loves Jesus will obey his teaching, and both the Father and the Son will love such disciples (John 14:23). This theme, resumed now in Revelation, reminds the victors that obedience to Jesus identifies them as fellow offspring of the woman. This makes them vulnerable to the dragon's attacks.

REFLECTIONS

REVELATION PORTRAYS THE REALITY of spiritual warfare in the Christian life. The dragon has proclaimed a declaration of war against all of God's children, so we are now combatants in that struggle, willing or not. The present eschatological period between Christ's two comings is often compared to two decisive events in World War II—D day and V day. D day marked the landing of Allied troops in Europe. This decisive operation guaranteed the final defeat of Germany. D day is therefore like the first coming of Jesus portrayed in Revelation 12. However, the final surrender of the Axis forces did not occur until almost a year later on V day. Christ's second coming—the V day for the church—remains a future event. Christians now live in this interim period, called by God to overcome the dragon and his forces by putting on the spiritual armor that he has given us (cf. Eph. 6:10–18).

The Two Beasts (13:1–18)

And I saw a beast coming out of the sea (13:1). John's next vision discloses the dragon's two agents who will make war against the saints. Satan and his two beasts form a counter unholy trinity. While the beast in 11:7 came up from the Abyss, here his origin is from the sea. There is no difference, however, because John draws on an early Old Testament tradition that beneath the earth was a subterranean sea (Ex. 20:4). Job 41:31 equates the abyss and the sea as the home of the monster Leviathan: "He makes the depths [abyss, LXX] churn like a boiling cauldron and stirs up the sea like a pot of ointment."

Geographically the province of Asia was oriented westward toward the sea. Ephesus and Smyrna were both major seaports on the Aegean. When the governor would arrive in Asia from Rome, his port of "First Landing" was Ephesus. The legend of coins dating from the third century A.D. affirms this long-standing right.

The four beasts of Daniel's vision also arise from the sea, and John's beast is the prophetic ten-horned beast who has devoured the leopard, bear, and lion (Dan. 7:3–7). The traditional view of Daniel holds that these four kingdoms are Babylon, Medo-Persia, Greece, and Rome. (The main alternative view believes the kingdoms are Babylon, Media, Persia, and Greece.) *Fourth Ezra* (c. 2d cent. A.D.) similarly identifies the fourth beast coming out of the sea as an eagle—the Roman empire (*4 Ezra* 12:10).

Seven heads, with ten crowns on his horns, and on each head a blasphemous name (13:1). The seven heads symbolize the rulers of the beast's kingdom, while the ten horns symbolize their client kings. The crowns, probably of gold, symbolize the authority of the beast. Domitian wore a gold crown engraved with the images of Rome's chief deities Jupiter, Juno, and Minerva. His priests representing Jupiter and the deified Flavian family also wore similar golden crowns, which

▶

THE HARBOR OF EPHESUS

Only an outline of the harbor is visible today due to the Cayster River filling it with silt.

were decorated with Domitian's likeness.[88] Imperial cult priests in Asia Minor normally wore golden crowns that displayed busts of the emperor and his family. The blasphemous name on each head no doubt alludes to the divine names such as lord (*kyrios*), which the emperors adopted.

One of the heads of the beast seemed to have had a fatal wound, but the fatal wound had been healed (13:3). The death and resurrection of one of the heads parodies that of the Lamb (5:6) and the two witnesses (11:7–11). While the earth dwellers react to the two witnesses with contempt and then terror, they are astonished by the beast's reappearance and follow him. Instead of worshiping the resurrected Lamb, they worship the resurrected beast. This imagery bears a strong resemblance to the *Nero redivivus* myth (see "The *Nero Redivivus* Myth").

The beast was given a mouth to utter proud words and blasphemies and to exercise his authority for forty-two months (13:5). The beast's reign is forty-two months, the same period the Gentiles are given to trample the holy city (11:2). This time frame is used exclusively for the period in which God's enemies persecute and oppress his people. The beast's persecution is a trampling on God's temple, which is to be identified as his people and represented by the two

◀

THE *RES GESTAE* INSCRIPTION

A portion of the inscription found at Pisidian Antioch.

▶ The *Res Gestae*

One of the most important inscriptions preserved from Roman antiquity is the Monumentum Ancyranum. Before his death in A.D. 14, Augustus deposited four documents with the Vestal Virgins in Rome, one of which was an account of his deeds (*Res Gestae*). The original brass tablets upon which his deeds were engraved have never been found. But most of the document has been recovered from the Greek and Latin versions found on the walls of the imperial cult temple at Ancyra (modern Ankara), which was the capital of the province of Galatia. The lengthy inscription reads like political propaganda. One paragraph mentions the province of Asia: "After my victory I replaced in the temples of all the communities of the province of Asia the ornaments which my adversary (Mark Antony) in the war had, after despoiling the temples, taken into his own possession." Fragments of the Res Gestae have also been found in Pisidian Apollonia and on the propylon at the entrance of Augustus square in Pisidian Antioch. The account of Augustus' deeds was probably displayed in the imperial cult temple at Pergamum as well as distributed among Asia's other leading cities.[A-50]

witnesses. The arrogance of the beast causes him to blaspheme God and his name. Like the Jews who blasphemed ("slander," NIV) the believers in Smyrna (2:9), the beast now blasphemes God and those dwelling in heaven with him. Because the beast has killed the saints, he appears to have triumphed over the church. Yet the audience already knows that those in heaven have overcome the devil through the blood of the Lamb (7:15; 12:11–12).

All whose names have not been written in the book of life belonging to the Lamb that was slain from the creation of the world (13:8). The beast's universal authority elicits worship from all his subjects. Unlike the victors who are assured a place in the book of life (3:5), the earth dwellers are excluded from this heavenly registry. The book of life relates to the doctrine of election. The time when God decided that his Son should die for the sins of the world was from "the creation of the world." Peter used this same phrase to assure his Anatolian readers that their redemption was secured by the precious

▶

NERO

A statue of the emperor from the Corinth Museum.

▶ The *Nero Redivivus* Myth

An unusual "urban legend" arose in the middle of the first century after Nero's death. Some residents of the eastern provinces refused to believe that this despotic, though popular, emperor was really dead. Rumors began to circulate that Nero's enemies had conspired to stage the whole event and that, after escaping to the East, he would return (Nero redux). Such speculation was fueled when imperial edicts continued to be circulated in his name. Others accepted that Nero had died but believed he would return to life (Nero redivivus).

In July 69 (after Nero had died), Asia became terrified over a report of Nero's arrival. His look-alike soon gathered a mob around him. Forced to land on the Aegean island of Cythnus, this slave from Pontus (or freedman from Italy, as some said) was confronted shortly by Calpurnius Asprenas. Calpurnius was the newly appointed governor of Galatia and Pamphylia and was sailing to assume his new post. This Roman official quickly captured and killed the pretender, whose body was first taken to Ephesus before being transported to Rome.

A second pretender named Tarentius Maximus appeared in Asia in 80. Gathering supporters as he moved eastward, he received the backing of Arta-panus IV, a pretender to the Parthian throne. The two tried to depose the emperor Titus, but his continued rule suggests they were unsuccessful.

A third pretender appeared during Domitian's reign (ca. A.D. 88/89) and received the support of the Parthian king Pacorus II. When the Romans demanded that the Parthians hand him over, they did so only with great reluctance.

Dio Chrysostom, a native of Prusa in Bithynia, summarized the popular expectations at the end of the first century: "Even now everyone wishes he (Nero) were alive, and most believe that he is."[A-51] We do not know when these Nero sightings ended, but the myth and its outworking is surely one of the most bizarre events in Roman imperial history.

▶ The Four *Hōde* Sayings

One popular view of Revelation believes that, since the church is never mentioned after chapter 3, it must be in heaven following the rapture.[A-52] The four *hōde* ("This calls . . .") sayings found in the second half of the book suggest otherwise. The first saying in 13:10 exhorts the saints to patient endurance and faithfulness, even though the beast is making war against them. The second saying in 13:18 calls for those with insight to calculate the meaning of the beast's name, 666. This and the fourth saying recall the parenthetical aside found in the Olivet Discourse—"let the reader understand" (Matt. 24:15). The third saying in 14:12 precedes the second beatitude and again encourages obedience and faithfulness. The persevering saints are to forgo the worship of the beast and his image, and to refuse his mark. The first three sayings also function as structural markers closing three of John's visions. The final saying in 17:9 invites the audience to have understanding about the symbolism of the seven heads and ten horns seen by John. More will be said about this complex imagery in chapter 17. Through these four *hōde* sayings, the Asian believers are exhorted to recognize and act on the spiritual implications of the present crisis. Therefore, Christians are still in view in these later chapters of Revelation.

blood of Christ the Lamb (1 Peter 1:20). Paul also used the phrase to assure his Gentile and Jewish audience concerning God's eternal plan of election for them (Eph. 1:4). The remarkable repetition of this theme is no doubt reassuring to the beleaguered Asian Christians, who were perhaps the same audience that received Ephesians. Christ's life, death, and resurrection on their behalf was no afterthought with God.

He who has an ear, let him hear (13:9). This modified hearing saying recalls the close of the seven prophetic messages (chaps. 2–3). The pronouncement of the unidentified speaker—"If anyone is to go into captivity . . . . If anyone is to be killed with the sword"—is drawn from a dirge in which God described the judgment of disobedient Judah at the hands of the Babylonians (Jer. 15:2; cf. 43:11). John's use of the saying is not deterministic, but a realistic warning for the saints to be prepared for future suffering. The beast's sword may appear to triumph, but only temporarily.

Then I saw another beast, coming out of the earth. He had two horns like a lamb, but he spoke like a dragon (13:11). John sees another beast, but this one comes

REFLECTIONS

WHAT DOES IT MEAN TO HAVE ENDURANCE AND faithfulness as believers today? This question is especially relevant for Christians living in countries where persecution exists. Survival may be a day-to-day matter, staying one step ahead of political and religious officials who are attempting to eliminate your faith or even your life. But what about those of us in the West, where freedom of religion exists and tolerance of Christianity prevails? Our beast is a subtle adversary who can work through culture, government, and false religion, all the while seeking to erode biblical faith and the eternal kingdom it represents. Both threats call for a mind of wisdom, which only the Holy Spirit can give.

from the earth, not the sea. Although its horns resemble those on the Lamb (5:6), when the beast speaks, his true colors are revealed. He is the mouthpiece of the dragon, a sheep in wolf's clothing (cf. Matt. 7:15). As the first provincial capital and the site of Asia's first imperial cult temple, Pergamum was also the seat of its league (*koinon*). Approximately 150 delegates—the leading citizens of the province—comprised the league. Because there was no separation of church and state in the Roman empire, the president of the league also served as the chief priest of the emperor cult. This was regarded as the most prestigious position in Asia. The high priest and league president is probably the individual represented as the second beast out of the earth.[89]

And he performed great and miraculous signs, even causing fire to come down from heaven to earth in full view of men (13:13). The second beast is the field representative for the dragon and the first beast, soliciting worship through deceptive signs and wonders. His activity fulfills Jesus' warning that false prophets would perform great signs and miracles (Matt. 24:24). Even as the two witnesses brought forth fire in the spirit of Elijah (see comments on 11:5), the second beast likewise produces fire. This power encounter is reminiscent of Moses' confrontation with the Egyptian magicians (Ex. 7:10–8:19). Trickery was commonly practiced by sorcerers in antiquity, and special-effects machines producing thunder and lightning were used in theatrical productions. In fact, the emperor Gaius had a device "by which he gave answering peals when it thundered and sent return flashes when it lightened."[90] Yet John seems to regard this supernatural

activity as genuine, although its source is demonic and not divine.

He ordered them to set up an image in honor of the beast (13:14). The Old Testament background is clearly Nebuchadnezzar's command to worship an image that he set up in Babylon. Because Shadrach, Meshach, and Abednego refused the order, they were thrown into the fiery furnace from which they were delivered (Dan. 3:1–17). People living in the Roman empire were quite accustomed to seeing images of the various Roman emperors.

He was given power to give breath to the image of the first beast, so that it could speak (13:15). Statues that spoke, typically in oracular utterances, were known in the Greco-Roman world. Plutarch noted that a particular statue spoke twice after it was erected in a temple. An omen pointing to Gaius's imminent murder occurred when a statue of Olympian Jupiter burst in laughter. Alexander of Abonuteichos (in Bithynia on the Black Sea coast) apparently erected an image of a serpent representing Glaucon-Asclepius that had a movable mouth and concealed speaking tubes.[91] Although no specific evidence of speech by imperial cult statues is extant, John again regards this activity as genuine since through it the nations were led astray (18:23).

No one could buy or sell unless he had the mark, which is the name of the beast or the number of his name (13:17). The mark given by the beast on the right hand and forehead is a parody of the seal received by the 144,000 (7:3). In order to buy and sell, the earth dwellers are forced to have the mark of the beast—his name or the number of his name (as grammatical appositives)—inscribed on their right hand or forehead. The position of this mark reflects that of the phylacteries worn by the Jews at the daily morning prayer. This Jewish practice reflects the divine command that God's word be bound on the hand and over the forehead (cf. Ex. 13:9; Deut. 6:8). The mark of the beast is a perversion of this custom, however, because the mark is on the right, not the left, hand and the mark on, not over, the forehead.[92] While the victors are promised that the name of God and the new name of Jesus will be inscribed on them (Rev. 3:12), the followers of the beast likewise have his name written on them. Two marks—one on the righteous and another on sinners—are likewise described in *Psalms of Solomon* 14:6, 9.

If anyone has insight, let him calculate the number of the beast, for it is man's number. His number is 666 (13:18). The use of codes in the Bible continues to provoke much interest, but there are

◀

IMAGES OF THE EMPEROR AUGUSTUS

Images of the emperor on Roman coins.

▶ Images of the Roman Emperor

The image (*eikōn*) of the emperor was a familiar sight in Asia. Such images were not necessarily realistic representations, but were standardized expressions of imperial ideology. About 250 portraits of Augustus survive from his forty-one year reign. Images of an emperor could be either busts or full statues. The imperial busts were set up in temples and could be so large that they were disproportionate to the size of the temple. The colossal head of Domitian (or Titus) in the Ephesus Museum gives the impression that this person was no ordinary human.

The full statues fell into three categories. First, cuirassed statues represented the emperor as a military conqueror. A coin from Pergamum shows Dea Roma crowning Augustus in his military dress inside the imperial cult temple. A second group of cult statues depicted the emperor naked, like the statues of Greek gods. This representation of the emperor suggested that he too was a divine being. An almost naked statue of Hadrian (A.D. 117–38), found in the imperial room of the Asclepium in Pergamum, had inscribed on its base the "god

Hadrian." The third category showed the emperor in civilian clothing, usually in a Roman toga but occasionally in Greek dress, the *himation*. The imperial cult temple in Smyrna contained a cult statue of Tiberius dressed in a toga.

Such images of the emperor were also placed in dedicated rooms in porticoes and gymnasiums. The north stoa of the agora in Ephesus' upper city had a basilica containing statues of Augustus and his wife Livia. There were also free-standing imperial buildings in the sanctuaries of other gods and goddesses. In Ephesus, within the sanctuary of the temple of Artemis stood a smaller building that served as an imperial shrine to Augustus. Approximately thirty temples, shrines, and porticoes containing images of the emperor stood in the province of Asia during the first century. Imperial images were also displayed publicly, being carried in processions that were part of imperial festivals and other important civic occasions. The emperor's image was well known to the early Christians in the seven churches.[A-53]

only a few clear examples where a code is used. Sheshach (Jer. 25:26; 51:41) and Leb Kamai (51:1) are atbash cryptograms used by Jeremiah to hide the name Babylon or its synonym Chaldea.[93] *Gematria* is the type of code used in Revelation. Hebrew and Greek lent themselves to *gematria* because the letters of their alphabets also represented numbers (a A = 1, b B = 2, g G = 3, etc.). In *gematria*, the name of a person is represented by a number whose sum is the numerical equivalent of its letters.

Examples of *gematria* have been found in graffiti at Pompeii (c. A.D. 79). One reads, "Amerimnus thought upon his lady Harmonia for good. The number of her honorable name is 45 (*me*)," while another states, "I love her whose number is 545 (*phme*)." After Nero murdered his mother in 59, a Greek verse circulated around Rome lampooning the emperor: "Nero, Orestes, Alcmeon their mothers slew/A calculation new. Nero his mother slew." The name Nero is the numerical equivalent of 1005 in Greek, the same as the phrase "his mother slew."[94] The *Sibylline Oracles* provide two examples of *gematria*. The emperors from Julius Caesar to Trajan are alluded to by the

gematria of their initials, and in a Christian passage Jesus is referred to by his number 888.[95] It is evident such a practice was well known in the ancient world.

The solution of the 666 riddle has puzzled Christians for centuries. By the time of Irenaeus (2d cent.), the exact identity of the beast was lost. His best guesses were "Teitan," the mythological Titans who rebelled against the gods, or "Lateinos," the Roman empire. Irenaeus records that a variant, 616, was already known in some versions.[96] Of the various solutions proposed for this cryptic cipher, Nero is the only first-century emperor whose name can be calculated to equal 666. Nero's Greek name *NERON KAISAR* was inscribed on the obverse of coins from Ephesus, Sardis, and Laodicea during this period.[97] John used this name to calculate the number of the beast in Hebrew (cf. Rev 16:16). Could John's audience have known the identity of the beast? Probably so, otherwise John would not have encouraged the Asian believers to calculate the beast's number. The Hebrew and Greek *gematria* associated with the calculation of the names of Nero and Jesus are shown in the chart below.

The Hebrew and Greek *Gematria* Associated with the Calculation of the Names of Nero and Jesus		
Neron Kaisar	**Nero Kaisar**	**Jesus**
נ = 50 N	נ = 50 N	
ר = 200 R	ר = 200 R	I = 10 I
ו = 6 O	ו = 6 O	η = 8 E
נ = 50 N		σ = 200 S
ק = 100 K	ק = 100 K	o = 70 O
ס = 60 S	ס = 60 S	υ = 400 U
ר = 200 R	ר = 200 R	ς = 200 S
666	616	888

REFLECTIONS

IN OUR DAY, ATTEMPTS HAVE BEEN made to link public figures with the number 666. Identifying persons like Henry Kissinger and Mikhail Gorbachev as 666 has proven embarrassingly futile. Because the English alphabet is not used to represent cardinal numbers, it is impracticable to calculate a name using gematria. The prophetic significance of 666 is to understand the political reality it represents—despotic individuals who use their power to persecute the church and oppress humanity. Rulers such as Adolph Hitler, Joseph Stalin, and Idi Amin are examples from the twentieth century.

The 144,000 and the Two Harvests (14:1–20)

Then I looked, and there before me was the Lamb, standing on Mount Zion (14:1). A threefold series of visions, which begin in heaven and move to earth, comprises chapter 14. The 144,000, introduced in chapter 7, now reappear with the Lamb around the heavenly Mount Zion. The earthly Zion was the mount in Jerusalem upon which the temple was built. This was the dwelling place of God: "Sing praises to the LORD, enthroned in Zion" (Ps. 9:11; cf. 132:13–14). Zion later became a synonym for the entire city of Jerusalem (cf. Isa. 4:3–4; 52:1–2). In Hebrews, Zion is viewed not as an earthly reality but as a heavenly city where God, the angels, and the church reside (Heb. 12:22–23; cf. 2 Esd. 2:42). Heavenly Zion has become the meeting point for the saints, even as earthly Zion was the meeting point for the tribes of Israel. John views Zion as the center of the eschatological kingdom, for Christ has been installed here to begin his messianic reign (cf. Ps. 2:6).

And with him 144,00 who had his name and his Father's name written on their foreheads (14:1). The names written on the foreheads of the 144,000 fulfills the promise given to the victors (3:12). These names are evidently the content of the seal mentioned in 7:3, whose nature has long been debated. Its Old Testament background is found in Ezekiel 9:3–11 where an angel is told to put a mark on the foreheads of Jerusalem's residents who grieve over evil. The angel is to slaughter those who do not receive the mark (Heb. *taw*; Ezek. 9:5). Taw is the last letter of the Hebrew alphabet, and in the Old Hebrew script used during Ezekiel's day until the New Testament period taw was written in the form of a cross (X). The Greek letter chi (C) was recognized as an equivalent to taw. Chi, the first letter of Χριστός, was a common abbreviation for this Greek word meaning Christ, or Anointed One. The *Damascus Document*, quoting Ezekiel, states that at the time of the Messiah's coming, the only ones to be spared the sword are those marked by the taw (CD 19.12).[98] A Jewish Christian told the third-century church father Origen that "the form of the Taw in the old [Hebrew] script resembles the cross, and it predicts the mark which is to be placed on the foreheads of the Christians."[99] The mark therefore signifies possession and protection because God's presence is with his people.

And they sang a new song before the throne and before the four living creatures and the elders (14:3). The elders sing a new song around the throne in 5:8; now the 144,000 sing their new song. Although its words are unstated, their quality is suggested through several metaphors: the roar of rushing waters, a loud peal of thunder, and harpists playing their harp. None of the heavenly creatures can learn this song because participation is restricted to those redeemed from the earth. Their praise undoubtedly centers on redemption by the Lamb and deliverance from the beast.

These are those who do did not defile themselves with women, for they kept themselves pure (14:4). Before going into battle, Israelite soldiers were required to maintain ritual purity including abstinence from sex (cf. Deut. 23:9–10; 1 Sam. 21:5; 2 Sam. 11:11). The Lamb's followers, literally called virgins (*parthenoi*), have kept themselves pure for the spiritual holy war. To interpret their continence literally is problematic, because the New Testament affirms the

role of sex in Christian marriage (cf. 1 Cor. 7:2–5). A figurative interpretation is preferred: The virgins are believers of either sex, who have not defiled themselves through spiritual fornication. Some at Sardis had not defiled their white garments (Rev. 3:4). Two women—Jezebel and the great prostitute—are the primary adversaries of the church. In Thyatira, the woman Jezebel threatened the churches with her false prophecy (2:20). And later Babylon/Rome is described as a woman who is the mother of all prostitutes (17:3, 4, 6, 7, 9, 18). Believers who have contact with either woman, Babylon or Jezebel, will soil their garments or, to change metaphors, lose their virginity.

They were purchased from among men and offered as firstfruits to God and the Lamb (14:4). Israel was the firstfruits of God's spiritual harvest (Jer. 2:3). Although firstfruits is used to describe a variety of spiritual blessings in the New Testament, Paul used the term to speak specifically of Israel as the spiritual root of the church (Rom. 11:16). Jewish believers in the Messiah comprised the firstfruits of God's new kingdom community (cf. James 1:18). The use of the term here helps to confirm the identification of the 144,000 as Jewish believers. This group that does not lie about the Lamb contrasts with those in the synagogue of Satan who are liars (Rev. 3:9).

Another angel . . . had the eternal gospel to proclaim to those who live on the earth (14:6). John's vision changes abruptly, and he next sees three angels flying in the middle heaven who have messages to deliver. The first angelic message is directed to individuals from every people group, who seem to be earthly

---

R E F L E C T I O N S

ACCORDING TO REVELATION, ALL PEOPLE ARE SEALED with one of two marks—that of God or that of the beast. The seals of water baptism and of the Holy Spirit have marked us spiritually as God's children. But what about the mark of the beast? Is it a physical stamp that will be implemented through modern technology? Some have suggested that retail bar codes and implanted computer chips are indications that the antichrist is soon to appear. Certainly there are disturbing trends in society that seek to depersonalize us and to deprive us of privacy. But we should not overreact to the information revolution that is fundamentally changing our world, for computer technology is allowing the church to preach the gospel in ways never before imagined. We need not fear the beast's mark since the seal marking us as God's possessions guarantees our divine inheritance (Eph. 1:13–14).

▶ The Emperor's "Gospel"

The white stone stele discussed in 2:17 was inscribed with an edict issued by the proconsul Fabius and approved by the assembly of Asia. It too contained a "gospel" message, which served as political propaganda celebrating the victories of the emperor Augustus and his generous benefactions to his subjects. The edict's language has several parallels in the New Testament. Providence sent Caesar as a savior that he might bring peace (cf. Titus 1:4). His coming is described as an appearing (cf. 2 Tim. 1:10). His birth is also said to be the beginning of life and breath (cf. Rev. 3:14). Likewise, the honor of Augustus is to remain forever (cf. 4:9; 5:13; 7:12). The decree closes by declaring that the birthday of the god Augustus "was the beginning for the world of the good tidings (*euangeliōn;* gospel) that came by reason of him."[A-54] When Paul and John proclaimed the gospel of Jesus Christ in Asia, it is no wonder that their message faced conflict with the imperial gospel. Jesus was both a political and a religious rival to the emperor in Rome and his ambassadors in the provinces.

representatives of the heavenly multitude seen in 7:9. This composite group living on the earth is specifically distinguished from the earth dwellers. The angel's announcement repeats that of the elders: The hour of judgment has come, bringing the positive rewards for the saints and the negative destruction of the wicked (cf. 11:18). The message of the eternal gospel is to fear and to worship God, something that only the saints do (cf. 15:4). This is the only use of the word "gospel" in Revelation.

A second angel followed and said, "Fallen! Fallen is Babylon the Great" (14:8). The second angel's announcement about Babylon's fall is proleptic because the city's actual destruction is not seen until chapter 18. From a heavenly perspective, Babylon's fall has already occurred. This is the first of six uses of the code name Babylon in Revelation (cf. 16:19; 17:5; 18:2, 10, 21). Babylon is used as a cipher in other contemporaneous Jewish literature (*4 Ezra* 15:46; *2 Bar.* 11:1; *Sib. Or.* 5.143). This dirge resembles similar pronouncements over Babylon spoken by Isaiah (Isa. 21:9) and Jeremiah (Jer. 51:8). Babylon was the capital of the Near Eastern empire that captured Jerusalem in 586 B.C. Jeremiah prophesied during this period of Judah's political instability, and twice he spoke judgment oracles against Babylon (25:12–38; 50:1–51:64). Babylon made the whole world of its day drunk when the nations drank her wine (51:7). Which first-century city does John refer to? Peter's use of Babylon (1 Peter 5:13) provides a clue. His probable referent is Rome, the place from which he is writing. Historical tradition dates Peter's martyrdom to the Neronic persecution of 65–66.[100] This would place the writing of 1 Peter before A.D. 70 and thereby attest to the use of Babylon for Rome before the destruction of the temple. Because of Rome's persecution, the early church named their adversary Babylon, a city opposed to God and his people.

A third angel followed them and said . . . "he, too, will drink of the wine of God's

fury, which has been poured full strength into the cup of his wrath" (14:9, 10). In the ancient world, wine was usually mixed with water before it was drunk. The typical ratio was one part wine to three parts water, depending on the type of wine. To drink wine full strength was considered a sign of debauchery and revelry. A cup of un-mixed wine became a metaphor for God's unmitigated judgment. God told Jeremiah: "Take from my hand this cup filled with the wine of my wrath and make all the nations to whom I send you drink it" (Jer. 25:15; cf. Ps. 75:8). Because Babylon destroyed Jerusalem, Jeremiah prophesied that it would be the primary nation to drink of God's wrath (Jer. 25: 26–28). Even as Babylon fell to the Persians in 539 B.C., so too Rome would one day be destroyed.

He will be tormented with burning sulfur in the presence of the holy angels and of the Lamb (14:10). Sulfur is a non-metallic yellowish element that burns with a blue flame while emitting a nox-ious, suffocating sulfur dioxide gas. The punishment of the wicked with burning sulfur is a common eschatological motif.

David wrote, "On the wicked he will rain fiery coals and burning sulfur" (Ps. 11:6). This is because the breath of the Lord is "like a stream of burning sulfur" (Isa. 30:33). God's destruction of Sodom and Gomorrah with burning sulfur is a para-digm of the final judgment (Gen. 19:24). For when Jesus returns, fire and sulfur will rain down from heaven as in the days of Lot (Luke 17:29–30). Burning sulfur is associated four times with punishment in Revelation (cf. 19:20; 20:10; 21:8).

"Blessed are the dead who die in the Lord from now on." "Yes," says the Spirit, "they will rest from their labor, for their deeds will follow them" (14:13). No beatitudes have been spoken since 1:3, so this is the first of the final six that occur in the second half of the book. The Asian audience is pulled from visions of the future back to their present situation, with those who will die being promised a special blessing. The Spirit who speaks to the seven churches in chapters 2–3 now speaks again. He promises the same rest ("wait," NIV) as that which is promised to the martyrs in 6:11. Unlike the idolatrous worshipers who receive no rest from their torments (9:4; 14:11), the saints receive rest from their work of tes-tifying for the Lamb.

There before me was a white cloud, and seated on the cloud was one "like a son of man" (14:14). In his initial vision, John sees someone called "a son of man" whose identity is clearly Jesus (1:13). Because the figure seen here receives orders and then acts as a harvester, he seems more angelic than divine. In 14:14–20 two har-vests are announced and completed—of grain and of grapes. In the parable of the weeds, Jesus compared the end of the age to a harvest in which the angels are the

SULPHUR
▼

harvesters. The angels will separate the weeds, representing the devil's sons, from the good seed, representing the sons of the kingdom (Matt. 13:30, 37–43).

Take your sickle and reap, because the time to reap has come, for the harvest of the earth is ripe (14:15). Sickle can refer to two types of curved knives used for agricultural purposes. Grain was harvested with a short-handled hand scythe, while the sickle used by vintagers was a small knife that could cut grape clusters from the vine. The time of ripeness depended on the crop. The wheat harvest occurred in June, while the harvest of grapes for wine production occurred in September. This agricultural analogy suggests that two groups are to be harvested—the righteous and the wicked. Two things in chapter 14 suggest that the grain harvest is of the righteous. The 144,000 are identified as firstfruits, an agricultural metaphor (14:4; cf. Lev. 2:14), and the audience addressed with the eternal gospel both fear and worship God (Rev. 14:7). Jesus likewise described the ingathering of the righteous as reaping the harvest (John 4:35–38).[101]

Take your sharp sickle and gather the cluster of grapes from the earth's vine, because its grape are ripe (14:18). The angel in charge of the fire on the heavenly incense altar commands another angel to gather the people like grapes. This second harvest is not for blessing but for judgment. Revelation's imagery follows that of Joel 3:13: "Swing the sickle, for the harvest is ripe. Come, trample the grapes for the winepress is full." The fullness of the winepress and its overflowing vats is not because of the abundance of the harvest, but because of the overwhelming wickedness of the nations.

They were trampled in the winepress outside the city (14:20). Archaeologists have discovered many winepresses in excavations throughout the Mediterranean world. Winepresses were square or circular pits, hewn out of rock or holes dug in the ground and then lined with rocks and sealed with plaster. The grapes would be placed in the press and then trampled by several individuals. The juice then flowed through a channel to a lower vessel called a winevat. Here the grape juice was collected and allowed to ferment. During his judgment of the nations, God is asked about his appearance: "Why are your garments red, like those of one treading the winepress?" (Isa. 63:2). This graphic description portrays the slaughter that will accompany the harvest of the unrighteous.

Joel located this final judgment in the valley of Jehoshaphat (Joel 3:2). The church historian Eusebius identified this valley as the Hinnom, which lies south of Jerusalem. This was the traditional valley of judgment in the Old Testament (Jer. 7:31–32; 19:5–6), and became the prototype for the concept of Gehenna seen in Jewish intertestamental literature (cf. 2 Esdras 7:36, NRSV note) and the New Testament (Matt. 5:22). Later Jewish,

WINEPRESS

The surface of a winepress in a village near Hebron.

Christian, and Muslim traditions came to identify the valley as the Kidron, east of Jerusalem. To secure a place in the resurrection, Muslims buried their dead on Kidron's western slope beneath the Golden Gate, while Jews buried their dead on the east beneath the Mount of Olives. John seems to delocalize purposely the valley from a Palestinian context by placing it outside the city—here Babylon—which is martyring the saints.

The Song of Moses and the Seven Last Plagues (15:1–8)

I saw in heaven another great and marvelous sign: seven angels with the seven last plagues (15:1). John's next series of visions, which run through chapter 18, replays through the final events that usher in the two harvests. The seven plagues are called last because with them God's wrath reaches its full measure. Before these plagues are revealed, John sees another vision of the victors in heaven.

Standing beside the sea, those who had been victorious over the beast and his **image and over the number of his name (15:2).** The clear sea of glass that John saw before the throne in 4:6 now has a fiery red hue. The color is ominous, foreboding the coming judgments of fire that will complete God's wrath (16:8; 18:8; 20:15). The victors find their ultimate deliverance at the sea of glass, just as Israel was delivered through the Red Sea. They have triumphed over the beast, the historical equivalent of the pharaoh.

They . . . sang the song of Moses the servant of God and the song of the Lamb (15:3). Like the 144,000 who sing a new song before the heavenly throne (14:1–3), the rest of the victors also sing a song of triumph. Their song imitates the heavenly song celebrating the triumph of the Lamb through his blood (cf. 5:5, 9–10). It has parallels with two songs of Moses recorded in the Old Testament. The first song celebrates God's triumph over the Egyptians (Ex. 15:1–18), while the second promises judgment to his enemies and reward to his servants (Deut. 32:1–43). The words of the song reflect a number of Old Testament texts including "Great are the works of the LORD" (Ps.

111:2) and "all his ways are just" (Deut. 32:4). This worship language carefully balances God's miraculous works with his moral attributes, both essential aspects of his nature. The question in verse 4 is drawn directly from Jeremiah 10:7: "Who should not revere you, O King of the nations?" There Jeremiah is contrasting the worship of God with idols, concluding that idolatry was foolishness. By refusing to worship the beast's image and receive his number, the victors have likewise rejected the temptation to idolatry.

For you alone are holy (15:4). Here and in 16:5 are the only occurrences of the distinctive Greek word *hosios,* translated "holy," which indicates the close relationship between the two songs. The language is drawn directly from the second Song of Moses: "just (*dikaios*) and holy (*hosios*) is the Lord" (Deut. 32:4 LXX). The linkage of these divine attributes is also found in these words of David: "The Lord is just in all his ways, and holy in all his works" (Ps. 145:17 LXX). The most unique gods worshiped in the Phrygian and Lydian regions of Asia (around Laodicea, Philadelphia, and Sardis) were called *Hosion kai Dikaion,* "Holy and Just." A funerary inscription from the area invokes Holy and Just to take vengeance on an individual if she does not return to the family some personal possessions left for safe keeping by the deceased. A limestone stele found in northeastern Asia depicts Holy and Just, one holding the scales of justice and the other the staff of authority.[102] John's insistence on the Lord as the only holy and just God would serve as a polemic against these popular indigenous deities.

All nations will come and worship before you (15:4). The universal worship of God is the great prophetic hope of the Old Testament. David cried, "All the nations you have made will come and worship before you, O LORD" (Ps. 86:9). In the new heavens and new earth "all mankind will come and bow down before me [God]" (Isa. 66:23; cf. Mal. 1:11). The victors echo this longing. However, there is no idea of mass conversion present in this language. Such worship is based on obedience to God's revealed righteousness and excludes the rebellious (Isa. 66:24). Representatives of all nations who have triumphed over the beast are among these worshipers (cf. Rev. 7:9; 14:6).

Out of the temple came the seven angels with the seven plagues (15:6). The visionary sign introduced in verse 1 is now fully revealed. After the seventh trumpet, John sees the ark of the covenant in the open temple (11:19). Again John sees the temple opened in heaven. This temple is also called the tabernacle of Testimony, a name that recalls the portable tabernacle that accompanied Israel in the desert (Ex. 38:21; cf. Acts 7:44). The Testimony refers to the two tablets of stone containing the ten commandments that were

THE TABERNACLE

A model of the tabernacle showing the entrance.

inscribed by the finger of God (Ex. 31:18). These stones were housed in the ark of the covenant along with the gold jar of manna and Aaron's staff that had budded (Heb. 9:4).

Then one of the four living creatures gave to the seven angels seven golden bowls filled with the wrath of God (15:7). The golden bowls seen in 5:8 and 8:3–5 are full of incense, which represent the prayers of the saints. This second set of golden bowls has a different function in both the earthly and the heavenly temple ritual. The use of the verb "pour out" in chapter 16 suggests that they are not censers but libation bowls. Moses made such sprinkling bowls for use at the altar of burnt offering (Ex. 27:3; Num. 4:14). For worship in the temple, Solomon had a hundred gold sprinkling bowls made for holding wine, which often accompanied sacrifices to God (2 Chron. 4:8; Hos. 9:4). These libation bowls now function as cups containing the wine of God's wrath (Rev. 14:10; 16:19).

And the temple was filled with smoke from the glory of God and from his power, and no one could enter the temple (15:8). On several occasions in the Old Testament, the glory of God was also heavy. After the tabernacle was erected,

Moses could not enter it because the divine cloud had settled upon it, and the glory of God had filled the tabernacle (Ex. 40:35). When Solomon brought the ark of the covenant into the temple, the cloud of God's glory so filled it that the priests could not perform their service (1 Kings 8:10–12; 2 Chron. 5:13–14). When Ezekiel saw the glory of the Lord filling the temple, he fell face down (Ezek. 44:4). The temple's closure until the plagues of the seven bowls are complete suggests that God's mercy is exhausted and that only his wrath remains for the earth dwellers.

The Seven Bowls of God's Wrath (16:1–21)

Ugly and painful sores broke out on the people who had the mark of the beast and worshiped his image (16:2). The outpouring of the seven bowls upon the worshipers of the beast completes the fullness of God's wrath announced in 14:10. The first bowl replicates the sixth Egyptian plague. Moses initiated the plague of boils by throwing soot from a furnace into the air. That soot spread as fine dust over Egypt to produce festering boils on both people and animals (Ex. 9:8–11). No medium like soot is mentioned in Revelation. Once the bowl is

▶ The Trumpet and Bowl Judgments and the Egyptian Plagues

The Exodus tradition is an important background for Revelation. The Passover typology was initially introduced in 5:6 when John sees a slain Lamb. The two witnesses, like Moses, were empowered to turn the waters into blood and to smite the earth with plagues (11:6). The song of Moses also became the song of the Lamb (15:3). The plagues against Egypt provide a prophetic background for the serial judgments of the seven trumpets and the seven bowls, with six of the ten being replicated in Revelation. Like Exodus, John arranges his judgments in increasing degrees of intensity. Like the pharaoh whose heart became hardened (Ex. 7–14 passim), the inhabitants of the earth refuse to repent (Rev. 9:20–21; 16:9, 11).

poured on the land, sores break out only on the earth dwellers. God warned Israel that one of the curses for disobedience would be painful boils covering the entire body (Deut. 28:35). Although it is impossible to determine medically the nature of the sores in Revelation, their appearance is repulsive and their festering pustules are extremely painful.

The sea . . . turned into blood like that of a dead man, and every living thing in the sea died. The third angel poured out his bowl on the rivers and springs of water . . . became blood (16:3, 4). The content of bowls two through four is comparable to that of the first three trumpets. Whereas only a third of the people are affected by the trumpet judgments, the destruction is total with the bowls. The sea turns to blood in the third bowl, while freshwater sources become blood in the fourth bowl. This parallels the first Egyptian plague; however, only the Nile River and freshwater sources were affected, not the sea (Ex. 7:17–21). From the perspective of John and his audience, the sea was the Mediterranean. The Old Testament frequently calls the Mediterranean "the sea" (e.g., Num. 34:5). Variations are "the Great Sea" (Num. 34:6) or "the western sea" (Deut. 11:24). The Romans, like the Greeks, called it "the inner sea" (Lat. *Mare Internum*). Several of the Asian cities were near the major rivers or their tributaries that drained western Anatolia: the Caicus River at Pergamum, the Hermus River at Sardis, the Cayster River at Ephesus, and the Lycus branch of the Meander River at Laodicea. These rivers provided valuable water resources for domestic and agricultural uses. Ephesus and Miletus were at the mouths of the Cayster and the Meander, but the ongoing deposit of silt from these rivers required regular dredging to keep the navigational channels of these great harbors open.

You have given them blood to drink as they deserve (16:6). Because the earth dwellers have shed innocent blood (cf. 17:6), God now pours out two blood judgments. Revelation's imagery is probably drawn from Isaiah 49:26: "They [your oppressors] will be drunk on their own blood, as with wine." This principle of juridical reciprocity is called *lex talionis*. It forms the foundation for the administration of biblical law: "You are to take life for life, eye for eye, tooth for tooth, hand for hand, foot for foot, burn for burn, wound for wound, bruise for bruise" (Ex. 21:23–25). Jesus' teaching in the Sermon on the Mount appears to overturn this concept that the punishment should fit the crime (Matt. 5:38). However, serious injury is not involved with any of the three examples he gives. Jesus is espousing the ethics of the citizens of the kingdom of God—a lifestyle demonstrated by the martyrs—and is not addressing the punishment of the wicked either by divine or secular justice.

And I heard the altar respond (16:7). John is not implying that an article of furniture now speaks. Rather, the sentence is better translated, "And I heard someone from the altar respond." The angel's declaration of God's justice elicits a response from a representative of those most affected—the martyrs themselves. These same saints under the altar cry out for justice in 6:10 and declare God's judgments true and just in 15:3.

The sun was given power to scorch people with fire (16:8). In the fourth bowl, the sun sears all people with unrelenting and oppressive heat (cf. 8:7). The earth dwellers for the first time now blaspheme ("cursed," 16:19 NIV) God, following the example of the beast (13:5–6). The earth dwellers' failure to repent and their blasphemy against God likewise serve as refrains to close the fifth and seventh bowls (16:11, 21).

His kingdom was plunged into darkness. Men gnawed their tongues in agony and cursed the God of heaven (16:10–11). With the outpouring of the fifth seal, total darkness descends on the beast's kingdom and his throne (cf. 8:12). The beast's seat of power in the first century was at Rome, while his localized throne in Asia was at Pergamum (2:13). The ninth plague on Egypt similarly covered the entire land in darkness for three days. Yet the Israelites had light where they lived (Ex. 10:21–23). Jesus often used a similar eschatological motif in his parables: "And throw that worthless servant outside, into the darkness, where there will be weeping and gnashing of teeth" (Matt. 25:30; cf. 22:13). Like the gnashing of teeth, gnawing the tongue represents the despair of the wicked.

The great river Euphrates . . . was dried up to prepare for the kings from the East (16:12). Babylon was captured in 539 B.C. when the Persians diverted the Euphrates River and marched into the city on the dried-up river bed.[103] In 9:14, the army gather at a ford on the Euphrates prepared for battle. Now that the river is dried up, perhaps because of drought, the crossing of the kings can occur anywhere. These kings are often identified with the Parthians who lived east of the Euphrates.

Then I saw three evil spirits that looked like frogs (16:13). The second plague on the Egyptians was a plague of frogs that covered the land. By using their magic arts, the Egyptian magicians were able to duplicate this miracle (Ex. 8:1–14). The same demonic deception employed by the magicians is now operating out of the mouths of the unholy trinity. The second

▶ Parthia and "The Kings from the East"

After Augustus became emperor in 27 B.C., the Romans began to vie with the Parthians for control of Armenia. Finally, Nero initiated a military campaign to secure Rome's eastern frontier. General Corbulo's conquest of Armenia (A.D. 59) and victory over the Parthians was total. Only through the folly of the Roman client king Tigranes in 60 and the ineptitude of Corbulo's replacement Paetus were the Parthians able to regroup and defeat the Romans at Rhandeia in 62. Once Corbulo reestablished the Roman position in 63, the Parthians again become suppliants with Tiridates and he was forced to travel to Rome in 65 to receive his crown. This new client king was treated as visiting royalty by Nero, and the emperor was hailed for restoring peace to the empire. Tiridates visited the cities of Asia on his return to Parthia. The civil war in 68–69 would have been an ideal time for the Parthians to strike against their longtime enemy. This was because Mucianus, the governor of Syria, had left the eastern frontier vulnerable when he led the sixth legion westward to depose Vitellius. However, neither Vologeses nor his brother Tiridates in Armenia desired to break the accord recently secured by Nero. In fact, Vologeses offered Vespasian 40,000 Parthian cavalry to help him secure the principate. The Flavian dynasty was therefore indebted to the Parthians for their cooperation during this tumultuous transition, and these kings in the east ceased to be a threat to Rome in the first century.[A-55]

beast is henceforth called the false prophet (cf. Rev. 19:20; 20:10). According to 1 John 4:1, "many false prophets have gone out into the world," whose false message about Jesus is "the spirit of the antichrist" (4:3). Although the word antichrist is not used in Revelation, the deceptive activity of the false prophet and the prophetess Jezebel (cf. 2:20) both have the demonic spirit of antichrist as their source. In the Old Testament, the prophet Micaiah saw a vision as to why the other prophets were prophesying falsely to the kings Ahab and Jehoshaphat. The Lord was enticing Ahab to die in battle by putting a lying spirit in the mouths of all the court prophets (1 Kings 22:1–28). God Almighty similarly allows the three evil spirits to deceive his opponents into believing they are prepared to fight him in battle.

They go out to the kings of the whole world (16:14). Through miraculous signs, these demonic spirits gather the kings of the whole world (*oikoumenē*; cf. 12:9). From a Roman perspective the *oikoumenē* was not only a geographical concept, but also a political and cultural one. The world consisted of its inhabited and civilized empire. The decree of Caesar Augustus that a census should be taken of the world is rightly translated in the NIV as "the entire Roman world" (Luke 2:1). Thus, Josephus could call Caesar "the lord of the universe," that is, of the *oikoumenē*.[104] The concept became idealized through the goddess Oikoumene. Her statues, sometimes used as lighthouses, served as useful propaganda symbols throughout the empire of Rome's global domination.[105]

The battle on the great day of God Almighty (16:14). Western Anatolia was the site of several important battles of the Greco-Roman period. Alexander the Great, the Macedonian leopard in Daniel's vision of four beasts (Dan. 6:6) who is also described as a one-horned goat (8:5–8), defeated the Persians for the first time in 334 B.C. at Granicus River. The battle site is just south of the Sea of Marmara near Biga in northwestern Turkey. Following Alexander's death, his successors fought one another at the "Battle of the Kings" at Ipsus (near modern Çay) in 301 B.C.; Antigonus and his son Demetrius confronted their rivals Lysimachus and Seleucus. The latter prevailed, and Alexander's great empire was broken up and divided among four successor states (cf. 11:4). In 190 B.C., the Romans defeated the Greek army near Smyrna at Magnesia and Sipylum (modern Manisa). Lucius Scipio Asiaticus was the Roman commander who gained control of the coastlands of western Anatolia and put an end to the insolence of Antiochus III (cf. 11:17–18). Such great historic battles will pale in comparison to the final battle of the Lord.

Behold, I come like a thief! Blessed is he who stays awake and keeps his clothes with him, so that he may not go naked and be shamefully exposed (16:15). Jesus suddenly speaks again in the midst of the sixth bowl, encouraging the Asian believers to persevere. Jesus uses imagery already introduced in the messages to Sardis and Laodicea. The believers were to remain watchful lest his coming be like a thief in the night (3:2–3) and to dress in white clothes to cover their shameful nakedness (3:18; see comments). Although the clothing/nakedness imagery is largely figurative here, it suggests an ancient cultural practice whereby people slept nude. There were varying opinions about nakedness in the ancient world. Greek athletes competed nude and introduced the gymnasium (from *gymnos*, "naked") to the Romans and Jews. The Romans were more conservative than the Greeks about public nudity. Males portrayed in Roman statues were usually clothed while their Greek counterparts were not.[106] When a gymnasium was established in Jerusalem and Jewish youth began to practice Greek customs such as nudity, traditional Jewish sensibilities were greatly offended (2 Macc. 4:9–15). This grievance was a background to the Maccabean rebellion.

Then they gathered the kings together to the place that in Hebrew is called Armageddon (16:16). Armageddon is popularly recognized as the place where the last battle between the forces of good and evil will take place. John appears to give a clue to its geographical location. Unlike 9:11 where John translates the Hebrew name *Abaddōn* into the approximate Greek form *Apollyōn*, here he simply provides the transliterated Hebrew word *Harmagedōn*. The closest Hebrew equivalent is *Har Megiddo*, meaning

"mountain of Megiddo." However, no such name exists in the Old Testament, although the plain of Megiddo is mentioned twice (2 Chron. 35:22; Zech. 12:11). Megiddo was a city in the Jezreel valley in lower Galilee that sat on the international highway connecting Egypt with Mesopotamia. It was the site of several major battles (cf. Judg. 5:19), including the one in 609 B.C. between the armies of Judah and Egypt. Pharaoh Neco, on his way to Carchemish on the Euphrates to reinforce the Assyrians, was engaged by King Josiah at Megiddo. Judah was defeated and her last good king was killed in the battle (2 Kings 23:29–30). Ezekiel locates the defeat of Gog in the final eschatological battle on the mountains of Israel (Ezek. 39:4). John combines these Old Testament battlefield traditions and delocalizes the future battle site by naming it *Harmagedōn* (Eng. "Armageddon"), a place without geographical reality. John has already done something similar in Revelation 1:7. There he takes Zechariah's comparison of Jerusalem's weeping at the coming of the pierced one with the weeping at Megiddo (Zech. 12:10–11) and universalizes that mourning to all the peoples of the earth.

Out of the temple came a loud voice from the throne, saying, "It is done!" (16:17). With the outpouring of the seventh bowl comes the completion of the bowl judgments. An *inclusio* involving cosmic phenomena occurs here as in the seal and bowl judgments (cf. 8:5; 11:19). However, the earthquake is unprecedented, splitting the great city into three parts and leveling all other cities. Babylon's demise through the cup of the Lord's wrath fulfills the angelic announcement in 14:8. Although the

R E F L E C T I O N S

JESUS OFTEN LIKENS HIS COMING TO THAT OF A THIEF in the night. His use of this simile suggests several attitudes for Christian living. The first is expectation. Since we know Jesus will return, meeting him at death or at the rapture should not be a surprise to us. Next is spiritual preparation. By living with a heart of repentance and faith, we will not be caught spiritually undressed but instead always be clothed with robes of righteousness. Finally, we are to be vigilant, "staying awake" to the voice of the Holy Spirit as he seeks to guide us through the spiritual hazards of life. Adopting such attitudes is the Christian's "security system" to avoid a surprise visit from the Lord.

◀

earthquake's damage is tremendous, it is not the final plague. A plague of large hailstones weighing a hundred pounds each falls on people (cf. 11:19). Hail was the seventh plague that fell upon Egypt (Ex. 9:22–26). For the earth dwellers, this is the third time in the chapter that they curse God because of the plagues. Because the plagues are done, their destiny at the judgment seat is finalized because they do not repent.

The Woman on the Beast (17:1–18)

Come, I will show you the punishment of the great prostitute, who sits on many waters (17:1). One of the seven angels who pours out the bowl judgments now shows John a detailed vision of the judgment against the church's foe personified as a prostitute. Although the great prostitute is not initially identified, her activities suggest she is a first-century Babylon. The angelic interpretation in verse 18 states that she symbolizes the great city that rules over the kings of the earth. Jerusalem (Isa. 1:21), Tyre (Isa. 23:16–17), and Nineveh (Nah. 3:4) were cities in the Old Testament called prostitutes because of their godlessness. Historical Babylon was a city of many waters because the Euphrates River flowed through the city from north to south (Jer. 51:13 [28:13 LXX]). Rome was similarly situated, with the Tiber River flowing through the city. It is not these literal waters, however, that the angel is talking about. They are interpreted in Revelation 17:15 as "peoples, multitudes, nations and languages," that is, her subjects throughout the empire. Such interpretive clues suggest that the imagery in this chapter is highly symbolic.

There I saw a woman sitting on a scarlet beast (17:3). For the third time, John finds himself "in the Spirit" (cf. 1:10; 4:2). In the desert he sees a second woman whose appearance (i.e., character) is the opposite of the woman he saw in the desert in 12:14. She sits on the same beast that was revealed in 13:1. Rome was named after Roma, the daughter of the site's first settler, Evander. Roma came to personify the city and was worshiped as a goddess. In 195 B.C., Smyrna became the first city anywhere to establish a cult to Rome by building a temple for the deity Roma.[107] By the time of Augustus, about twenty cults of Roma existed in Asia Minor. When Augustus visited Ephesus in 30 B.C., he gave permission for a temple to Dea Roma and Divus Julius to be built for the city's Roman residents.[108] Archaeologists have located this temple between the Boule-

terion and the Prytaneion, two important civic structures in the upper city. The original imperial cult temple to Augustus built in Pergamum in 29 B.C. was jointly dedicated to Roma. Most of the seven cities had active cults to Roma in them. A coin issued in Asia during the reign of Vespasian (A.D. 69–79) shows his image on the obverse and that of Dea Roma seated on seven hills on the reverse. In her left hand is a small sword whose tip rests on her left knee, symbolizing Rome's military might. At the feet of the goddess is a representation of the river god Tiber, while beneath her is a she-wolf suckling Romulus and Remus. Since imperial coin engravers normally copied real statues and structures, it is likely that this portrait of Roma is a copy of an actual marble or bronze relief.[109] Therefore, John sees an image probably known to him.

The woman was dressed in purple and scarlet (17:4). The woman dressed in bright, expensive clothing and adorned with precious jewels is a stock descrip-

▶
THE GODDESS ROMA

An image of the goddess on a Roman coin.

▶
TEMPLE OF ROMA

The remains of the temple in Ephesus.

tion of a prostitute in antiquity. God asked wayward Jerusalem: "Why dress yourself in scarlet and put on jewels of gold? . . . You adorn yourself in vain. Your lovers despise you" (Jer. 4:30). Purple also signified wealth and nobility in the ancient world. Daniel was awarded the right to wear purple by King Belshazzar (Dan. 5:16, 29). Purple was a color associated with Thyatira (cf. Acts 16:14). A number of inscriptions attest to the presence of a guild of purple dyers in the city.[110] The purple dye used there was derived from the madder root and of lesser quality than that derived from several types of mollusks found in the eastern Mediterranean. This superior dye, known as Tyrian purple, was extracted from the throat of the shellfish with each one producing a single drop. The resulting colors fell in the violet-scarlet range. Because such dyes were expensive, purple came to represent social status on the togas worn by all male Roman citizens. Senators displayed a broad purple stripe on their togas and equestrians a narrow purple stripe. Emperors wore togas entirely of purple. The woman's purple dress symbolizes her connection to Rome and its political elite.[111]

She held a golden cup in her hand, filled with abominable things (17:4). First-century Jews well understood the meaning of abominations, for this unusual word (bdelygma) had a rich history in second-temple Judaism. Daniel prophesied about an abomination that would be set up and desolate the temple (Dan. 9:27; 11:31; 12:11).

In 167 B.C., the Seleucid ruler Antiochus IV Epiphanes erected the abomination of desolation—an altar to the Greek god Zeus Olympius—in the Jerusalem temple (1 Macc. 1:54). This and other sacrileges against the Jews sparked the Maccabean rebellion. When Jerusalem was recaptured in 164 B.C., the abomination in the temple was immediately destroyed (1 Macc. 6:7). The cleansing and rededication of the temple was celebrated annually at the Feast of Hanukkah (cf. John 10:22).

Jewish freedom ended in 61 B.C. when the Roman army under Pompey captured Judea and Jerusalem. Pompey desolated the temple by entering the Holy of Holies, forbidden to everyone but the high priest. Pompey's defeat by Julius Caesar and subsequent assassination fifteen years later was attributed by one Jewish writer to his insolence and contempt in despising God (*Pss. Sol.* 2:26–27).

Augustus and the emperors that followed largely respected the sacred status of Jerusalem. Roman military standards, which bore the imperial image, were banned from the city to avoid breaking the second commandment against graven images. In A.D. 40, however, the megalomaniac Caligula provoked the Jews by issuing an order that his image be erected in the temple. Only the persuasive intervention of King Agrippa prevented an insurrection against Rome.[112]

Jesus prophesied that the abomination causing desolation would appear before the destruction of Jerusalem. In Luke's version that desolation is related to Jerusalem's encirclement by Roman armies (Luke 21:20). The Jerusalem church took this as a sign to flee the city in A.D. 66. Matthew's version locates the abomination as standing in the holy place of the temple (Matt. 24:15; cf. Mark 13:14).

Josephus attributed the defilement of the temple to the Zealots who first shed their blood in it and later stopped its daily sacrifice. After the Roman general Titus led his troops into Jerusalem, a confrontation broke out between the Jews and the Romans in the temple area. On August 30, A.D. 70 Roman soldiers set the temple on fire. When Titus entered the temple and saw the splendor of the holy place, he attempted to put out the flames. However, the fire was too far advanced to be extinguished.[113] The desolation of the temple was complete and it was never rebuilt.

Certain Jewish and Christian activists today are mobilizing resources to rebuild the temple in Jerusalem. However, the el-Aksa Mosque and the Dome of the Rock now stand on the temple mount, and any attempt to remove these Muslim holy places would provoke a holy war.

This title was written on her forehead (17:5). The mark of the beast worn by the earth dwellers on their foreheads (cf. 13:16) reflects what the woman herself has on her forehead. The word "mystery" is probably not part of the title, as in the NIV, but rather describes the nature of the name that follows (see 17:7). This is the third and final mystery revealed in the book (cf. 1:20; 10:7). This woman, finally identified as Babylon the Great, is the mother of prostitutes and source of the earth's idolatrous abominations. Again, she stands in contrast to the woman who bore the male child and the other offspring who followed him (12:13, 17). It is inevitable that the descendants of these two lineages would clash. John sees that this woman for the moment has the upper hand in the struggle, for she is intoxicated not with wine, but with the blood of the saints.

The beast, which you saw, once was, now is not, and will come up out of the Abyss (17:8). John's reaction to seeing the woman on the beast is astonishment. For the rest of the chapter, the angel explains the vision he has shown John. The span of the beast's finite rule parodies that of the eternal Father who is and was and is to come (cf. 1:4, 8). When the earth dwellers finally realize his true nature, they too will be astonished, for their names are not written in the book of life. This language is nearly identical to 13:8, except the stress here is on God's eternal election of a people rather than his eternal redemption through the Lamb.

The seven heads are seven hills (17:9). The angel's explanation continues with this final *hōde* saying directed to the original audience. These believers are to discern two things related to the significance of the beast's seven heads. First, they represent seven hills. Rome was known throughout the ancient world as the city of seven hills, whose names are: Capitoline, Aventine, Caelian, Esquiline, Quirinal, Viminal, and Palantine. Numerous Roman writers used the phrase "seven hills" as a locution for Rome.[114] The names of the seven hills are inscribed on the base of a second-century A.D. statue found in Corinth. The statue apparently depicted Dea Roma sitting or standing on Rome's seven hills.[115]

They are also seven kings (17:10). The heads also represent seven emperors, whose identity is problematic. Some scholars have questioned whether John is even referring to actual individuals. While the number seven undoubtedly symbolizes the full sequence of Roman emperors, to interpret it as exclusively symbolic is problematic, since both the seven churches and the seven hills represent literal realities. If it is a historical reference, which emperor is the first?

The Roman historian Suetonius began his *The Twelve Caesars* with Julius Caesar. However, his contemporary Tacitus started his *Annals* with Augustus. From a Roman historiographical tradition, the evidence is inconclusive.

For John and the Asian churches, Augustus, called Octavian until 27 B.C., seems the better starting point. Augustus had a strong link to Asia through his slave Zoilos. In 39 B.C., Octavian influenced the Senate to grant special status to Zoilos's native town Aphrodisias, near Laodicea. Around 35 B.C., Octavian guaranteed the right of the Asian Jews to send the temple tax to Jerusalem. He was the ruler who introduced imperial cult worship to the province in 29 B.C.

Augustus made a personal visit to Asia in 20 B.C. during a tour of Asia Minor. In 9 B.C. the Asian calendar was changed to begin on Augustus's birthday. Jesus was born during the reign of Augustus (Luke 2:1; ca. 4 B.C.). The epigraphical record shows that Augustus still had a pervasive influence over the lives of the Ephesians at the end of the first century A.D.[116]

During Julius's lifetime, the only provincial cities to issue coinage with his portrait were the Anatolian cities of Nicea and Lampsacus. However, the coming of the principate brought a major change to this pattern. Suddenly the portrait of Augustus began to dominate the obverse of provincial coinage. During his reign, seventy-three Asian mints (out of the ninety-seven for the Anatolian peninsula) issued Augustan bronze coins. Augustus' face was as familiar in Asia as the portrait of Atatürk, the founder of the Turkish republic, is today in the region. Because Suetonius called the brief reigns of Galba, Otho, and Vitellius a rebellion,[117] some interpreters omit these three from the sequence of seven. Such lists ignore the ancient literary evidence because the three are recognized as legitimate emperors by Suetonius, the *Sibylline Oracles* (5:12–51), and *4 Ezra* (chs. 11–12). Numismatic evidence demonstrates that the three were recognized as legitimate emperors in the provinces. Galba's representation on Asian coinage shows specifically that his rule was recognized there.[118] Therefore, any identification that omits the three ignores that evidence. Interpreters who date Revelation to Domitian's reign must begin with an emperor later than either Julius or Augustus to make Domitian the current emperor. Or they must develop

---

▶ **The Eight Emperors**

Revelation presents the eight emperors in a distinctive numerical pattern: 5 + 1 + 1 = 7 + 1 = 8. Five have died, one is currently reigning, another is yet to come. The eighth is the beast, an emperor *redivivus* or *redux*, who will go to his destruction. Nero was the likely head with the mortal wound who was and now is not (see comments on 13:3). Since he would be dead, Nero could not be the reigning emperor ("one is"). Numerous interpretations of the eight emperors have been proposed, but the Principate view that begins with Augustus is now presented:

> *Five Fallen*—1. Augustus, 2. Tiberius, 3. Gaius, 4. Claudius, 5. Nero
> *One is*—6. Galba
> *One not yet*—7. Otho
> *Beast or Nero redivivus*—8.

Revelation would date approximately to the early months of 69, if this model were correct.

an alternate criterion for the list, such as emperors who were deified or died violently.

The ten horns you saw are ten kings (17:12). Rome was the temporary home of many foreign notables who awaited appointments as rulers over client kingdoms throughout the empire. Herod the Great received his appointment as King of Judea there from Antony, Octavian, and the Senate in 40 B.C. Herod's descendants—Archelaus, Antipas, Philip, Agrippa I, and Agrippa II—who ruled various kingdoms in Palestine after Herod's death in 4 B.C. either were reared in Rome or were appointed to their rule there. The ten kings receive authority to rule for one hour. During this brief period they mobilize their kingdoms to join the beast in fighting one final battle.

The Lamb will overcome them because he is Lord of lords and King of kings (17:14). The allied forces of the beast and the kings take the offensive against the Lamb by crossing the Euphrates and gathering at Armageddon (16:12, 16). However, they cannot prevail against the Lamb "because he is Lord of lords and King of kings." While God is called "God of gods and Lord of lords" in the Old Testament (Deut. 10:17; Dan. 2:47), the singular title "King of kings" does not occur until the intertestamental period (2 Macc. 13:4; *3 Macc.* 5:35). Paul is the only other New Testament writer to use this dual title. Mentioning the Parousia, he writes that "God will bring [it] about in his own time—God, the blessed and only Ruler, the King of kings and Lord of lords" (1 Tim. 6:15). The allies of the Lamb in this last battle are his followers said to be called, chosen, and faithful.

This is the only place in Revelation where believers are described as called and chosen, both familiar designations in the New Testament (cf. Rom. 8:28; Col. 3:12; 2 Tim. 2:10). Faithfulness, commanded to the Christians in Smyrna about to suffer (Rev. 2:10), is rewarded by association with the Lamb at the end.

The Fall of Babylon (18:1–24)

Fallen! Fallen is Babylon the Great! (18:2). Like the angel's announcement in 14:8, this one also speaks of Babylon's fall as if it had already occurred. In fact, for the six different voices heard in this chapter, either lamenting or celebrating the city's demise, Babylon's fall is still future. Jeremiah's prophetic description of the fall of historical Babylon (Jer. 50–51) provides an important backdrop for this chapter. There are at least twelve allusions to Jeremiah in its language and imagery. The angel's opening lament in verses 2–3 mentions several reasons for Babylon's devastation.

A haunt for every evil spirit, a haunt for every unclean and detestable bird (18:2). The Jewish belief that evil spirits lived in desolate places is reflected in the teaching of Jesus (Luke 11:24). He healed a demoniac who lived in the hill country southeast of the Sea of Galilee (Mark 5:5). Jerusalem is described as a ruined city that had become a habitation for unclean spirits (Bar. 4:35). The levitical law identifies twenty different species of birds as unclean (Lev. 11:13–19). The majority of these are birds of prey that drink blood and whose diet consists mainly of carrion or flesh. Isaiah (Isa. 13:21) and Jeremiah (Jer. 50:39) both prophesied that Babylon would be devastated and that owls—an unclean bird—would inhabit the site. Unclean birds, probably carnivorous vultures, are again mentioned in Revelation 19:21.

The merchants of the earth grew rich from her excessive luxuries (18:3). The potential for great profits enticed many merchants to bring their commodities to Rome. However, the risks were also enormous. Storms on the Mediterranean caused many ships to sink, bankrupting the merchants who had laid out a life's savings for the cargo. The business interests of Asian merchants in Rome are attested through an inscription found on the tomb of T. Flavius Zeuxis in Hierapolis. Dating from the first century, the inscription in part reads: "a merchant had rounded Cape Malea [the tip of Greece] seventy-two times on voyages to Italy."[119] To complete such an ambitious itinerary,

Flavius Zeuxis must have averaged two trips a year from Asia to Rome. This merchant probably dealt in the textiles for which the Lycus valley was famous.

Revelation 18 is the only New Testament text to use the Greek word group that speaks of living in luxury and sensuality (18:3, 7, 9). One scholar calls the economic critique in this chapter "one of the fiercest attacks on Rome and one of the most effective pieces of political

DENARIUS

A Tyrian silver denarius with the image of Alexander the Great.

▸Roman Money

The common unit of Roman money was the sesterce. Calculating the exchange rate of the sesterce to modern currencies, such as the dollar, is difficult because of inflation and the differences in buying power between ancient and modern society. However, such equivalencies can be approximated. During Julius Caesar's time (50 B.C.), foot soldiers received 900 sesterces a year and day laborers earned about 1000 sesterces. Around A.D. 100, Roman soldiers received 1200 sesterces a year, and day laborers, given the same percentage increase, would receive approximately 1333 sesterces. Since four sesterces equaled a denarius, laborers in Rome would receive approximately one denarius a day, the salary of a day laborer in Palestine (Matt. 20:2).

Today the salary of a person receiving a wage of $6 would be $48 a day (approximately $12,500 a year). A denarius would therefore equal approximately $48, and a sesterce $12. Such wages were barely subsistence level in first-century Rome, even as they are at the poverty line in America today. The Roman lower class received monthly grain handouts to supplement their meager wages. The disparity between the rich and poor becomes apparent when we read that Pliny the Younger purchased one piece of property for 3 million sesterces, Cicero paid 500,000 sesterces for a single table, or Vitellius, during his brief reign from May to December 69, spent approximately 900 million sesterces on banquets.[A-56]

resistance literature from the period of the early empire."[120] The wanton luxury of several Caesars is well known. Both Tacitus and Suetonius document the licentious living of Nero and record all manner of his debaucheries. Roman writers during the Neronian period, such as Lucan, Petronius, and Seneca, routinely issued diatribes against wanton luxury.[121] The extravagances of the emperor Vitellius were notable. The menu for one banquet was 2000 fish and 7000 birds.[122] The list of edibles procured from every corner of the empire for the banquet resembles remarkably the cargoes mentioned in this chapter. To feed Rome's appetites generated great riches, and her destruction would be particularly sobering to the Laodicean church, which was flush with wealth (3:17–18). That church is again reminded to desist from its false prosperity, lest the judgment pronounced on Rome's economic system would also come upon it.

Come out of her, my people, so that you will not share in her sins (18:4). The readers are jarred from the prophetic future to present reality by another voice, probably that of God. For this is the only place in the book where the saints are called "my people" (contrast "his people" in 21:3). God frequently calls Israel "my people" in the Old Testament, particularly in the Prophets. Jeremiah issued a similar exhortation to the Jews living in exile to flee Babylon before it was destroyed (Jer. 51:6). In Revelation, however, to come out is not so much to have physical separation, but to be separate spiritually from Rome's sins. The plagues, already poured out prophetically in chapter 16, have only been received in part by Babylon as judgment. Those believers who have failed to repent still

have time to spare themselves from the remaining plagues.

The kings of the earth . . . will stand far off and cry: "Woe! Woe, O great city" (18:9–10). Three groups of Babylon's allies—the kings, the merchants, and the seafarers—now recognize her inevitable doom and cry over her fate. Their mourning is not in repentance, but over lost revenues. Each of their laments begins with "Woe! Woe, O great city" and ends with a declaration of the suddenness of her end. The client kings, who have shared Babylon's power, are now terrified at her fate. As co-conspirators against the Almighty, their doom is likewise imminent. Although they stand apart still hoping to escape, soon the evil trinity will deceive them into joining the great battle at Armageddon (16:12–16).

The smoke of her burning (18:9, 18). Rome, the city on seven hills (17:9), was

REFLECTIONS

WHAT DOES JOHN'S INCISIVE CRI- tique of Roman luxury say to Christians today, particularly those in the West? With household debt and personal bankruptcies rising and personal savings and charitable giving on the decline among Christians, perhaps the "good life" has become an idol to many. The situation of the Laodicean church demonstrates that financial prosperity does not necessarily mean spiritual prosperity. What is our responsibility to our brothers and sisters who are living in poverty conditions? Given the excessive materialism in Western culture, maybe the Holy Spirit is now speaking to the church, "Come out of it, my people."

accessible to the sea through its port Ostia at the mouth of the Tiber. A repeated image in this chapter is a city being destroyed by fire whose smoke is seen miles away by sea captains (17:17–19). This description of an apocalyptic conflagration has a historical antecedent in the fire at Rome in A.D. 64. Rumored to have been started by Nero himself, it was certainly of the massive scale described in this chapter. After burning for six days and seven nights, the fire left only four of Rome's fourteen districts still standing.[123] During Titus' reign (A.D. 79–81), a smaller fire in Rome burned three days and nights, consuming the area from the Capitol to the Pantheon.[124] There is no record of any destructive fire in Rome during Domitian's reign.

The merchants of the earth will weep and mourn over her because no one buys their cargoes any more (18:11). John provides a detailed list of the cargoes carried from the emporia of the world to Rome by ship. Such products were very costly and affordable only to the wealthy of Roman society. The list resembles that of the merchandise brought to Tyre by merchants before its destruction (Ezek. 27:12–24). Of the twenty-eight trade

items listed in Revelation, seventeen are found in Ezekiel. Unlike Ezekiel, John does not give the products' origination point or its middleman to market. Asia was one of the richest provinces in the empire and exported many of its products to Rome. It was noted for its wine, marble, olive oil, textiles, and parchment.

Bodies and souls of men (18:13). The final, and only human, commodity on the list is slaves. The Greek word for bodies (*sōma*) is an idiom meaning slaves. Slaves played an important role in the Roman economic system. In the first century A.D., slaves, most of whom were men, numbered about ten million, approximately twenty percent of the population of the empire. People became slaves for various reasons—sale by parents, indebtedness, self-sale for economic stability, and kidnapping by slave traders. Another important source was prisoners of war. During the Jewish revolt, 97,000 Jewish captives were sent into slavery.[125] Perhaps the most unusual and important source was foundlings—those children who were unwanted and left exposed by their parents. The interior of Asia Minor was an important source of slaves, and many of these would pass through the slave markets in Ephesus before being shipped to Rome. Many slaves were numbered among the members of the early church. Of the twenty-six Roman Christians greeted by Paul (Rom. 16:3–16), it is estimated that two-thirds were of slave origin. Unlike race-based slavery in the antebellum South, the Roman slaves were from every race, nationality, economic class, and educational background. And most slaves had the expectation of manumission by age thirty. Roman slavery was a temporary process, not a permanent condition.[126]

◀ *left*

MERCHANT SHIP

A coin from the reign of Nero depicting a galley ship from Alexandria, Egypt.

Every sea captain . . . and all who earn their living from the sea, will stand far off (18:17). The final group of profiteers is the mariners. Aelius Aristides, the Greek rhetorician from Mysia in Asia, described the scene in Rome: "So many merchant ships arrive here, conveying every kind of goods from every people every hour and every day, so that the city is like a factory common to the whole earth. . . . The arrivals and departures of the ships never stop, so that one would express admiration for the harbor, but even the sea."[127] What John describes is a total disruption of such frenetic activity.

They will throw dust on their heads (18:19). Throwing dust on your head was a sign of mourning in the ancient world. After thirty-six Israelites were killed by the men of Ai, the elders of Israel sprinkled dust on their heads (Josh. 7:6). When the mariners and seamen saw the destruction of Tyre, they sprinkled dust on their heads and rolled in ashes (Ezek. 27:30). The seafarers similarly show their grief.

Rejoice over her, O heaven! (18:20). The speaker, whose identity is probably the same as that in verses 1–4, abruptly changes (not brought out in the NIV). He exhorts those in heaven and on earth to rejoice over Babylon's judgment. Three groups of believers are singled out— saints, apostles, and prophets. In the parallel verse 24, the reference to apostles is omitted. This is the first mention of true apostles in the book (cf. 2:20).

Then a mighty angel picked up a boulder the size of a large millstone and threw it into the sea (18:21). An angel now seals the fate of Babylon by performing the symbolic act of hurling a boulder into the sea. The violence of the act symbolizes the violence with which Babylon would be destroyed. Jeremiah performed a similar act by tying a stone to a scroll of judgment oracles against Babylon and throwing it into the Euphrates. He then declared, "So will Babylon sink to rise no more because of the disaster I will bring upon her. And her people will fall" (Jer. 51:64). Such is Babylon's fate here as well.

Will never be heard in you again . . . will be found in you again (18:22–23). This refrain, with the variation "will never shine in you again," is echoed six times in these verses. The normal activities of life—music, work, and marriage—will forever disappear from the streets of Babylon. However, Babylon's dark under-

ROME AND ITALY

▼

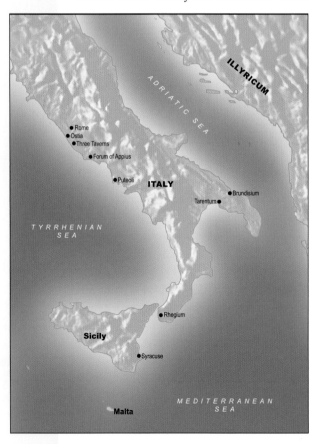

belly is also exposed—her economic exploitation and political control through deceptive magic. The language and imagery again resemble that in the judgment oracles against Tyre in Isaiah 23 (v. 8) and Ezekiel 26 (vv. 13, 21). There is an eeriness to this picture, like the modern visitor to Pompeii who sees time frozen upon streets that one day vibrated with life and the next were sepulchers of ash from Mount Vesuvius.

In her was found the blood of prophets and of the saints (18:24). The shift from the second to the third person in this closing verse suggests that again a direct address to believers is spoken. Its explanatory nature clarifies and complements verse 20. The refrain in verses 22–23 says there is no longer life "in you" (Babylon) because the blood of Christians was found "in her." Babylon's persecution of the church is the primary cause of her downfall. "All who have been killed on the earth" does not refer to a group distinct from the prophets and saints, but simply explains where their blood was shed. These martyrs are identical to the slain seen earlier who also had shed their blood (6:9–10).

The Hallelujah Chorus (19:1–10)

The roar of a great multitude in heaven shouting: "Hallelujah!" (19:1). With the destruction of Babylon, a hallelujah chorus is heard in heaven. The great multitude reappears for the first time by name since 7:9. Responding to the exhortation to "Rejoice" in 18:20, this multitude shouts its praise to God for two mighty acts of judgment: the condemnation of the great prostitute and his avenging the blood of the saints. This chapter records the only four uses in the New Testament

of *hallelujah*, a Hebrew word meaning "Praise the Lord!" that is found frequently in the book of Psalms. David likewise rejoices over divine judgment: "But may sinners vanish from the earth and the wicked be no more. . . . Hallelujah" (Ps. 104:35; see NIV note). Tobit 13:17 states that in the eternal Jerusalem the houses of the holy city will cry, "Hallelujah!"

The smoke from her goes up for ever and ever (19:3). The great multitude's second hallelujah focuses on the eternal nature of Babylon's judgment. The phrase "for ever and ever" is used a number of times in Revelation both positively and negatively. God (15:7) and Jesus (1:18) are both eternal, and praise to them is everlasting (5:13). The reign of Jesus (11:15) and the saints (22:5) is forever. Conversely, fallen Babylon, those who worshiped the beast (14:11), and the devil, the beast, and the false prophet (20:10) must suffer the smoke of eternal torment. This continued emphasis on the kingdom's eternal nature serves to shift the audience's attention from the temporary trials being experienced in this life to the blessings they will enjoy forever.

The twenty–four elders and the four living creatures . . . cried: "Amen, Hallelujah!" (19:4). The response given by the elders and living creatures resembles that given in 5:14 and 7:12, to which is added hallelujah. The focus of their worship is still God seated on his heavenly throne. Their amen concludes the heavenly response concerning Babylon's judgment.

Then a voice came from the throne, saying: "Praise our God" (19:5). This unidentified voice enjoins God's servants to praise God. The focus of praise shifts from Babylon's judgment to the long-anticipated rewards of the saints. The twenty-four elders offer similar praise proleptically in 11:18 because the time has come for the saints to be rewarded.

For the wedding of the Lamb has come, and his bride has made herself ready (19:7). The great multitude shouts the final hallelujah hymn. The focus of their joy is that God's eternal reign has begun and the moment of the Lamb's wedding to his bride has arrived. The Greek word translated "bride" here is literally "wife" (cf. Eph. 5:23). It reflects the Jewish custom in which the formal wedding is preceded by a legally binding betrothal. During this period, which normally lasted no longer than a year, the pair were called husband and wife. To dissolve the betrothal required a formal divorce, which Joseph briefly considered doing with Mary (Matt. 1:18–20). As part of the betrothal, gifts were exchanged between the families. The bridegroom paid a bride-price to the family of the bride (Ex. 22:16–17), while the bride's father presented a dowry to his daughter (Judg. 1:14–15). When the wedding day arrived, the bride prepared herself by dressing in finery, such as an embroidered garment (Ps. 45:13–14), jewels (Isa. 61:10), ornaments (Jer. 2:32), and a veil (Gen. 24:65).[128] The wedding is a familiar metaphor used in Scripture to describe God's relationship with his people. God likened Israel to a bride in the Prophets (Isa. 49:18; Jer. 2:2). In the Gospels, John the Baptist compared Jesus to a bridegroom (John 3:29) as does Jesus himself (Luke 5:35). In the eschatological parable of the ten virgins, the bridegroom (unnamed but surely Jesus) found only five virgins prepared to attend the wedding banquet (Matt. 25:1–13). Paul

explicitly identified the church as the bride (2 Cor. 11:2). Revelation's four references to the church as the bride of Christ are the most in the New Testament (cf. Rev. 21:2, 9; 22:17).

Fine linen, bright and clean, was given her to wear (19:8). The bride's garment, which she receives for her wedding with the Lamb, is clean shining linen. Her apparel contrasts with the purple and scarlet linen in which the harlot was dressed (17:4; 18:16). The victors are likewise promised to be dressed in white if they were worthy (3:4–5). John adds an explanatory note interpreting the spiritual meaning of fine linen: It represents the righteous acts of the saints. The plural "acts" suggests that those who overcame had a lifestyle of worthy deeds. These worthy deeds flow out of justification, that is, washing one's robes in the blood of the Lamb (7:14). The antonym of righteous acts is used in 18:5. Because of the volume of Babylon's sins, God has remembered her unrighteous acts ("crimes," NIV). As the day of the Lord's return draws near, the behavior of the saints and the sinners becomes set. As 22:11 declares, the wicked are to continue in their wickedness while the righteous (i.e., the justified) are to continue to do righteous deeds.

Blessed are those invited to the wedding supper of the Lamb (19:9). An angel announces the fourth beatitude, which gives a blessing to those participating in the messianic banquet. The Laodiceans who repented and opened the door to eat with Jesus are now eligible to participate in this wedding supper (3:20). The idea of an end-time feast is found in Isaiah 25:6, where the menu is aged wines and fine meats and the invitation list includes guests from all peoples. The location of this banquet—Mount Zion—is seen in 14:1 with the Lamb and the 144,000 already gathered on it. Before he went to the cross, Jesus had a last supper with his disciples. He announced at the meal's conclusion, "I will not drink of this fruit of the vine from now on until that day when I drink it anew with you in my Father's kingdom" (Matt. 26:29). The church's ongoing celebration of the Eucharist, or communion, is an eschatological event looking forward to that time. As Paul wrote, "For whenever you eat this bread and drink this cup, you proclaim the Lord's death until he comes" (1 Cor. 11:26). The wedding supper thus becomes a reunion dinner when for the first time his bride can drink the cup and break bread together with him.

At this I fell at his feet to worship him (19:10). John's reaction is to prostrate himself before the angel whom he believes is divine. The angel, however, rebukes him and identifies himself as a fellow servant with John and the Asian believers. Angels similarly forbid worship and focus attention on God in other apocalyptic literature (cf. Tobit 12:16–22; *Mart. Ascen. Isa.* 7:21). The worship of angels was a problem in the Asian churches, and Paul condemns the practice in Colossians 2:18. A similar incident of attempted angel worship occurs in Revelation 22:8–9, where again John is rebuked. Rather than attribute John's strange behavior to memory loss, the double rebuke perhaps serves as a strong repudiation of angel worship and a reminder that only God is to be worshiped.

For the testimony of Jesus is the spirit of prophecy (19:10). The phrase, "the testimony of Jesus," was discussed in 1:9 and is common in Revelation. The interpretation of "the spirit of prophecy" is difficult. The NIV translation suggests that the testimony of Jesus is the spirit (uncapitalized), or essence, of all prophetic utterance. While this is true generally for all Christian prophecy, it fails to account for the context in Revelation. By capitalizing Spirit and inserting the untranslated article "the" from the Greek text—"For the testimony of Jesus is the Spirit of the prophecy"—a more viable interpretation can emerge. The seven messages (chaps. 2–3) strongly link the words of Jesus with "what the Spirit says to the churches." Although the Spirit is clearly referred to only nine times in Revelation (the adjective Holy is never added), this text is probably another reference. To paraphrase, the testimony that Jesus is speaking to the churches is the same message that the Holy Spirit is speaking through the rest of the prophecy in Revelation.[129]

The Battle with the Rider on the White Horse (19:11–21)

Before me was a white horse, whose rider is called Faithful and True (19:11). For the second time, John sees heaven opened. The first occasion in 4:1 forms a major transition in the book. There John is caught up to heaven to see God on his heavenly throne and to view the opening of the scroll of destiny. Now John sees another divine figure poised to descend to earth for the final judgment of its inhabitants. The great battle of Armageddon, announced in 16:12–16, finally occurs. The rider is presented using imagery that is introduced earlier in Revelation. His appearance shares aspects with a Roman general returning from a successful triumph over his enemies. White was a color of victory in the ancient world, and the appearance of four snow-white horses was viewed as an omen of victory.[130] The Roman Senate granted Julius Caesar permission to drive a chariot drawn by white horses through Rome to celebrate his victory in north Africa.[131] During such triumphs, Rome became a *candida urbs,* a "city in white," which Juvenal describes as "the imposing procession of white-robed citizens marching."[132] The conquering horseman of the first seal—the false messiah—also rode a white horse (6:1–2).

And on his head are many crowns (19:12). Many diadems ("crowns," NIV) sit upon the Rider's head. Isaiah associated the diadem with royalty (Isa. 62:3), and Esther received a diadem when she became queen of Persia (Est. 2:17). The Greeks and Romans adopted the diadem as a regal badge from the Persians, distinguishing it from the wreath, or crown (cf. Rev. 2:10). Diadem appears two other times in the Greek text. The dragon had a diadem on each of his seven heads (Rev. 12:3), and the beast had a diadem on each of his ten horns (Rev. 13:1), which represent ten kings (Rev. 17:12). After Ptolemy VI Philometer conquered Antioch around 169 B.C., he wore two diadems on his head, one representing his sovereignty over Egypt and the other over Asia (1 Macc. 11:13). Upon the rider's diadem is a name known only to himself. Israel's high priest wore a diadem upon which was inscribed the phrase, "Holy to the LORD" (Ex. 39:30). The many diadems on the rider's head suggest his superior strength, and contrast with the finite number belonging to the dragon and the beast. The diadems visually validate his claim to be King of kings and Lords of lords.

His name is the Word of God (19:13). Of the three names mentioned in this section, only "Word of God" is new to the audience. "Faithful and True" and "King of kings and Lords of lords" have already been named (cf. 1:5; 3:7, 14; 17:14). Although the phrase "word of God" is found in 1:2 and 9, it is not used as a personal name there. The personified Word (*logos*) of God is likewise used as a name for Jesus in the Gospel of John (John 1:1, 14). Word as a title coupled with the imagery of the sword out of his mouth emphasizes the authority by which he declares that the nations are destroyed. The Wisdom of Solomon portrays a similar image, describing the all-powerful word leaping from the heavenly throne as "a stern warrior, carrying the sharp sword of your authentic command" (Wisd. Sol. 18:15–16 NRSV). In Hebraic thought, the concept of word conveys both idea and action (cf. Heb. 4:12), and now the eternal Word moves into action as the divine warrior.

The armies of heaven were following him (19:14). Several clues suggest the identity of this heavenly army. In the preview of this battle in 17:14, the Lamb was accompanied by his faithful followers. And the uniform of these mounted troops—clean white linen—is the same apparel worn by the saints at the messianic banquet (19:8). The army is thus to be identified as the bride, the saints, and not as an angelic host. Their white horses indicate that they are the victors who have triumphed over the beast.

"He will rule them with an iron scepter." He treads the winepress (19:15). The destiny of the male child is to rule all nations with an iron scepter (12:5). Now that time has come when the messianic prophecy of Psalm 2:9 is fulfilled. Not only will Jesus rule the nations, but the victors will rule with him, as the Thyatirans were promised (Rev. 2:26–27). The winepress imagery depicting the harvest of wrath for the earth is first introduced in 14:17–20. There the vintner is unnamed; here Jesus himself is identified as the one who treads the winepress.

On his robe and on his thigh he has this name written: KING OF KINGS AND LORD OF LORDS (19:16). This is the name written on him that no one knows but he himself (19:12), and it is probably the new name that Jesus promises he would write upon the victors (3:12). It is introduced in 17:14, although in reverse order, in a brief preview of the battle. While the image is perplexing, it cannot be interpreted as a body tattoo because the Jews prohibited permanent body markings (Lev. 19:28). Inscriptions were sometimes placed on the thighs of statues that stood in the Greco-Roman cities. Cicero mentions a statue of Apollo that had a name written on it in small silver letters. At Altis, the sacred precinct of Zeus at Olympia, Pausanius saw a statue with this couplet written on its thigh: "To Zeus, king of the gods, as first-fruits I placed here, by the Mendeans / who reduced Sipte by might of hand."[133] The portrait of the Rider contrasts with that of the beast, who is covered with blasphemous names, and the woman sitting upon it, who has various titles on her forehead (Rev. 17:3–5). This title emphatically declares that the beast is not the ultimate head of the kings of the earth, but that Jesus is.

Come, gather together for the great supper of God (19:17). Two banquets are presented in this chapter and implicitly contrasted. The first banquet is the wedding supper of the Lamb and serves as a blessing for the saints. The second is the great supper of God and results from the outpouring of his wrath. The slaughter that occurs is complete and excludes no one who has taken the mark of the beast (cf. 6:15; 13:16). The guests are the carnivorous birds who are invited to feast on the carcasses of the victims. These birds are probably not eagles (cf. 8:13), because the Greek word can also be translated to "vulture." It is translated this way in Jesus' proverb which describes his coming: "Wherever there is a carcass, there the vultures will gather" (Matt. 24:28). That proverb is literally fulfilled in the devastation portrayed here.

But the beast was captured, and with him the false prophet (19:20). The armies of the beast and the kings are gathered at Armageddon to battle the rider of the white horse and his army. Interestingly, no battle is described, for the struggle is over before it begins. Only two prisoners are taken alive—the beast and the false prophet. The false prophet is particularly singled out for his role in working false miracles to delude the earth dwellers. The two are then thrown alive into the lake of burning sulfur. This is the first mention of this fiery lake, composed of burning sulfur or brimstone. In the Olivet Discourse, Jesus made a curious statement about the last judgment: The King will ask the cursed to depart from him into the eternal fire prepared for the devil and his angels (Matt. 25:41). Whereas God was forced to provide a place of punishment for Satan and his rebellious angels, that abode was never intended for man and woman who were created for fellowship in the eternal kingdom. But after the Fall, those who choose to rebel likewise find themselves destined for the eternal fire.

All the birds gorged themselves on their flesh (19:21). The earth dwellers are killed en masse by the Rider's sword, that is, his word of judgment. The resulting carnage resembles Ezekiel's graphic description of the slaughter associated with Gog's destruction. There God also issued an invitation to carnivorous birds: "At my table you will eat your fill of horses and riders, mighty men and solders of every kind" (Ezek. 39:20). The defeat of Gog's army serves as a prophetic antecedent to the battle of Armageddon.

The Thousand Years and the First Resurrection (20:1–6)

And I saw an angel coming down out of heaven, having the key to the Abyss and holding in his hand a great chain (20:1). This is the second time that the Abyss is opened with a key. In 9:1, a "star" opens the Abyss to release a plague of demonic locusts. Here an angel is dispatched from heaven, not to release, but to imprison. Fallen angels are likewise bound with chains as they await the day of judgment (Jude 6; cf. 2 Peter 2:4). Chains binding Satan and his fallen angels is a motif found in other apocalyptic literature (cf.

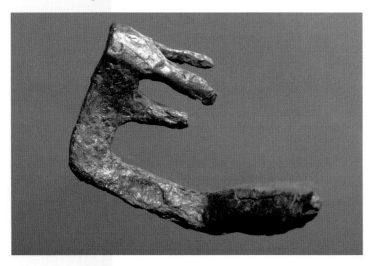

1 En. 54:3–6; *2 Bar.* 13; *Sib. Or.* 2.289). That such a large chain is required suggests the great demonic power of the one being bound.

He seized the dragon . . . and bound him for a thousand years (20:2). The visions from chapters 13–19 trace the activities of the beast and the false prophet. Except for four brief references (13:2, 4, 11; 16:13), the dragon has been out of the picture since his introduction in chapter 12. The relationship between chapters 12 and 20 is apparent. His names are in the same order—dragon, ancient serpent, devil, and Satan (12:9; 20:2), his activity is deceiving (or not) the nations of the world (12:9, 12; 20:3), and the heavenly action either casts him to earth (12:13–17) or into the abyss (20:3). Six times in 20:2–7 a thousand years is mentioned. During this period, the devil is bound and prevented from deceiving the nations (vv. 2, 3), the martyrs live again and reign with Christ (vv. 4, 6), and the unbelieving dead wait in their graves (v. 5).

A thousand years is mentioned in two familiar verses—Psalm 90:4 and 2 Peter 3:8—in which a thousand years is compared to a day, a brief period from a divine perspective. Jewish rabbis speculated about the length of the messianic age, and Eliezer ben Hyrcanus (ca. A.D. 90) estimated the period to be a thousand years.[134] The book of *Jubilees* (ca. 150 B.C.) mentions a thousand years, but this is said to be the life span of persons in the messianic age (*Jub.* 24:15, 27). An early Christian document, the *Epistle of Barnabas*, allegorizes the Genesis account of a six-day creation to signify that there are six thousand years of human history. The Sabbath day signifies the seventh and final thousand-year period when the Son comes and judges the ungodly (*Barn.* 15:4–5). Barnabas's use of a thousand years comes closest to that in Revelation, where John likewise uses the number as a cipher to describe the final period of divine activity.

He threw him into the Abyss . . . to keep him from deceiving the nations anymore until the thousand years were ended (20:3). The dragon's mission is described in 12:9 as leading astray the whole world. He accomplishes this through the great signs and miracles performed by the false prophet. However, "if those days had not been cut short, no one would survive, but for the sake of the elect those days will be shortened" (Matt. 24:22, 24). The binding of Satan suspends his deceptive activity so that the saints might be preserved. The chronicle of Satan's demise is resumed in verse 7.

I saw thrones on which were seated those who had been given authority to judge (20:4). John's vision abruptly changes from the Abyss to heaven, where he sees the martyred souls depicted in 6:4. The martyrs are rewarded with thrones and given authority to judge, fulfilling the promises given to the victors (2:26; 3:21). Judgment by the saints is a familiar theme in the New Testament. Jesus promised the apostles that they would "sit on thrones, judging the twelve tribes of Israel" (Luke 22:30). And Paul reminded the Corinthians, "Do you not know that the saints will judge the world? . . . Do you not know that we will judge angels?" (1 Cor. 6:2–3). While the martyrs are given authority to judge, they are never shown judging. No judgment actually occurs until that of the great white throne when the dead are judged (Rev. 20:11–12). The scene serves to encourage the Asian Christians that one day the power to judge will no longer be in the hands of their oppressors.

And I saw the souls of those who had been beheaded (20:4). Roman law provided two forms of capital punishment. The first was vindictive and involved crucifixion, exposure to wild animals, or burning at the stake. Such punishment was meted out to persons of low social

▶ The Meaning of the Millennium

The thousand years of Revelation 20 is often called the millennium (Lat. *mille* = thousand, and *annus* = year). Chiliasm, from the Greek word *chilia* meaning a thousand, is the belief in a literal thousand-year reign on earth. Three basic understandings of the millennium are current. Premillennialism is the belief that Jesus will return before the millennium; and after Satan is bound, the saints will then reign on this earth with Christ for a thousand years. Amillennialists believe that the millennium is a present spiritual reality instituted by Christ at his first coming, at which time Satan was bound. The thousand-year reign is now occurring as the souls of deceased believers rule with Christ in heaven. Postmillennialism is the belief that the church with its evangelistic outreach has a direct role in bringing in the millennium. As the nations become progressively more Christian and the kingdom of God is established more fully on earth, the millennial period is ushered in. After the thousand years of peace and prosperity on earth, Jesus will then return. There are, of course, variations on these three positions, which have been held by Christians throughout church history. Each position has its strengths and weaknesses, as its advocates attempt to understand this difficult concept of the thousand years.

117

Revelation

status. Jesus, of course, died by crucifixion (John 19:18) as did Peter, according to tradition (*Acts of Peter* 37–38). Some Christians killed during Nero's persecution were dressed in wild animal skins and torn to pieces by dogs at the Roman Circus. Others were crucified along the public streets or wrapped in tunics soaked with oil to be lit as human torches in Nero's private gardens.[135] John's disciple Polycarp was burned at the stake in Smyrna. The death penalty was uncommon for persons of the upper classes. Their punishment usually involved exile or deportation. John's exile to Patmos suggests that his social influence was considerable (Rev. 1:9). However, when capital punishment was proscribed for them, it took a second form—beheading either with a sword or an axe. The governor of Asia could execute only with the sword (cf. 2:12). Probably Antipas had been killed this way in Pergamum, and Paul traditionally died by beheading in Rome (*Acts of Paul* 11.5). Christians who died by beheading were either Roman citizens or persons of social status. This vision probably preserves a memory of John's own brother James, who was the first apostolic martyr and beheaded with the sword by Herod Antipas I in the early 40s (Acts 12:2). Beheading is the only method for the death of the saints mentioned in Revelation.

They came to life and reigned with Christ a thousand years. . . . This is the first resurrection (20:4–5). Jesus is the first to die and come to life again (2:8). The testimony of the angels to the women in Gethsemane was: "Why do you look for the living [One] among the dead?" (Luke 24:5). Through his death and return to life, Jesus became the Lord and Judge, before whose judgment seat all believers will stand one day (Rom. 14:9–12). The beast's power to deceive results from his counterfeit resurrection that occurs following his fatal wound (13:14). Such scriptures suggest that this resurrection should be interpreted as physical, not spiritual, as amillennialists suggest. While the martyrs who epitomize the righteous dead are included in the first resurrection, another group does not come back to life until after the thousand years. This implied "second resurrection" is for the unrighteous dead, who are not the recipients of the beatitude that follows, but whose fate is the second death. This is the third pair of images that contrast the destiny of the righteous and unrighteous—two harvests, two banquets, and two resurrections.

Blessed and holy are those who have part in the first resurrection (20:6). This is the fifth beatitude directed to all of the Asian believers. Sin's juridical authority to produce death is now broken for those who participate in the first resurrection. Here the second death is contrasted with the first resurrection. The implied "first death" is universal, except for those raptured at Christ's coming. The time of the first resurrection is neither the believer's spiritual resurrection following a decision of faith (John 11:25–26), nor the intermediate state with Christ after death (Phil. 1:23). Rather, the first resurrection occurs at Christ's return during the "thousand years." This perspective accords with Paul's teaching on the resurrection of the saints (1 Thess. 4:16–17; 1 Cor. 15:51–52).

They will be priests of God and of Christ and will reign with him for a thousand years (20:6). The reign of the saints was prophesied by Daniel: "Then the sovereignty, power and greatness of the king-

R E F L E C T I O N S

FOR JOHN AND THE OTHER NEW
Testament writers, the threat of persecution and martyrdom was constant. Yet many Christians today live free of tribulation and die peaceful deaths. How do we maintain our spiritual edge when life is relatively easy and our faith goes largely unchallenged? Jesus calls us as his disciples to deny ourselves and take up his cross daily and follow him (Luke 9:23). In principle, every Christian must be a living martyr, ready to lay down his or her life for the faith. Martyrdom then is an attitude rather than an act for Christians in safe countries.

doms under the whole heaven will be handed over to the saints" (Dan. 7:27). The identity of those who reign is sometimes questioned. Are they only the martyrs or all the righteous dead? Two things suggest the latter. First, the beatitudes are addressed to all Asian believers, and John never suggests that everyone will be martyred. Second, this priestly reign of the saints fulfills the new song of the elders that people from every language and nation would be a kingdom and priests (Rev. 5:10; cf. 1:6). This group is a universal, not a select, one. The inclusive nature of this beatitude is echoed in one of Paul's trustworthy sayings: "If we died with him, we will also live with him; if we endure, we will also reign with him" (2 Tim. 2:11–12).

The Judgment of Satan and the Dead (20:7–15).

Satan . . . will go out to deceive the nations in the four corners of the earth—

Gog and Magog (20:7, 8). After Satan's release, he resumes his deception of the nations, which is described in 16:13–16 as leading to the battle of Armageddon. Here that last battle is called Gog and Magog. "The sand of the seashore" is a figure of speech used to describe a large army (cf. Josh. 11:4; 2 Sam. 17:11). The background of the language and sequence here lies in the eschatological restoration and battle described in Ezekiel 37–39. First, there is the resurrection of the dry bones and the return of Israel to the land (Ezek. 37:1–14; cf. the first resurrection). The covenantal restoration that follows in 37:15–28 is not portrayed by John until chapters 21–22. Next, Israel is attacked from the north by the armies of Gog and Magog (Ezek. 38:1–16). The early Lydian king Gyges of Sardis (ca. 700 B.C.) is thought to be the historical figure behind the Jewish tradition of Gog, a tradition undoubtedly familiar to the Asian Christians. Known in Assyrian inscriptions as Gugu, Gog came to personify the evil forces that would come against Israel in the last days. Gyges is buried in a conspicuous necropolis of tumuli, or burial mounds, called Bin Tepe ("a thousand mounds") about five miles north of Sardis. Gyges' mound is set on the highest point of the bedrock and is one of three mounds that rises higher than the other hundred tumuli. Gog's attack against Israel arouses God's anger, and he sends judgments of sword, plague, and hailstones against the nations mobilized against his people (Ezek. 38:17–39:6). That judgment culminates when God sends fire on Magog (39:6). The clean-up of Gog's armies is accomplished by the carnivores, birds and beasts who feed on the rotting corpses (39:4, 17–20), a scene already depicted in Revelation 19:17–21.

The shared tradition in Ezekiel that underlies these scenes in Revelation 19 and 20 shows that the battles are one and the same.

They . . . surrounded the camp of God's people, the city he loves (20:9). "Camp" refers to a fortified military facility, such as the Roman barracks in which Paul was incarcerated in Jerusalem (cf. Acts 21:34). Using a related word, Jesus warned that Jerusalem would be surrounded by army camps before its desolation (cf. Luke 19:43; 21:20). The Romans established several camps around the city to quarter the four legions that besieged Jerusalem and brought its fall. "Camp" can also be translated as "army" (cf. Judg. 8:11 LXX). God's people as an army are portrayed in Revelation 19:14 where they are seen accompanying the Rider. While the Rider's sword (i.e., word) causes the destruction of the armies in chapter 19, here heavenly fire devours them. The link between the two is seen in God's question to Jeremiah, "Is not my word like fire?" (Jer. 23:29; cf. 5:14). God's army of saints is also compared to a beloved city, whose nature is fully revealed in chapter 21.

And the devil . . . was thrown into the lake of burning sulfur (20:10). The source of the lake of fire imagery is obscure. Gehenna, the usual biblical expression for hell (cf. Matt. 5:29–30; Mark 9:43–49), is missing in Revelation. The linkage with brimstone/sulfur suggests the destruction of Sodom and Gomorrah (Gen. 19:24; cf. Luke 17:29) by a God who will rain fire and brimstone upon sinners (Ps. 11:6). The final verse of Isaiah 1 (v. 31) and the book's final verse (Isa. 66:24) both state that the fate of the wicked is to burn, and no one can quench the fire (cf. 34:9; Mark 9:48). Burning sulfur was one of the elements God used to destroy Gog and his armies (Ezek. 38:22). Similar themes are found in the intertestamental book of *1 Enoch*. The unrighteous burn and die for eternity as their punishment on the great day of judgment (*1 En.* 10:12–13; cf. 103:8), while suffering in the presence of the righteous (48:9). The lake of burning sulfur—the end of the beast and the false prophet following the great battle (Rev. 19:20)—is likewise the fate of the devil. Eternal torment is the final destiny of this unholy trinity, who never appear again in Revelation. Their judgment occurs before that of the unrighteous dead, which follows.

The Judgment of the Dead (20:11–15)

Then I saw a great white throne and him who was seated on it (20:11). The judgment scene that follows resembles that in Daniel 7:9–10. There the Ancient of Days, seated on his throne, executes judgment as the heavenly books are opened. Although John sees the heavenly throne many times, only here does he describe it as large and white. The color white suggests the triumph of God's righteousness, and the large throne suggests the great task of final judgment. The judgment of the great and small, announced in Revelation 11:18, involves all those in the second resurrection. The dead are judged according to their individual deeds as recorded in the books. *Second Baruch* 24:1 likewise speaks of books that will be opened "in which are written the sins of all those who have sinned." In Revelation, salvation is never based on good works, but always related to the blood of the Lamb.[136] Jesus spoke of a judgment of the nations at the Parousia (Matt. 25:31–46). As the nations are gathered before his throne, Jesus will separate the righteous from the unrighteous, as a shepherd separates sheep from goats. Although the people are first gathered collectively in nations, they are judged individually. The wicked receive eternal punishment, while the righteous go to eternal life (v. 46). The disappearance of the earth and sky signals the passing away of the first heaven and earth (cf. Rev. 21:1).

Another book was opened, which is the book of life (20:12). Daniel prophesied that "everyone whose name is found written in the book—will be delivered" (Dan. 12:1). The deliverance promised to the righteous dead is everlasting life (12:2). The victors in Sardis are promised that their names would not be erased from the book of life (Rev. 3:5). The primary act disqualifying the earth dwellers from inclusion in the book of life is worshiping the beast rather than the Lamb (cf. 13:8; 17:8). The consequence of

omission from the book of life is being thrown into the lake of fire. An angel has earlier warned those who worship the beast that eternal torment with burning sulfur would be their fate (14:10–11). That moment has finally arrived.

Then death and Hades were thrown into the lake of fire. The lake of fire is the second death (20:14). The second death is eternal, and to suggest it is annihilation introduces a theological concept absent from the text. The language of eternity here forbids thinking of a dissolution into nothingness. Whatever its specific outworking in the divine plan, for John's audience the lake of fire was meant to be a hard saying to dissuade false teachers and to frighten potential apostates. The dead, who are excluded from the first resurrection, are the multitudes spoken of by Daniel who will awaken to shame and eternal contempt (Dan. 12:2). Upon hearing the voice of the Son of Man, those practicing evil will come out of their graves to be condemned to the resurrection of judgment (John 5:28–29). The second death is the punishment Jesus warned about: "Rather, be afraid of the One who can destroy both soul and body in hell" (Matt. 10:28). Death and Hades are the last to be thrown into the lake of fire. He who holds the keys of death and Hades has finally turned the lock (cf. Rev. 1:18). This picture accords with Paul's statement, "The last enemy to be destroyed is death" (1 Cor. 15:26).

The New Jerusalem (21:1–22:6a)

Then I saw a new heaven and a new earth (21:1). The transformation of the universe was prophesied by Isaiah: "Behold, I will create new heavens and a

◀ *left*

CENSUS DOCUMENT

A first-century A.D. papyrus census list from Egypt.

new earth" (Isa. 65:17; cf. 66:22). Its inhabitants would be the nations from the far corners of the earth, including Lydia and Javan ("Greece," NIV; 66:19). Ionia, a region on Anatolia's western coast, is the Greek equivalent of Javan. Ephesus and Smyrna were geographically located in ancient Ionia; Sardis and Philadelphia in Lydia. This Old Testament prophecy was being fulfilled through the believers in these churches. Following the day of God, the early church was "looking forward to a new heaven and a new earth" (2 Peter 3:13). "New" (*kainos*) is an eschatological catch-word in Revelation that speaks of the kingdom of God and the coming age when all things become new (Rev. 21:5). Other "new" spiritual realities include a new name (2:17; 3:12) and the new Jerusalem (3:12; 21:2). Irenaeus likened the new order to the resurrection body,[137] an apt analogy since John deals with it first in Revelation 20:5–6. The spiritual body has both continuity and discontinuity with the natural body, according to Paul (1 Cor. 15:42–44). The spiritual body necessarily follows the natural body (15:46), but they are of two different worlds—the first heavenly, the second earthly (15:48). Heaven and earth will undergo a similar transformation when the new order arrives.

I saw the Holy City, the new Jerusalem, coming down out of heaven from God (21:2). From the new heaven the Holy City descends. The descent of the new Jerusalem is described twice in this chapter. Here it is compared to a bride, while verse 10 begins its full description as a city. The bridal imagery resumes from 19:7–9, where the wedding of the Lamb and his bride is announced. The use of this image suggests that the new Jerusalem is a people, the church. In 11:2, God's people are portrayed using the figure of a holy city that was trampled; here "Holy City" describes their heavenly destination where safety and security are assured (cf. 21:10; 22:19). The participation of the saints in this city fulfills the promise to be a part of the new Jerusalem (3:12). The coming of a new, second Jerusalem thus implies the passing away of an old, first Jerusalem. This newness suggests more than renewal or renovation, but, in fact, replacement.

Now the dwelling of God is with men, and he will live with them (21:3). God's desire to live with his people in covenant relationship is first stated in Leviticus 26:11–12. This hope, unrealized because of Israel's disobedience, was again expressed in the Prophets. "My dwelling place will be with them; I will be their God, and they will be my people" (Ezek.

R E F L E C T I O N S

PROPHETIC MOVEMENTS HAVE OFTEN SOUGHT TO locate the site where the new Jerusalem will descend from heaven. The Montanist movement, which began around A.D. 170, had its origins fifteen miles east of Philadelphia at Ardabav. Its founder Montanus, with his two prophetesses Prisca and Maximilla, taught that the Paraclete (Holy Spirit) would come just before the second advent. The Montanists believed that the new Jerusalem would descend at Pepuza, also near Philadelphia.[A-57] Recently a Korean prophet moved his followers to the Dallas, Texas area, where he believed Jesus would return and establish his eternal kingdom. Needless to say, his prediction was never fulfilled. Such attempts throughout church history to locate the site of the new Jerusalem have proven futile. Even relocation to Jerusalem to be present at the supposed site of Christ's return is misguided. For his return will be seen globally before his kingdom is established on the new earth (1:7).

37:27) and "Many nations . . . will become my people. I will live among you" (Zech. 2:11). The announcement in Revelation, given prophetically in the Old Testament and proleptically to the martyrs in Revelation 7:15–17, is now fully realized. God's transcendence, which was part of the old heaven and earth, has given way to his immanence as he now lives with his people. He is a personal comforter, particularly to those who have endured much hardship for their faith. Death, mourning, crying, and pain—all associated with the old order—have passed away for the saints. Just as salvation is assured for the saints with Jesus' declaration, "It is finished" (John 19:30), here their glorification is accomplished with God's pronouncement, "It is done" (Rev. 21:6).

To him who is thirsty I will give to drink without cost from the spring of the water of life (21:6). A final promise saying resembling those in Revelation 2–3 is now presented. This eighth saying completes and summarizes the rest. It is introduced by the epithets, "I am the Alpha and the Omega, the Beginning and the End" (cf. 1:8). The Lord God Almighty is the speaker here, not Jesus who addressed the seven churches. The victors are promised three things: the water of life, an inheritance, and adoption as children. Several of the beatitudes given by Jesus reflect these same themes: Those who thirst will be filled, the pure will see God, and the peacemakers will be called sons of God (Matt. 5:6, 8, 9). Water and thirst are familiar metaphors for spiritual life. The psalmist declares that all the righteous will drink from God's river, because with him is the fountain of life (Ps. 36:8–9). Enoch saw a fountain of righteousness that never becomes depleted: "All the thirsty ones drink (of the water) and become filled with wisdom" (*1 En.* 48:1). The promise of the water of life complements the earlier "life" promises—tree of life (Rev. 2:7), crown of life (Rev. 2:10), and book of life (3:5). Such metaphors emphasize that a high quality of life will be a hallmark of the new Jerusalem.

He who overcomes will inherit all this (21:7). Inheritance was an important matter in ancient society. In Israel, the father's inheritance was passed on to the sons, although daughters could obtain the inheritance if there was no male heir (Num. 27:4–11). Such social legislation protected a family's inheritance. The firstborn son, as the first sign of his father's strength, was given twice as much property as the other sons (Deut. 21:15–17). Greek society did not practice primogeniture; rather, the father's estate was divided equally among the surviving sons by lot. In Roman society, the father was the undisputed family head and retained full legal authority over his male children of any age until his death. A father could make his will as he determined, so the fear of disinheritance was a great motivation to filial obedience. Only with the father's death could full manhood be attained and one's inheritance enjoyed. This is the only reference to inheritance and sonship in Revelation. Paul developed the theme similarly: "And since you are a son, God has made you also an heir" (Gal. 4:7) and "Now if we are children, then we are heirs—heirs of God and co-heirs with Christ" (Rom. 8:17). The victors' inheritance—the sum of all the promises—relates directly to the promise of adoption as sons.

And I will be his God and he will be my son (21:7). This promise closely parallels

Nathan's promise to David that God would raise up his offspring to reign forever (2 Sam. 7:14). A similar covenant promise was made by God to Israel: "They will be my people, and I will be their God" (Jer. 32:38). Paul quotes these texts from 2 Samuel and Jeremiah to convince the Corinthian believers that they are now God's temple (2 Cor. 6:16, 18). This adoption formula also resembles the legal language of the covenants that God made with Abraham (Gen. 17:7–8) and Solomon (2 Chron. 7:18). There are varied traditions of adoptions in the ancient world. The Old Testament records three cases of adoption in Egypt and Persia—Moses (Ex. 2:10), Genubath (1 Kings 11:20), and Esther (Est. 2:7, 15). No specific examples of adoption are found in Israel, although the frequent use of such adoption language in the Old Testament suggests that such an institution existed.

A Greek man, either while he was alive or by will after his death, could adopt any male citizen as a son. The only condition was that the adopted son fulfill his legal and religious obligations. The Roman situation was basically the same for males who were fatherless. At age four, Augustus lost his father. Following the assassination of his great uncle Julius Caesar, he was designated the heir in Julius's will and adopted into the Caesar family.[138] However, when a father was still living, given his unique role in Roman society, adoption was more complicated. The natural father, using an adoption agreement, transferred his legal rights to the adoptive father. It was unlawful for the adoptive father ever to disinherit his new son or to reduce him to slavery. The use of adoption language here emphasizes the special relationship the victors will enjoy with God in the new Jerusalem.

But the cowardly, the unbelieving, the vile, the murderers, the sexually immoral, those who practice magic arts, the idolaters and all liars (21:8). This is the first, and most complete, of the vice lists found in the final two chapters (cf. 9:20–21). The parallel list in 22:15 omits only cowardice, unbelief, and vileness, while 21:27 mentions two sins—vileness and lying ("shameful or deceitful," NIV). Many of the sins denounced relate to the situation of the Asian churches. Cowardice and faithlessness were temptations to those facing persecution and possible death (cf. 2:10; 3:11); sexual immorality and idolatry were apparently advocated by the Nicolaitans and Jezebel (cf. 2:14, 20–21). To preserve their lives, some Christians had compromised by resuming the evil practices of their unbelieving friends. However, the warning is clear: Do this and you will experience the second death in the lake of burning fire and brimstone.

"Come, I will show you the bride, the wife of the Lamb." And he carried me away in the Spirit to a mountain great and high, and showed me the Holy City, Jerusalem (21:9–10). John now sees another vision of the heavenly city. However, the order of the images is reversed. John first sees the new Jerusalem prepared as a bride; here the bride is announced before John sees the holy city descending from God. Such a reversal of images suggests that for John, the New Jerusalem is both a people and a place (cf. John 14:2–4). This picture of a renewed city fulfills numerous Old Testament prophecies where Zion is now the "City of the LORD" (Isa. 60:14) and the "City No Longer Deserted" (62:12). Much of its imagery is specifically drawn from Ezekiel's vision of the renewed temple, land, and city in Ezekiel 40–48. This vision is contrasted deliberately with the vision of Babylon, the mother of prostitutes. Both are introduced by one of the seven angels who holds the seven bowls (Rev. 17:1; 21:9) who then takes John up in the Spirit to see the visions (17:3; 21:10). The earthly city Babylon is a prostitute while the heavenly Jerusalem, also called the "holy city" (21:2, 10), is a bride and wife. A similar connection between city, bride, and wife is found in *Joseph and Aseneth*. Aseneth is renamed the City of Refuge because many nations will find refuge in her (*Jos. Asen.* 15:7). She is promised as a bride for Joseph (15:9; 18:11) and later becomes his wife after Pharaoh blesses their union and stages a seven-day wedding feast in their behalf (21:4–9). Imagery related to a city now predominates in John's vision.

It had a great, high wall (21:12). Of the approximate one thousand cities in the Roman empire, most were founded as Hellenistic cities. Greek cities were usually walled for defensive purposes. The wall around Ephesus, part of which can still be seen on Mounts Koressos and Pion, was constructed by Lysimachus (3d cent. B.C.). Pergamum, Smyrna, and Sardis each had an acropolis surrounded by a wall. After Laodicea was ravaged by multiple earthquakes in the first century, it is doubtful that its wall was restored. Cities built during the Roman period often lacked defensive walls because of Rome's military might. The defensive walls found in Philadelphia today date to the later Byzantine period. Herodian Jerusalem was surrounded by three defensive walls; and after Titus captured the city in A.D. 70, he ordered that the walls be razed. He allowed the towers of

Hippicus, Mariamne, and Phasael to remain,[139] and the lower portion of Phasael forms part of the Jaffa Gate today. The present walls around the old city were constructed by the Ottoman sultan Suleyman the Magnificent in 1537–40. The image of a walled city thus suggests safety and security for those allowed inside.

On the gates were written the names of the twelve tribes of Israel (21:12). This is the first use of the number twelve, used repeatedly in chapter 21 to speak of gates (vv. 12, 21), angels and tribes (v. 12), foundations and apostles (v. 14), and pearls (v. 21). Twelve signifies completion and perfection and is the product of the sacred numbers three and four. The gates were the only means of entrance to an ancient city. Ancient Babylon had eight massive gates, while Jerusalem in the time of Jesus had four gates through its outer defensive walls. Ephesus also had four outer gates—Magnesian, Harbor, Koressos, and Agora. The visionary city seen by Ezekiel likewise had twelve gates, three on each side, which were named after the twelve tribes (Ezek. 48:31–34). These twelve sons of Jacob differ from the list in Revelation 7:4–8 where Manasseh is mentioned and Dan omitted. The more general nature of John's description suggests that it is symbolic. Entrance through these gates guarded by angels is not based on Israelite lineage but through moral purity (cf. Rev. 21:27; 22:14). Gates were closed at night for protection but, because there is no night in the Holy City, its gates are forever open (21:25). The twelve open gates suggest unlimited access to God and the Lamb for the victors/kings who will forever offer up their glorious praise (21:24; cf. Isa. 60:11).

Twelve foundations, and on them were the names of the twelve apostles of the Lamb (21:14). The names of the twelve apostles are given in the Synoptics (Matt. 10:2–4; Mark 3:16–18; Luke 6:14–16). John—son of Zebedee, brother of James, a Son of Thunder—is named among the first four apostles in all three lists. Judas Iscariot is also named, but after Judas's betrayal and death, Matthias was chosen by lot to be added to the eleven apostles (Acts 1:15–26). Paul also considered himself an apostolic builder who laid the foundation of Jesus Christ (1 Cor. 3:10), but because he had not walked with Jesus during his earthly ministry, he could never be considered one of the Twelve (cf. Acts. 1:21–22). The church was the finished structure to be "built on the foundation of the apostles and prophets, with Christ Jesus himself as the chief cornerstone" (Eph. 2:20). The twelve tribes and the twelve apostles represent the collective people of God (see comments on Rev. 4:4).

The city was laid out like a square (21:16). In 11:2, John measures the temple of God; here an angel uses a golden rod to measure the city. The square was an important shape in Judaism. The breastplate of the high priest was square (Ex. 28:16), as was the Most Holy Place in Solomon's temple (2 Chron. 3:8). The angelic figure who measured the inner court of the eschatological temple found it to be a square of 500 cubits per side (Ezek. 42:16–20). Many hellenistic cities had square agoras. The lower agora in Ephesus is called the Square (*tetragona*) Agora, measuring approximately 365 feet per side. The length of each side of the heavenly Jerusalem measures 12,000 stadia (12 x 1000), while the walls are 144 (12 x 12) cubits thick. The previous

use of the numbers 12, 144, and 1000 in Revelation plus the unreality of the precise measurements—1400 miles for the city and 200 feet for the walls—point to a figurative understanding of these numbers. The city is further given an identical height measurement of 12,000 cubits, making it a perfect cube. The description of the Most Holy Place in the temple is also of a cube (1 Kings 6:20). This portrayal of the eternal dwelling place of God and his people suggests perfection and completeness.

The wall was made of jasper, and the city of pure gold, as pure as glass (21:18). Jasper is a precious stone previously associated with God (cf. 4:3). The purity of the city and its streets is compared to two other precious commodities—gold and glass. Gold in antiquity was typically alloyed with another mineral such as silver, hence pure gold was especially valuable. The use of glass proliferated after the discovery of glassblowing near Sidon around 50 B.C. Glass tableware and vessels soon became common in households around the Roman empire. Impurities in the ingredients or air bubbles left during production commonly produced glass that was colored or translucent. Pure glass was thus highly valued. Sardis was a center both for the production of gold and glass. The gold deposits found along the Pactolus River valley provided the raw material for the gold refineries that archaeologists have discovered at the site. Although these date to the Lydian period of Croesus (6th century B.C.), inscriptions that speak of goldsmiths and gold gilding on public buildings suggest that the tradition of "Golden Sardis" continued into the Roman period. Sardis also emerged as a center of glass production in Asia, particularly in late Roman times (ca. A.D. 400). The Asian believers would associate wealth and splendor with this description of the new Jerusalem's building materials.

The foundations of the city walls were decorated with every kind of precious stone (21:19). Isaiah described the future Zion as a city whose foundations, walls, and gates are composed of precious stones (Isa. 54:11–12). Tobit likewise portrayed the restored Jerusalem as built with precious stones (Tobit 13:16–18). The square breastplate worn by the high priest contained twelve precious stones, each engraved with the names of one of the twelve tribes (Ex. 28:17–20; 39:10–13). The Septuagint reading of Ezekiel 28:13 gives a virtually identical list as that of the breastplate's twelve stones. However, these stones adorned the king of Tyre in the garden of paradise. As John does with other Old Testament borrowings, he adapts this list for his own purposes. His order is different than these other Old Testament lists, and he changes three stones: Chalcedony, chrysophase, and jacinth are substituted for carbuncle, ligurion, and agate, although these may be semantic equivalents. The colors of the stones represent different shades of yellow, red, blue, and green. The stones represent a city not only of majestic beauty and glory, but also one of great value to be desired by its future residents.

I did not see a temple in the city, because the Lord God Almighty and the Lamb are its temple (21:22). The activity in the heavenly city is described in the closing verses of this section using two divine metaphors—temple and throne (22:3). The temple symbolizes the eternal worship of God. The nations of redeemed peoples both worship and reign in the heavenly city. The transformed nations coming into a new Jerusalem is a popular prophetic theme. Isaiah wrote, "And they will bring all your brothers, from all the nations, to my holy mountain in Jerusalem as an offering to the Lord" (Isa. 66:20; cf. Zech. 14:16–19; Tobit 14:6–7). The destruction of the second temple in Jerusalem by the Romans in A.D. 70 was prophesied by Jesus (Matt. 24:1–2). For almost two thousand years, the Jews have not had a central sanctuary for worship and sacrifice. While many prophecy teachers believe that the temple must be rebuilt before the return of Christ, the New Testament never explicitly states that. Instead, the Gospel of John teaches that when the Word became flesh, the divine tabernacle was now with humanity (John 1:14). Because his own body was now the temple (2:19–22), Jesus taught that true worship would be spiritual rather than located at a physical temple either in Samaria or Jerusalem (4:21–24). The temple imagery suggests that

TWELVE PRECIOUS STONES

These are the twelve stones used in the breastplate of the high priest.

eternal worship will center on God and the Lamb.

The city does not need the sun or the moon to shine on it, for the glory of God gives it light, and the Lamb is its lamp (21:23). Heaven is portrayed here and in 22:5 as a place of perpetual light generated by God and the Lamb. The ongoing activity of the redeemed—worshiping and reigning—takes place in such an environment. The association of God with light is common in Scripture. God manifested his glory as a pillar of fiery light throughout Israel's travels in the desert (Ex. 40:38). David declared, "The LORD is my light and my salvation" (Ps. 27:1). In one of his "I am" sayings, Jesus declared, "I am the light of the world" (John 8:12). And John wrote, "God is light; in him there is no darkness at all" (1 John 1:5). Because of this constant light in the city, no evil or impurity can ever enter its gates.

The river of the water of life (22:1). The new heaven is a restored and renovated Eden, and several images from the original paradise now appear. A river flowed from Eden that watered the garden (Gen. 2:10). After Eden was barred to humanity after the Fall, renewed access to its blessings formed part of Israel's prophetic hope. Joel declared that on the Day of the Lord a fountain would flow out of the Lord's house (Joel 3:18). Both Ezekiel and Zechariah saw waters of life flowing out of the eschatological Jerusalem (Ezek. 47:1–10; Zech. 14:8). The source of these living waters changed from a place to a person with the Incarnation. At the Feast of Tabernacles, Jesus named himself as the source of the streams of living water and identified the Holy Spirit as the spiritual reality, for which living water was a metaphor (John 7:37–39). The coming of the Spirit at Pentecost was the deposit guaranteeing the church's future eschatological inheritance (cf. Eph. 1:13–14), which in Revelation is the restored Eden. That the source of the river is the throne of God and the Lamb suggests that "water of life" is also used as a metaphor for the Holy Spirit. *Epistle of Barnabas* 6:13 summarizes the imagery found here: "He made a second creation in the last days. And the Lord says: 'Behold, I make the last things as the first.'"

On each side of the river stood the tree of life . . . . No longer will there be any curse (22:2–3). When Eve ate the fruit from the tree of the knowledge of good and evil, a curse came upon humanity and the created order (Gen. 3:1–19). The effects of that curse are at last reversed, and the victors are permitted unlimited access to the tree. John's imagery comes directly from Ezekiel, who saw fruit trees lining the banks of the river flowing from the temple. These trees produced fruit monthly for food, and their leaves were for healing (Ezek. 47:12). In *4 Ezra* 2:18, the single tree of life likewise becomes twelve trees, each loaded with various fruits. The perpetual fruitbearing in the new order epitomizes the transformation of the normal seasonal cycles of seedtime and harvest (Eccl. 3:2). It also symbolizes the ongoing renewal that exists in the eternal city. The healing provided for the nations takes away the mourning, crying, and pain experienced under the curse in the old earth (Rev. 21:4). The abundant fruit and medicinal leaves symbolize the completeness of Christ's salvation for the victors.

The throne of God and of the Lamb will be in the city, and his servants will serve him (22:3). The second eternal activity of the redeemed besides worship (21:22) is service around the heavenly throne, which symbolizes God's eternal rule. Because the effects of sin are reversed, the saints are now free to reign eternally. To see God's face is an idiom suggesting personal contact and fellowship. Although Jesus' time on earth was brief, he promised that in heaven his disciples would be with him forever (John 14:2–3). God's servants continue to be identified as those marked with his name on their foreheads (Rev. 7:3; 14:1). The reign begun by the martyrs during the thousand years (20:4–6) now continues for eternity.

These words are trustworthy and true (22:6a). The angel mediating the heavenly vision affirms its truthfulness for a third time in the closing chapters (cf. 19:9; 21:5). Jesus likewise concluded his Olivet Discourse with an oath: "I tell you the truth .... Heaven and earth will pass away, but my words will never pass away" (Mark 13:30–31). Greco-Roman divinatory charms also emphasized the truthfulness of their revelation. This oath formula serves to validate the content of John's revelation to his audience.

The Coming of Christ (22:6b–21)

The Lord, the God of the spirits of the prophets, sent his angel (22:6b). The closing, or epilogue, of Revelation begins with the reintroduction of the angel who first appears in 1:1 and interprets the visions in the book. Since God superintends the spirits of the prophets, the readers are assured of the divine authority behind John's prophecy. Likewise, 2 Peter 1:21 affirms this: "For prophecy never had its origin in the will of man,

but men spoke from God as they were carried along by the Holy Spirit." It is God's intention to show his servants in the seven churches what was soon to take place (cf. Rev. 1:1). "Soon" is used four times as a catchword in these closing verses, signaling prophetic, not chronological, time.

Behold, I am coming soon! (22:7). Jesus has not spoken since 3:22, but now speaks three times in closing (cf. 22:12–16, 20). The final two beatitudes are also spoken by Jesus at this time. Like the threefold oath formula spoken by the angel, Jesus' three statements epitomize the principle that all testimony must be validated by two or three witnesses (cf.

Deut. 19:15; Matt. 18:16). Each begins with the declaration that he is coming soon. For the Asian believers who have not repented, his coming in judgment is imminent (cf. Rev. 2–3).

Blessed is he who keeps the words of the prophecy in this book (22:7). The sixth beatitude blesses those who keep the words of the prophecy, that is, the book of Revelation. This essentially repeats the first beatitude (1:3), which blesses those who keep ("take to heart," NIV) what is written in this prophecy. Keep is a key word in Revelation and means to trust and obey God and his commandments. Each of its eleven uses refers directly to the believers in the seven churches who must keep the word in order to overcome.

Your brothers the prophets (22:9). Here the angel calls the prophets John's brothers. John clearly regards himself as a prophet, for six times he calls his book a prophecy. In 10:11, he is told to prophesy in a ministry like other New Testament prophets (cf. 1 Cor. 14:29–32). Apostles and prophets were closely linked in the early church, since ministry was charismatic and functional (cf. Eph. 2:20; 3:5). Paul himself functioned in both offices during his ministry (Acts 13:1; 1 Cor 1:1; Eph. 1:1). John likewise ministered among the seven churches as both an apostle and a prophet.

Do not seal up the words of the prophecy of this book (22:10). The scroll that John sees in 5:1 has seven seals, which need divine authorization to be broken. In 10:4, John is told to seal up what the seven thunders said to him. Since the contents of the scroll and the words of the thunders have been revealed to John, the angel now

commands John to reveal them also to the churches. The only extrabibilical Jewish apocalypse to have a similar command to conceal and reveal is *4 Ezra*. Ezra is told to write what he has seen in a book and hide it, but he is to teach its contents to those who are wise and able to keep its secrets (*4 Ezra* 12:37–38; cf. 14:5–6, 45–46). John's prophecy must be communicated to all believers because the time of its fulfillment is near.

Let him who does wrong continue to do wrong . . . and let him who is holy continue to be holy (22:11). Four parallel commands follow, the first two to sinners, and the last two to the victors. This contrast between the righteous and unrighteous is likewise depicted at the conclusion of Daniel: "Many will be purified, made spotless and are refined, but the wicked will continue to be wicked" (Dan. 12:10). *Didache* 10:6 gives a similar exhortation to early Christians: "If anyone is holy, let him come; if anyone is not, let him repent." This and the hearing saying that follows in Revelation 22:17 are designed to stir the churches from their spiritual lethargy and to sharpen the divide between the faithful and the apostate in their midst.

I am the Alpha and the Omega, the First and the Last, the Beginning and the End (22:13). Jesus promises that the reward for the victors for their faithful deeds will be distributed at his coming. He affirms his declarations here and in verse 16 by describing himself by five epithets, all previously introduced in the book. "Alpha and Omega" and "Beginning and End" are used as epithets of the Lord God (cf. 1:8; 21:6). Jesus can claim these same titles because he shares God's nature. The meaning of the three epithets in verse 13 is synonymous: Jesus is the eternal One who spans all time. As "the Root and Offspring of David" (cf. 3:7; 5:5), Jesus is the king whose reign will never end; he is likewise the "bright Morning Star" promised to the victors in Thyatira (cf. 2:28).

Blessed are those who wash their robes (22:14). The final beatitude commends those washing their robes, which is the positive aspect of those who have not defiled their garments (3:4; 14:4). This is another version of Jesus' beatitude, "Blessed are the pure in heart, for they will see God" (Matt. 5:8). Meeting this condition is a prerequisite for realizing two other promises—partaking of the tree of life and entering the holy city, the new Jerusalem. This exhortation is a final reminder to the Asian believers to purify themselves, lest they defile themselves with those practicing the sins that follow.

Outside are the dogs (22:15). Dogs is a pejorative term based on the contemptible attitude of ancient Jews towards dogs (1 Sam. 17:43). Jesus, tongue in

▶ The Alpha and Omega Puzzle

In A.D. 79, the city of Pompeii was buried by the ash of nearby Mount Vesuvius. When archaeologists excavated the city, many fascinating discoveries were made including what some scholars believe is an early Christian puzzle. In the form of a square it reads in Latin:

```
R O T A S
O P E R A
T E N E T
A R E P O
S A T O R
```

The translation of these five words is: "Arepo the reaper holds the wheels with care." Those who have studied the puzzle observe that its simple meaning must go beyond the obvious. First, note that the words read the same no matter from which corner one begins. Second, the letters of the square spell out the opening words of the Lord's prayer, Pater Noster, if the letter N is used twice. Third, with the double use of N the letters must be spelled out in the form of a cross, which leaves four letters left over—two As and two Os. The diagram reads as shown below.

Back to the square, observe next that the central letter in each side is the letter T. Early Christian tradition saw significance in this shape: "And because the cross, which is shaped like the T, was destined to convey grace" (*Barn.* 9:8). Also note that the T is flanked on all sides by the A and O, the letters representing alpha and omega in Latin. The remarkable nature of the square suggests that these relationships are not merely coincidental, although some scholars question whether this Christian interpretation is viable. But if it is, G. R. Beasley-Murray is right to observe that "the significance of the square lies in its embodiment of the faith that he who is the Alpha and Omega of all things has been revealed as 'our Father' in the Christ who died on the cross."[A-58]

```
                    A
                    P
                    A
                    T
                    E
                    R
A  P A T E R N O S T E R   O
                    O
                    S
                    T
                    E
                    R
                    O
```

cheek, used the euphemism for Gentiles in general (Matt. 15:26–27).[140] It is also used to denigrate specific individuals: Paul called his Judaizing opponents dogs (Phil. 3:2) and Ignatius called false teachers mad dogs (*Eph.* 7:1). Deuteronomy 23:18 (see NIV note) uses dog as a euphemism for a male temple prostitute. The link with fornicators (NRSV) in this vice list suggests that sexual sin is being denounced. Pederasty was common in the Greek world, and older men routinely took boys as their lovers. The poetess Sappho, from the Aegean island of Lesbos (hence lesbianism), celebrated the beauty of her female students. Although Plato regarded homosexuality as unnatural,[141] intellectuals like Sophocles and Socrates had male lovers even in old age.

The Roman experience with homosexuality accelerated with Greek acculturation in the second century B.C. To describe these new sexual practices, the Romans had to adopt many Greek terms. A law passed in Rome in 149 B.C. made pederasty illegal. The Roman orator and statesman Cicero (d. 43 B.C.) provides two vignettes related to the sexual practices in Asia. Cicero discredited the character of a litigant from Pergamum by using as evidence his virtual kidnapping of a young man from Temnos. And while in Laodicea, a young man named Hortensius propositioned Cicero to have sexual relations.[142] Plutarch was a Roman author who denounced homosexuality as against nature.[143] His fellow critics used such terms as vile (cf. Rev. 21:8; 22:11) and filthy to attack homosexuality. Paul was a Christian voice that likewise inveighed against such "shameful lusts," calling these indecent acts a "perversion" (Rom. 1:26–27). In spite of negative cultural attitudes, Roman aristocrats began to indulge in same-sex relationships.

Julius Caesar's reputation was tarnished because of an affair with Nicomedes, king of Bithynia.[144] Of the eleven emperors in the first century, most were bisexual. The Roman historians Suetonius and Tacitus recorded numerous accounts of the sexual deviancy of these Caesars, particularly Nero who "married" young men on two occasions.[145] Homosexuality was a prevailing vice of Rome and its rulers.

The sexually immoral (22:15). Promiscuous heterosexual activity was even more common in antiquity. The orator Demosthenes, in summarizing the Greek view of sexuality, stated that men should have "mistresses for our enjoyment, concubines to serve our person, and wives for the bearing of legitimate offspring."[146] The mistresses, or *hetairai*, were a regular feature of the male-only Greek banquets and provided sexual pleasures on the dining couches following the meal. Among the Roman aristocracy, adultery was considered an illegal act, not because it broke a divine law but because it violated property rights (wives were considered property). Infidelity also worked against one's self-interest by compromising familial loyalty (Lat. *fides*). Marital sex was primarily for producing children and not for pleasure. Hence slaves were often used for sexual gratification both by the master and the mistress of the household. For the general population sexual intercourse was indulged in freely because it was regarded as a bodily function like eating and drinking (cf. 1 Cor. 6:12–13).[147] Few physical consequences, such as AIDS or sexually transmitted diseases, existed for promiscuous behavior in antiquity. Syphilis was first introduced to Europe in 1494 following Columbus's voyage to America. Jesus' warning of exclusion from the heavenly city because of immorality therefore flew in the face of the prevailing societal mores about sex.

I, Jesus, have sent my angel to give you this testimony for the churches (22:16). This is the only place in Revelation where Jesus identifies himself using the first person. He attests that he is the One who has sent the angel to give this prophetic witness to the churches. This is also the first explicit reference to the seven churches since chapters 2–3, although the original audience has been in view throughout the prophecy.

The Spirit and the bride say, "Come!" (22:17). For the second time, the Holy Spirit speaks directly (cf. 14:13). He is joined by the church presented again as the bride. Responding to Jesus' threefold announcement that he is coming soon, the church now answers three times in a crescendo that builds until the end of the book (22:20). The first invitation to "Come" begins with that of the Spirit and the bride. The Spirit, echoing the words of Jesus, speaks to the churches in the hearing sayings in Revelation 2–3 (cf. Ezek. 3:27). The second "Come" issues from those who are hearing in the seven churches. This same group is now itself invited to come and partake of the spiritual blessing of the water of life.

Whoever is thirsty, let him come; and whoever wishes, let him take the free gift of the water of life (22:17). Isaiah's water metaphor (Isa. 55:1) is now used to symbolize God's restored covenant with the victors, who are the new remnant Israel. This metaphor is likewise found in the invitation in *Odes of Solomon* 30:1–2, "Fill for yourselves water from the living spring of the Lord, because it has been opened for you. And come all you thirsty and take a drink, and rest beside the spring of the Lord." The divine promise to quench the thirst of the saints (Rev. 7:16; 21:6) is finally realized. This saying echoes a familiar word of Jesus in John 7:37: "If anyone is thirsty, let him come to me and drink" (cf. John 6:35). For the Laodiceans who were spiritually parched but did not know it, this final promise to quench their thirst would have been especially significant.

I warn everyone who hears the words of the prophecy of this book (22:18). The warning formula that closes the book is given to protect the integrity of the document. Such formulas, common in ancient sacred texts, acted in lieu of modern copyright laws. A similar injunction concerning God's commandments is found in Deuteronomy 4:2: "Do not add to what I command you and do not subtract from it" (cf. Deut. 12:32). The translators of the Pentateuch into Greek "commanded that a curse should be laid, as was their custom, on anyone who should alter the version by any addition or change to any part of the written text, or any deletion either" (*Let. Aris.* 311). The

REFLECTIONS

CHRISTIANS ARE AGAIN SURROUNDED BY A SOCIETY that has abandoned biblical teaching on sexuality and promotes a promiscuous lifestyle. How do we maintain purity of thought and body when we are constantly confronted by salacious images on television and the Internet, and in movies and magazines? This assault is already negatively impacting the church. The percentage of divorces among Christians approximates that of non-Christians. And several denominations are allowing homosexuals to serve in ministry. Revelation speaks prophetically against such moral compromise and warns that the failure to overcome sexual sin risks exclusion from the heavenly new Jerusalem.

translators of the Pentateuch into Greek "commanded that a curse should be laid, as was their custom, on anyone who should alter the version by any addition or change to any part of the written text, or any deletion either" (*Let. Aris.* 311).[148] And Barnabas warned his readers: "You shall guard what you have received, neither adding nor subtracting anything" (*Barn.* 19:11). This warning is addressed particularly to the Nicolaitans and the followers of Jezebel. Those who add or subtract, that is, distort or minimize, the words of this prophecy, God will add plagues or remove participation in the tree of life and in the holy city. The opposition parties in the seven churches are warned

a final time that failure to heed John's prophetic word will result in eternal exclusion from the new Jerusalem.

Amen. Come, Lord Jesus. The grace of the Lord Jesus be with God's people. Amen (22:20–21). This invitation is the equivalent of the Aramaic words *marana tha* meaning "Our Lord, come!" That this word came into the vocabulary of the Greek-speaking churches shows its early use among Palestinian Christians. Paul closed 1 Corinthians with a curse upon those who did not love the Lord followed by the cry *Marana tha*, "Come, O Lord!" (1 Cor. 16:22). This language suggests that the Apocalypse was perhaps later

▶ The Seven Churches Today

Pilgrimages to the sites of the seven churches have been popular for over three centuries. In 1678, Tho. Smith wrote an account of his visit in A Survey of the Seven Churches of Asia, as they now lye in their ruins. Alexander Svoboda provided one of the earliest photographic records during his visit in 1869. Through the years, other famous travelers, such as Mark Twain, Lord Kinross, and Freya Stark, have recorded their impressions of the seven churches.[A-59]

What is the state of these sites today? For over a century, the Austrian Archaeological Institute has been excavating in Ephesus. Its team of archaeologists has completed extensive restoration to the city, making it the premier archaeological site in Turkey today. The site of ancient Smyrna is now occupied by Izmir, Turkey's third largest city. A two-story state agora with a vaulted basement is well preserved in the city center, and Roman ruins remain on the acropolis called the Kadifekale, which overlooks the city. Pergamum attracts many visitors because of its archaeological treasures. Although the altar of Zeus has been removed to the Staatliche Museum in

Berlin, the Germans have done extensive restorations to the other remains on the acropolis. The theater that appears to hang from its hillside is one of the most spectacular in the ancient world. The Asclepium there has also been restored.

Thyatira has only a few ruins to see near the city center. Important inscriptions from the city must be viewed at the nearby regional museum at Manisa. At Sardis, an American archaeological team has done extensive restoration, most notably at the gymnasium complex. Its restored synagogue is the most elaborate outside of Israel. Columns from a temple of Artemis still stand below the acropolis. At Philadelphia, visitors can see the pillars of a Byzantine church and sections of a Roman wall running through the modern city of Alasehir. The ruins of a theater and a stadium on the acropolis are unexcavated. Laodicea's large, deserted site is normally bypassed today for the popular hot springs at Pamukkale and its nearby ruins of Hierapolis. However, Laodicea does offer the extensive remains of Greek and Roman theaters, a stadium, an aqueduct system, and the Ephesian gate.

read in the Asian churches when they celebrated the Eucharist. In *Didache* 9–10, the liturgy for communion closes with a prayer of thanksgiving that ends similarly, "Maranatha! Amen" (*Did.* 10:6). Revelation ends with a typical letter closing, "The grace . . . ," a phrase that concludes most of Paul's letters (e.g., Rom. 16:20; Gal. 6:18). The final word "Amen" in the NIV is not found in some manuscripts of Revelation and may be a scribal addition. If original, it would also be the last word in the New Testament and in the Bible, and stand like a divine punctuation mark underscoring the extraordinary revelation that precedes it.

ANNOTATED BIBLIOGRAPHY

Ekrem Akurgal. *Ancient Civilizations and Ruins of Turkey.* 8th ed. Istanbul, 1993.

This is the most complete work on the historical background and archaeological excavations for many of the biblical sites in Turkey. Numerous photographs and diagrams are included.

David E. Aune. *Revelation.* 3 volumes. WBC 52A. B. C. Dallas: Word; and Nashville: Thomas Nelson, 1997–1998.

Aune is one of the foremost interpreters of Revelation today and provides invaluable historical background, although the amount of information may be overwhelming.

Richard J. Bauckham. *The Theology of the Book of Revelation.* Cambridge: Cambridge University Press, 1993.

Bauckham, another outstanding interpreter of Revelation, carefully examines the book's theological themes in this volume. His collected essays on Revelation are found in *The Climax of Prophecy* (Edinburgh: T. & T. Clark, 1993).

G. K. Beale. *The Book of Revelation.* NIGTC. Grand Rapids: Eerdmans, 1999.

Based on the Greek text, this large commentary provides a thorough, up-to-date discussion of Revelation's theological issues as well as its background in Old Testament literature.

Colin J. Hemer. *The Letters to the Seven Churches of Asia in their Local Setting.* Grand Rapids: Eerdmans, 2000 repr.

W. M. Ramsay's foundational work is updated in this study, which surveys literary, epigraphical, archaeological, and numismatic sources.

J. Ramsey Michaels. *Interpreting the Book of Revelation.* Grand Rapids: Baker, 1992.

This incisive guide introduces readers to the various issues involved in interpreting Revelation. Michaels's volume *Revelation* (Downers Grove, Ill.: InterVarsity, 1997) is an insightful and readable commentary for lay readers.

S. R. F. Price. *Rituals and Power: The Roman Imperial Cult in Asia Minor.* Cambridge University Press, 1986.

This definitive and richly illustrated work thoroughly surveys the background and influence of emperor worship in Asia Minor.

William M. Ramsay. *The Letters to the Seven Churches.* Edited by Mark Wilson. Peabody, Mass.: Hendrickson, 1993.

Written by a pioneer epigrapher and archaeologist in Turkey, this is the classic work on the seven churches, particularly in his development of local references.

Main Text Notes

1. For an excellent overview of the development of Christianity in Asia Minor, see R. E. Oster Jr., "Christianity in Asia Minor," *ABD*, 1:938–54.

2. Irenaeus, *Haer.* 5.30.3.

3. Suetonius, *Dom.* 10; Eusebius, *Eccl. Hist.* 3.17–20.

4. See L. L. Thompson, *The Book of Revelation: Apocalypse and Empire* (New York: Oxford, 1990), 103–4; B. W. Jones, *The Emperor Domitian* (London: Routledge, 1992), 117.

5. Josephus, *J.W.* 6.9.3 §420.

6. The Roman poets Statius, *Theb.* 1.22–22; *Silv.* 1.1.79–81, and Martial, 5.5.7, describe Domitian's role during this period. Statius claims that it was Domitian who ended Jupiter's war (the battle for the Capitol) and other hostilities; Martial states that Domitian for a time held the reins formerly held by the Julians and then handed them to his father and brother to be third in the world. Suetonius, *Dom.* 13.1, likewise states that Domitian had "given" the empire to his father.

7. Cited in C. E. Arnold, *The Colossian Syncretism* (Grand Rapids: Baker, 1996), 80; see 61–89 for a full discussion of angel texts with numerous examples; cf. S. Mitchell, *Anatolia: Land, Men, and Gods in Asia Minor* (Oxford: Clarendon, 1993), 2:45–46.

8. Justin Martyr, *Dial.* 81.4; Irenaeus, *Haer.* 3.1.1; 4.20.11; 4.30.4; 5.35.2.

9. Eusebius, *Eccl. Hist.* 7.25.

10. Ibid., 3.39.2–4.

11. W. V. Harris, *Ancient Literacy* (Cambridge, Mass.: Harvard Univ. Press, 1989), 272–74; for the inscriptional evidence see G. H. R. Horsley, "The Inscriptions of Ephesos and the New Testament," in *NovT* 34 (1992): 105–68.

12. Horsley, "Inscriptions of Ephesos," 125.

13. Tacitus, *An.* 14.50; 15:71; cf. Eusebius, *Eccl. Hist.* 3.18.

14. This is the view held by Tertullian, *Praescr. Haer.* 36; cf. G. B. Caird, *The Revelation of St. John the Divine* (New York: Harper & Row, 1966), 21–23.

15. J. R. Michaels, *Revelation* (Downers Grove, Ill.: InterVarsity, 1997), 26–32.

16. W. M. Ramsay, *The Letters to the Seven Churches* (Peabody, Mass.: Hendrickson, 1994), 134. Ramsay's classic study of the seven churches along with C. J. Hemer's updated discussion in *The Letters to the Seven Churches of Asia in their Local Setting* (Grand Rapids: Eerdmans, repr. 2000) provide a comprehensive introduction to each church. Therefore, these foundational secondary sources will not be cited as references for the churches individually.

17. Josephus, *J.W.* 7.5.5 §§148–49.

18. See D. F. Watson, "Nicolaitans," *ABD*, 4:1106–7; D. E. Aune, *Revelation 1–5* (WBC; Dallas: Word, 1997), 1:148–49; Hemer, *Letters to the Seven Churches of Asia*, 87–94.

19. Strabo, *Geog.* 14.1.5, 20.

20. F. F. Bruce, *The Gospel of John* (Grand Rapids: Eerdmans, 1983), 46.

21. Philo, *Vit. Apoll.* 4.7; Aristides, *Or.* 15.20–22; cf. Aune, *Revelation*, 1:171–75.

22. Homer, *Iliad* 24.602–17; Ovid, *Met.* 6.310–12; Pausanius 1.21.3; Quintus of Smyrna 1.292–306. See J. R. March, "Niobe," *OCD*[3], 1045.

23. Tacitus, *Hist.* 3.68; Suetonius, *Galb.* 11; Dio Cassius, 42.37.

24. Eusebius, *Eccl. Hist.* 2.23.11–18.

25. For a full discussion of this important word, see L. Coenen and A. A. Trites, "Witness, Testimony" in *NIDNTT*, ed. Brown (Grand Rapids: Zondervan, 1978): 3:1038–51.

26. W. M. Ramsay, *Historical Commentary on First Corinthians*, ed. M. Wilson (Grand Rapids: Kregel, 1996), 119.

27. The text of this decree, *OGIS* 458, is published in A. C. Johnson, P. R. Coleman-Norton, and F. C. Bourne, *Ancient Roman Statutes* (Austin: University of Texas Press, 1961), §142.

28. *CIG* 300. See Hemer, *Letters to the Seven Churches*, 110–11; G. K. Beale, *The Book of Revelation* (NIGTC; Grand Rapids: Eerdmans, 1999), 259–60.

29. Eusebius, *Eccl. Hist.* 3.31; cf. 5.17. The tradition is confused as to whether Philip the apostle or the deacon is meant or perhaps both.

30. For the Gnostics, see Irenaeus, *Haer.* 1.24.5; Justin, *Dial.* 35; Eusebius, *Eccl. Hist.* 4.7; for Cerinthus, see Eusebius, *Eccl. Hist.* 4.14.6; cf. 3.28.6.

31. See *T. Levi* 18:3; *T. Jud.* 24:1; 1QM 11:6–7; 4QTestim. 9–13; CD 7:18–20.

32. Herodotus, *Hist.* 1.47–49, 71–91.

33. Dio Chrysostom, *Or.* 31.84; Xenophon, *Hell.* 2.3.51.

34. J. A. T. Robinson, *The Priority of John* (Oak Park, Ill.: Meyer-Stone, 1987), 72–81. See also W. Horbury, "The Benediciton of the *Minim* and the Early Jewish-Christian Controversy," *JTS* 33 (1982): 19–61.

35. Pliny, *Nat. Hist.* 36.95; cf. B. Ashmole, *Architect and Sculptor in Classical Greece* (New York: New York Univ., 1972), 7.

36. See Hemer, *Letters to the Seven Churches of Asia*, 186–91; M. J. S. Rudwick and E. M. B. Green, "The Laodicean Lukewarmness," *ET* 69 (1957–58): 263–64.

37. Strabo, *Geog.* 12.8.18; Suetonius, *Tib.* 8; Tacitus, *Ann.* 14.27.1.

38. Strabo, *Geog.* 12.8.16; Vitruvius, 8.3.14.

39. Pliny, *Nat. Hist.* 8.73.190.

40. Strabo, *Geog.* 12.8.20.

41. Pliny, *Nat. Hist.* 36.36.145ff.; Celsus, 5.2; see Hemer, *Letters to the Seven Churches*, 196–99.

42. Strabo, *Geog.* 14.2.24; Appian, *Bell. Civ.* 5.75; Dio Cassius, 49.25.4; Plutarch, *Ant.* 38.3.

43. Pliny, *Nat. Hist.* 37.9–10.

44. R. K. Harrison, "Cherubim," *ISBE*, 642–43. See also J. E. Pritchard, *The Ancient Near East in Pictures* (Princeton: Princeton Univ. Press, 1969), Plates 128, 456, 458, 644–56.

45. Philo, *Alleg. Interp.* 114–16.

46. Josephus, *Ant.* 14.3.1 §35; 14.12.2 §304; 14.12.3 §313; 16.9.4 §296.

47. Josephus, *J.W.* 7.5.2 §§105–6.

48. For Gaius, Philo, *Alleg. Interp.* 353; Suetonius, *Cal.* 22.2; Dio Cassius, 59.28.5; for Nero, Martial, 7.45.7; Suetonius, *Nero* 11.2; for Domitian, Martial, 5.8.1; 7.34.8; 9.66.3; Statius, 1.1.62; 3.3.103, 110; 4.2.6; 5.1.42, 112, 261; Suetonius, *Dom.* 13.2; cf. Dio Cassius, 67.5.7; 67.13.4; Dio Chrysostom, *Or.* 45.1.

49. Pliny, *Nat. Hist.* 13.21–22.

50. See E. J. Goodspeed and I. A. Sparks, "Papyrus," *ISBE*, 3:651–55; I. A. Sparks, "Parchment," *ISBE*, 3:663; F. G. Kenyon, *Books and Readers in Ancient Rome and Greece* (Oxford: Clarendon, 1932); H. Y. Gamble, *Books and Readers in the Early Church* (New Haven, Conn.: Yale Univ. Press, 1995), 42–81.

51. Interestingly the *Testament of Judah* (2d cent. B.C.), which purports to be the last words of that patriarch, omits mentions of the lion in its eschatological imagery and instead focuses on the Shoot of God and scepter images (*T. Judah* 24:5; cf. Isa. 11:1, 10).

52. O. Michel, "σφάζω," *TDNT*, 7:934–35.

53. Cicero, *In Verr.* 3.81; Suetonius, *Nero* 45.

54. Tacitus, *Ann.* 12.43.

55. Josephus, *J.W.* 6.3.3–5 §§193–219.

56. Suetonius, *Dom.* 7.2; Philo, *Vit. Apoll.* 6.42; M. Rostovtzeff, *The Social and Economic History of the Roman Empire*, 2 vols. (Oxford: Clarendon, 1957), 1:201, 147.

57. Thucydides, *Hist.* 2.50.1; for the plague, see 2.47–55.

58. For Rome, Suetonius, *Nero* 38; for Jerusalem, Josephus, *J.W.* 6.9.3 §421.

59. For Nero, Tacitus, *Ann.* 12.64; 14.12; 15.47.; for A.D. 69, Tacitus, *Hist.* 1.3.3.

60. Josephus, *J.W.* 6.5.3 §§289–90; see also Tacitus, *Hist.* 5.11.

61. K. Wellesley, *The Long Year AD 69*, 2d ed. (Bristol: Bristol Classical Press, 1989), 140–41.

62. Irenaeus, *Haer.* 5.30.2.

63. Juvenal, *Sat.* 3.62; see also M. Reasoner, "Rome and Roman Christianity," *DPL*, 851.

64. Tacitus, *An.* 15.44; Clement, *1 Clem.* 6:1.

65. Pausanius, 8.48.2–3.

66. A. Burnett, M. Amandry, and P. P. Ripollès, *Roman Provincial Coinage* (London: British Museum/Paris: Bibliothèque Nationale, 1992). Examples from Asia are Smyrna (left 2465/1; right 2473), Sardis (left 3010), Laodicea (left 4403A–14), and Colossae (right 2891). In fact, Burnett et al. list thirty-seven coin issues of Nike that include a palm branch.

67. ΤΟ ΘΥΧΙΑΤΗΡΙΟΝ; see C. Foss, *Ephesus in Antiquity* (Cambridge: Cambridge Univ. Press, 1979), 45.

68. S. R. F. Price, *Rituals and Power: The Roman Imperial Cult in Asia Minor* (Cambridge: Cambridge Univ. Press, 1986), 214–15, Plate 3a.

69. Pliny, *Ep.* 10.96.

70. Josephus, *J.W.* 3.5.3 §86

71. Pliny, *Ep.* 6.16, 20.

72. Dioscorides Pedanius, *Mat. Med.* 3.23.1–4.

73. Seneca, *Apol.* 4.1.22–23; Suetonius, *Nero* 53; Cassius Dio, 61.20.5; 62.20.5.

74. Suetonius, *Dom.* 4.4; 15.3; Cassius Dio, 67:1.2; 67.16.2 [Athena]. For a coin type of Domitian showing a sacrifice to Minerva, see M. Grant, *Roman History from Coins* (New York: Barnes & Noble, 1968), Pl 4, #2.

75. P. Connolly, *Greece and Rome at War* (Englewood Cliffs, N.J.: Prentice Hall, 1981), 259.

76. Guy M. Rogers, *The Sacred Identity of Ephesos* (London: Routledge, 1991), 110–11.

77. For eye healing, see Pliny, *Nat. Hist.* 28.5.28–29; for the chariot curse, *ILS* 8753.

78. On magic, see C. E. Arnold, "Magic and Astrology," *DLNT*, 701–5; F. Graf, *Magic in the Ancient World* (Cambridge, Mass.: Harvard Univ. Press, 1997); H. D. Betz, ed., *The Greek Magical Papyri in Translation* (Chicago: University of Chicago Press, 1999); J. G. Gager, *Curse Tablets and Binding Spells from the Ancient World* (New York: Oxford Univ. Press, 1992).

79. Pliny, *Nat. Hist.* 34.41; Strabo, *Geog.* 14.2.5.

80. The early date of 70 is adopted rather than the traditional one of 96; cf. J. A. T. Robinson, *Redating the New Testament* (London: SCM, 1976), 327–34.

81. Eusebius, *Eccl. Hist.* 2.25.7–8

82. Plutarch, *Pomp.* 80; cf. *Pss. Sol.* 2:27.
83. From Paulus' *Opinions*, J. Shelton, *As the Romans Did* (Oxford: Oxford Univ. Press, 1988), 97.
84. Josephus, *J.W.* 4.6.3 §§381–83.
85. Tacitus, *Ann.* 14.21.
86. See F. Graf, "Apollo," *OCD³*, 122–23; F. Graf, "Leto," *OCD³*, 845–46; "Python," *DCM*, 343.
87. Eusebius, *Eccl. Hist.* 3.5.3; Epiphanius, *Haer.* 29.7; 30.2. Although Josephus does not specifically mention the Christians, he does state that many distinguished Jews abandoned Jerusalem at this time (*J.W.* 2.13.3 §556).
88. Suetonius, *Dom.* 4.4.
89. See D. E. Aune, "The Provincial League (Koinon) of Asia," *Revelation*, 2:773–75; R. A. Kearsley, "Asiarchs," *ABD*, 1:495–97; D. Magie, *Roman Rule in Asia Minor* (Princeton: Princeton Univ. Press, 1950), 1:447–52, 2:1295–1301.
90. Dio Cassius, 59.28.6.
91. Plutarch, *Cor.* 37.3; Suetonius, *Gaius* 57.1; Lucian, *Alex.* 12–26.
92. J. Finnegan, *The Archaeology of the New Testament* (Princeton: Princeton Univ. Press, 1992), 346.
93. The *Atbash* system of encipherment substitutes the last letter of the Hebrew alphabet for the first, the next to the last for the second, and so on through all the Hebrew alphabet. The three Hebrew consonants in Sheshach are decoded in this manner: sh=b (2x) and ch (or k)=l, hence bbl or Babel, the Hebrew word for Babylon. Cf. Charles L. Feinberg, *EBC*, 6:534–35.
94. For the Pompeii graffiti, see A. F. Johnson, "Revelation," *EBC*, 12:533; for the Nero verse see Suetonius, *Nero* 39.2.
95. *Sib. Or.* 5.12–42.
96. Irenaeus, *Haer.* 5.28.2.
97. Burnett et al., *Roman Provincial Coinage*, Nos. 2626, 3011, and 2917.
98. Finnegan, *Archaeology of the New Testament*, 344.
99. Origen, *Sel. Ezek.* 9.13.801.
100. Eusebius, *Eccl. Hist.* 2.25.5–7; cf. F. H. Chase, *HDB*, 3:769.
101. Many commentators believe both harvests are of the unrighteous. For a discussion of the arguments pro and con, see David E. Aune, *Revelation 6–16* (WBC; Nashville: Nelson, 1998), 2:801–3.
102. Mitchell, *Anatolia*, 2:25–26.
103. Herodotus, *Hist.* 1.191.
104. Josephus, *J.W.* 1.32.3 §633.
105. For examples, see Cornelius C. Vermeule, *Roman Imperial Art in Greece and Asia Minor* (Cambridge, Mass.: Belknap/Harvard Univ. Press, 1968), 35–37.
106. Pliny, *Nat. Hist.* 34.18.
107. Tacitus, *Ann.* 4.56.
108. Cassius Dio, 51.20.6–7.
109. For a full description of this figure, see Aune, *Revelation 17–22*, 3:920–23.
110. E.g., *CIG* 3496–98.
111. Pliny (*Nat. Hist.* 9.61–64) gives a description of the purple-dyeing process; see also L. A. Moritz, "Purple," *OCD³*, 1280.
112. Josephus, *Ant.* 18.8.2 §§261–3
113. Josephus, *J.W.* 4.3.12 §202; 4.6.3 §388; 6.2.1 §95; 6.4.5–7 §§250–66.
114. Juvenal, *Sat.* 9.130; Horace, *Carm. Saec.* 5; Ovid, *Trist.* 1.5.69; Pliny, *Nat. Hist.* 3.66–67.
115. H. S. Robinson, "A Monument of Roma in Corinth," *Hesperia* 43 (1974): 470–84.
116. Rogers, *Ephesos*, 94.
117. Suetonius, *Vesp.* 1.
118. A. Burnett et al., *Roman Imperial Coinage*, 1:386, 392, 518; 2:735.
119. *IGRR*, 4:841.
120. R. Bauckham, *The Climax of Prophecy* (Edinburgh: T. & T. Clark, 1993), 338.
121. Lucan, 10.110–21; Petronius, *Sat.* 55, 119; Seneca, *Ep.* 60.2; 89.22.
122. Suetonius, *Vit.* 13.
123. Tacitus, *Ann.* 15.40.
124. Suetonius, *Tit.* 11.8.
125. Josephus, *J.W.* 6.9.3 §420.
126. See K. R. Bradley, "Slavery," *OCD³*, 1415–17; E. Ferguson, *Background of Early Christianity²*, 56–59; S. S. Bartchy, "Slavery," *ABD*, 6:65–73; T. Wiedemann, *Greek and Roman Slavery* (Baltimore: Johns Hopkins, 1981).
127. Aelius Aristides, *Or.* 26.11, 12.
128. See A. Edersheim, *Sketches of Jewish Social Life* (London: James Clarke, repr. 1961), 147–55; P. Trutza, "Marriage," *ZPEB*, 4:92–97.
129. This interpretation differs from the one I expressed earlier in "Revelation 19.10 and Contemporary Interpretation," in *Spirit and Renewal*, ed. Mark W. Wilson (Sheffield: Sheffield Academic Press, 1994), 191–202.
130. Virgil, *Aen.* 3.537.
131. Cassius Dio 43.14.3; the Roman poet Tibullus writes similarly: "The Fates sang true, and today Rome celebrates new triumphs,/ while the shackled Gallic chiefs pass, pair by pair./ In an ivory chariot drawn by matched and milk-white horses,/ Messalla wears the laurel that victors wear" (1.7.5–8).
132. Juvenal, *Sat.* 10.45.
133. Cicero, *Verr.* 4.43; Pausanius, 5.27.12.
134. *Midr. Ps.* 90.17
135. Tacitus, *An.* 15.43.

136. Contrarily, in the *T. Abr.* 13:9–14, two angels weigh the righteous deeds against the sins of each individual. Those whose deeds are burned up by fire are consigned to punishment with other sinners, while those whose works survive are placed with the other righteous.

137. Irenaeus, *Haer.* 5.36.1.

138. Suetonius, *Jul.* 83; *Aug.* 8.

139. Josephus, *J.W.* 7.1.1 §1.

140. For other examples in Jewish literature, see W. L. Lane, *Mark* (Grand Rapids: Eerdmans, 1974), 262 n. 63.

141. Plato, *Phaed.* 251a; *Leg.* 1.6363b–d; 8.841d–e.

142. Cicero, *Flac.* 21.51; 29.70; *Att.* 6.3.9; 10.4.6.

143. Plutarch, *Am.* 751c–d.

144. Suetonius, *Jul.* 49.

145. Suetonius, *Nero* 28, 29.

146. Demosthenes, *Or.* 59.118–22.

147. See A. Richlin, "Sexuality," *OCD*³, 1399; P. Veyne, "The Roman Empire," P. Veyne, ed., *A History of Private Life* (Cambridge: Belknap, 1987), 33–49, 202–5; Shelton, *As the Romans Did*, 37–58; A. A. Bell, Jr., *Exploring the New Testament World* (Nashville: Nelson, 1998), 221–38.

148. Similar curses have been found on Jewish gravestones found in Phrygia dating from around A.D. 250. One example reads: "And if anyone after their burial, if anyone shall inter another corpse or do injury in the way of purchase, there shall be on him the curses which are written in Deuteronomy"; see W. M. Ramsay, "The Old Testament in Roman Phrygia," in *The Bearing of Recent Discovery on the Trustworthiness of the New Testament* (London: Hodder & Stoughton, 1915), 358.

Sidebar and Chart Notes

A-1. See S. T. Carroll, "Patmos," *ABD*, 5:178–79; O. F. A. Meinardus, *St. John of Patmos* (New Rochelle, N.Y.: Caratzas, 1979), 7–22; S. A. Papadopoulos, *The Monastery of Saint John the Theologian* (Patmos: Monastery of St. John the Theologian, 1993), 4–8.

A-2. Tacitus, *An.* 2.54.

A-3. For the translation of one of these inscriptions, see Arnold, *The Colossian Syncretism*, 12–13, 118–19.

A-4. For a fascinating discussion of how oracles at Claros and Didyma functioned, see R. L. Fox, *Pagans and Christians* (New York: Alfred A. Knopf, 1988), 200–61; cf. G. E. Bean, *Aegean Turkey* (London: John Murray, 1989), 155–60, 192–201; H. W. Parke, *The Oracles of Apollo in Asia* (London: Croom Helm, 1985).

A-5. S. Friesen, *Twice Neokorus* (Leiden: Brill, 1993), 25ff.

A-6. See R. E. Oster, Jr., "Ephesus," *ABD*, 2:542–49; C. E. Arnold, "Ephesus," *DPL*, 249–53; P. Trebilco, "Asia," in D. W. J. Gill and C. Gempf, eds., *The Book of Acts in its First Century Setting: Greco-Roman Setting* (Grand Rapids: Eerdmans, 1994), 302–57; H. Koester, ed., *Ephesos, Metropolis of Asia* (Valley Forge, Pa.: Trinity, 1995).

A-7. Ramsay, *Letters* 29–33.

A-8. D. L. Barr, "The Apocalypse of John as Oral Enactment," *Int* 40˙(1986): 245–46 n. 9.

A-9. Cicero, *Phil.* 11.2.5.

A-10. Tacitus, *An.* 4.56; cf. R. Mellor, QEA RWMHÇ: *The Worship of the Goddess Roma in the Greek World* (Göttingen: Vandenhoeck & Ruprecht, 1975), 16.

A-11. See D. S. Potter, "Smyrna," *ABD*, 6:73–75; E. M. Yamauchi, *New Testament Cities in Western Asia Minor* (Grand Rapids: Baker, 1980), 55–62; C. J. Cadoux, *Ancient Smyrna* (Oxford: Oxford Univ. Press, 1938).

A-12. Josephus, *Ant.* 12.3.4 §149; 14.10.17 §235; 16.6.6 §171.

A-13. See A. R. Seager and A. T. Kraabel, "The Synagogue and the Jewish Community," in G. M. A. Hanfmann, *Sardis from Prehistoric to Roman Times* (Cambridge, Mass.: Harvard Univ. Press, 1983), 168–90.

A-14. Josephus, *Ant.* 14.10.11–12, 13, 16, 19, 25 §§223–27, 228–29, 230, 234, 238–40, 262–64; 14.12.2–3, 4 §§301–13, 314–17; 16.2.3 §§427–65; *Ag. Ap.* 2.4 §39.

A-15. Cicero, *Flac.* 28.68; cf. Josephus, *Ant.* 14.10.22 §§247–55.

A-16. For further information on the Jews in Asia Minor, see Aune, *Revelation*, 1:168–72; Mitchell, *Anatolia*, 2:30–37; P. Trebilco, *Jewish Communities in Asia Minor* (Cambridge: Cambridge Univ. Press, 1991).

A-17. See K. W. Arafat, "Nike" in *OCD*³, 1044; Jenny March, *Dictionary of Classical Mythology* (London: Cassell, 1998), s.v.

A-18. *IG*², 2311.

A-19. Pliny, *Nat. Hist.* 5.126.

A-20. See M. Grant, "Pergamum," in *A Guide to the Ancient World* (New York: Barnes & Noble, repr. 1997), 484–86; R. North, "Pergamum," *ISBE*, 3:768–70; D. S. Potter, "Pergamum," *ABD*, 5:228–30; H. Koester, ed., *Pergamon: Citadel of the Gods* (Harrisburg: Trinity, 1998).

A-21. See E. M. Blaiklock, "Thyatira," *ZPEB*, 5:743–44; R. North, "Thyatira," *ISBE*, 4:846; E. C. Blake and A. G. Edmonds, *Biblical Sites in Turkey* (Istanbul: Redhouse, 1996), 131–33.

A-22. Tacitus, *An.* 2.37; 4.56.

A-23. See J. G. Pedley, "Sardis," *ABD*, 5:982–84; J. G. Pedley, *Ancient Literary Sources on Sardis* (Cambridge, Mass.: Harvard Univ. Press, 1972); G. M. A. Hanfmann et al., *Sardis from Prehistoric to Roman Times* (Cambridge, Mass.: Harvard Univ. Press, 1975).

A-24. Eusebius, *Eccl. Hist.* 4.13.1–8.

A-25. Polybius, 30:1–3; 31.1; 32.1.

A-26. M. E. Boring, K. Berger, and C. Colpe, *Hellenistic Commentary to the New Testament* (Nashville: Abingdon, 1995), §771.

A-27. Strabo, *Geog.* 12.8.18; 13.4.10.

A-28. See W. W. Gasque, "Philadelphia," *ABD*, 5:304–5; M. J. S. Rudwick and C. J. Hemer, "Philadelphia," *IBD*, 3:1210–11; Magie, *Roman Rule*, 1:124–25; 2:982–83.

A-29. See F. F. Bruce, "Laodicea," *ABD*, 4:229–31; G. E. Bean, *Turkey Beyond the Maeander* (London: John Murray, 1989), 213–21; E. M. Yamauchi, *New Testament Cities*, 134–46.

A-30. Cicero, *Att.* 5.15; *Fam.* 3.5.

A-31. Irenaeus, *Haer.* 3.11.8.

A-32. The others are found in 5:9, 12, 13, 14; 7:10, 12; 11:15, 17–18; 12:10–12; 15:3–4; 16:5–6, 7; 19:1–2, 3, 4, 5, 6.

A-33. Price, *Rituals and Power*, 61, 90, 105, 118.

A-34. F. M. Cross, Jr., "The Discovery of the Samaria Papyri," *BA* 26:4 (1963): 110–21.

A-35. T. T. Packer, "Greek Religion," in J. Boardman, J. Griffin, O. Murray, eds., *The Oxford History of the Classical World* (New York: Oxford, 1986), 262–63.

A-36. Pliny, *Ep.* 10.96.

A-37. Josephus, *J.W.* 6.5.3 §§300–309.

A-38. Paul Rycaut, the British consul at Smyrna (1667–78) who rediscovered the site of Thyatira, provided an early account of the Sabbatai affair in an anonymous contribution to John Evelyn's *History of the Three Late Famous Impostors* published in 1669. Later in 1679, Rycaut incorporated this account into his *The History of the Turkish Empire from the Year 1623 to 1677*. The story of Sabbatai Zevi and other messianic movements is recounted in M. O. Wise's *The First Messiah* (San Francisco: HarperSanFrancisco, 1999).

A-39. Shelton, *As the Romans Did*, 6–17, 206–31; E. Ferguson, *BEC*, 45–60.

A-40. See Bell, *Exploring the New Testament World*, 185–219; J. Matthews, "Roman Life and Society," 748–70; Veyne, *A History of Private Life*, 51–159; F. Dupont, *Daily Life in Ancient Rome* (Oxford: Blackwell, 1992).

A-41. On the principal views regarding the Tribulation, see W. H. Baker, "Tribulation," *EDT*, 1110–11; R. H. Gundry, *The Church and Tribulation* (Grand Rapids: Zondervan, 1987); G. A. Archer, Jr., P. D. Feinberg, D. J. Moo, R. R. Reiter, *The Rapture: Pre-, Mid-, or Post-Tribulational* (Grand Rapids: Zondervan, 1984).

A-42. Diogenes Laertius, 4.5.27.

A-43. *Sib. Or.*, 5.3.18.

A-44. Strabo, *Geog.* 13.4.14; cf. Dio Cassius, 68.27.3.

A-45. See N. W. Lund, *Chiasmus in the New Testament* (Peabody, Mass.: Hendrickson, repr. 1992 and its updated "Preface" by D. M. Scholer and K. R. Snodgrass). See also M. W. Wilson, "The Structure of Revelation and the Seven Letters," *A Pie in a Very Bleak Sky?* (University of South Africa: D.Litt. et Phil. thesis, 1996), 102–28.

A-46. D. H. Lawrence, *Apocalypse* (New York: Penguin, [1931] 1976), 85.

A-47. Epiphanius, *Pan* 3.78.11.

A-48. W. M. Ramsay, "The Worship of the Virgin Mary at Ephesus," in *Pauline and Other Studies* (London: Hodder and Stoughton, 1906), 125–59; G. E. Bean, *Aegean Turkey*, 146–48; V. Limberis, "The Council of Ephesos," H. Koester, ed., *Ephesos*, 321–40.

A-49. This inscription comes from the Asclepium at Epidaurus; E. J. Edelstein & L. Edelstein, *Asclepius* (Baltimore: Johns Hopkins Univ. Press, 1945), 1.§423.17; cf. Hippocrates, *Ep.* 15.

A-50. For the complete text, see C. K. Barrett, *The New Testament Background*, rev. ed. (San Francisco: HarperSanFrancisco, 1989), 1–5.

A-51. The sources for this myth are Tacitus, *Hist.* 2.8–9; John of Antioch, Fr. 104; Suetonius, *Nero* 57; Dio Chrysostom, *Or.* 21.10.

A-52. For example, H. Lindsay, *There's a New World Coming* (Santa Ana, Calif.: Vision House, 1973), 78.

A-53. This paragraph summarizes information drawn from the chapter "Images," in Price, *Rituals and Power*, 170–206.

A-54. Boring et al., *Hellenistic Commentary to the New Testament*, 225.

A-55. See B. W. Henderson, *The Life and Principate of the Emperor Nero* (London: Macmillan, 1903), 153–95; D. E. Aune, "Rome and Parthia," *Revelation*, 2:891–94; cf. F. Millar, *The Roman Near East 31 BC–AD 337* (Cambridge, Mass.: Harvard Univ. Press, 1993), 66–68.

A-56. Shelton, *As the Romans Did*, 129–37, 459; cf. Aune, *Revelation*, 3:1000.

A-57. See W. Tabbernee, *Montanist Inscriptions and Testimonia* (Macon, Ga.: Mercer Univ. Press, 1997).

A-58. G. R. Beasley-Murray, *Revelation* (NCBC; Grand Rapids: Eerdmans, 1978), 62. Other examples of the Rota-Sator square have been found in Cirencester, England and in Dura Europos on the Euphrates; see F. F. Bruce, *The Spreading Flame* (Grand Rapids: Eerdmans, 1958), 356–57; D. Fishwick, "On the Origin of the Rotas-Sator Square," *HThR* 57 (1974): 39–53.

A-59. These impressions are found in Mark Twain's *Innocents Abroad*, Freya Stark's *Ionia: A Quest*, and Lord Kinross's *Europa Minor*.

CREDITS FOR PHOTOS AND MAPS

ALSO AVAILABLE

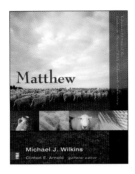

Matthew

Michael J. Wilkins

Clinton E. Arnold general editor

Mark

David E. Garland

Clinton E. Arnold general editor

Luke

Mark L. Strauss

Clinton E. Arnold general editor

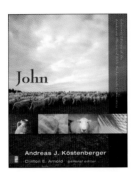

John

Andreas J. Köstenberger

Clinton E. Arnold general editor

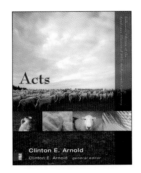

Acts

Clinton E. Arnold

Clinton E. Arnold general editor

Romans
Galatians

Douglas J. Moo
Ralph P. Martin
Julie L. Wu

Clinton E. Arnold general editor

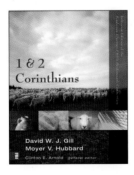

1 & 2
Corinthians

David W. J. Gill
Moyer V. Hubbard

Clinton E. Arnold general editor

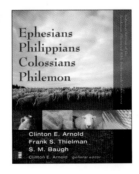

Ephesians
Philippians
Colossians
Philemon

Clinton E. Arnold
Frank S. Thielman
S. M. Baugh

Clinton E. Arnold general editor

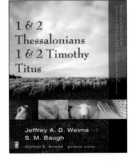

1 & 2
Thessalonians
1 & 2 Timothy
Titus

Jeffrey A. D. Weima
S. M. Baugh

Clinton E. Arnold general editor

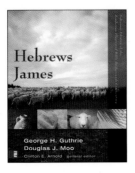

Hebrews
James

George H. Guthrie
Douglas J. Moo

Clinton E. Arnold general editor

1 & 2 Peter
1, 2, & 3 John
Jude

Peter H. Davids
Douglas J. Moo
Robert W. Yarbrough

Clinton E. Arnold general editor

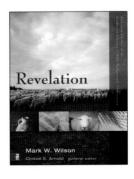

Revelation

Mark W. Wilson

Clinton E. Arnold general editor

We want to hear from you. Please send your comments about this book to us in care of zreview@zondervan.com. Thank you.

ZONDERVAN.com/
AUTHORTRACKER
follow your favorite authors